You Can Unde

Paul's
First Letters:
Galatians

and

I & II
Thessalonians

Bob Utley

BIBLE LESSONS INTERNATIONAL

Study Guide Commentary Series
New Testament, Vol. 7
Bible Lessons International, Marshall, Texas

ISBN 0-9661098-0-5

Bible Lessons International
P. O. Box 1289
Marshall, TX 75671
1-800-785-1005

The basic biblical text used in this commentary is:
New American Standard Bible (Update;1995)
Copyright ©1960, 1962, 1963, 1968, 1971, 1972, 1973, 1975, 1977, 1995
by the Lockman Foundation
P. O. Box 2279
La Habra, CA 90632-2279

The paragraph divisions and summary captions as well as selected phrases are from:
1. The Greek New Testament, Fourth Revised Edition
   Copyright ©1993 Deutsche Bibelgesellschaft, O Stuttgart
2. The New King James Version
   Copyright ©1979, 1980, 1982 by Thomas Nelson, Inc.
   Used by permission. All rights reserved.
3. The New Revised Standard Version of the Bible
   Copyright ©1989 by the Division of Christian Education of National
   Council of the Churches of Christ in the U. S. A. Used by
   permission. All rights reserved.
4. Today's English Version is used by permission of the copyright owner, The
   American Bible Society, ©1966, 1971. Used by permission.
5. The Jerusalem Bible, copyright ©1966 by Darton, Longman & Todd, Ltd.
   and Doubleday, a division of Bantam Doubleday Dell Publishing
   Group, Inc. Reprinted by permission.

STUDY GUIDE COMMENTARY

These detailed study guide commentaries are being published by Bible Lessons International beginning in 1997 with Volume 7:

Paul's First Letters (Galatians and I & II Thessalonians)

The other New Testament books will be available in the near future.

Why Use The New American Standard Bible Update - 1995?

Easier to read:
❖Passages with Old English "thee's" and "thou's" etc. have been updated to modern English.

❖Words and phrases that could be misunderstood due to changes in their meaning during the past 20 years have been updated to current English.

❖Verses with difficult word order or vocabulary have been retranslated into smoother English.

❖Sentences beginning with "And" have often been retranslated for better English, in recognition of differences in style between the ancient languages and modern English. The original Greek and Hebrew did not have punctuation as is found in English, and in many cases modern English punctuation serves as a substitute for "And" in the original. In some other cases, "and" is translated by a different word such as "then" or "but" as called for by the context, when the word in the original language allows such translation.

More accurate than ever:
❖Recent research on the oldest and best Greek manuscripts of the New Testament has been reviewed, and some passages have been updated for even greater fidelity to the original manuscripts.

❖Parallel passages have been compared and reviewed.

❖Verbs that have a wide range of meaning have been retranslated in some passages to better account for their use in the context.

And still the NASB:
❖The NASB update is not a change-for-the-sake-of-change translation. The original NASB stands the test of time, and change has been kept to a minimum in recognition of the standard that has been set by the New American Standard Bible.

❖The NASB update continues the NASB's tradition of literal translation of the original Greek and Hebrew without compromise. Changes in the text have been kept within the strict parameters set forth by the Lockman Foundation's Fourfold Aim.

❖The translators and consultants who have contributed to the NASB update are conservative Bible scholars who have doctorates in Biblical languages, theology, or other advanced degrees. They represent a variety of denominational backgrounds.

Continuing a tradition:
The original NASB has earned the reputation of being the most accurate English Bible translation. Other translations in recent years have sometimes made a claim to both accuracy and ease of reading, but any reader with an eye for detail eventually discovers that these translations are consistently inconsistent. While sometimes literal, they frequently resort to paraphrase of the original, often gaining little in readability and sacrificing much in terms of fidelity. Paraphrasing is not by nature a bad thing; it can and should clarify the meaning of a passage as the translators understand and interpret. In the end, however, a paraphrase is as much a commentary on the Bible as it is a translation. The NASB update carries on the NASB tradition of being a true Bible translation, revealing what the original manuscripts actually say— not merely what the translator believes they mean.

—The Lockman Foundation

This first volume is dedicated to

Henry "Ted" and Eileen Beyer and their family

whose trust, prayers, encouragement,
and generous financial help
through the years have made this series possible.

I would like to thank my colleagues at East Texas Baptist
University and other friends
who read through the text of this commentary at different stages
of its development
and offered such encouraging and helpful suggestions:

Franklin Atkinson
Robert Ellison
John Harris
David King
Don Rominger
Jerry Summers
Bruce Tankersley
Wallace Watkins

I also want to thank those who have typed these notes as they
have developed through the years:

Bettye Hughes
Jodell Logan
LeAnn Malone
Peggi Powers
Doris Spraberry
Peggy Utley
Helen Whitmire

TABLE OF CONTENTS

A Word From the Author:

How Can This Commentary Help You?

Biblical interpretation is a rational and spiritual process that attempts to understand an ancient inspired writer in such a way that the message from God may be understood and applied in our day.

The spiritual process is difficult to define. It does involve a yieldedness and openness to God. There must be a hunger for Him, to know Him, to serve Him. This process involves prayer, confession and the willingness for lifestyle change. The Spirit is crucial in the interpretive process but why sincere, godly Christians understand the Bible differently is a mystery.

The rational process is easier to describe. The problem is consistency and fairness to the text and not our personal, denominational biases. We are all historically conditioned. None of us are objective, neutral interpreters. This commentary offers a careful rational process containing three interpretive principles structured to help us overcome our biases.

The first principle is to note the historical setting in which a biblical book was written and the particular historical occasion that caused the writing. The original author had a purpose, a message to communicate. The text cannot mean something to us that it never meant to the original, ancient, inspired author. His intent—not our historical, emotional, cultural, personal or denominational need—is the key. Application is an integral partner to interpretation but proper interpretation must always precede application. It needs to be stated again and again that every biblical text has one and only one meaning. This meaning is what the original biblical author intended through the Spirit's leadership to communicate to his day. This one meaning may have many possible applications to different cultures and situations. These applications must be linked to the central truth of the original author. Thus, this study guide commentary is designed to provide an introduction to each book of the Bible.

The second principle is to identify the literary units. Every biblical book is a unified document. Interpreters have no right to isolate one aspect or truth by excluding others. Therefore, we must strive to understand the purpose of the whole before we interpret the individual literary units. The individual parts, be they chapters, paragraphs, or verses, cannot mean what the whole does not mean. Interpretation must move from a deductive approach of the whole to an inductive approach to the parts. Therefore, this study guide commentary is designed to help the student analyze the structure of each literary unit by paragraphs. Paragraph divisions are not inspired, but they do aid us in identifying thought units.

Interpreting at a paragraph level—not sentence, clause, phrase or word level—is the key in following the intended meaning of the biblical author. Paragraphs are based on a unified topic, often called the theme or topic sentence. Every word, phrase, clause, and sentence in the paragraph relates somehow to this unified theme. They limit it, expand it, explain it, and question it. A real key to proper interpretation is to follow the original author's thought on a paragraph-by-paragraph basis through the individual literary units that make up the biblical book. This study guide commentary is designed to help the student do that by comparing modern English translations. The following translations have been selected because they employ different theories of translations:

1. The United Bible Society's Greek text is the revised fourth edition. This text was paragraphed by modern textual scholars.

2. The New King James Version is a word-for-word literal translation based on the Greek manuscript tradition known as the Textus Receptus. Its paragraph divisions are longer than the other translations. These longer units help the student to see the unified topics.

3. The New Revised Standard Version is a modified word-for-word translation. It forms a mid point between the following two modern versions. Its paragraph divisions are quite helpful in identifying subjects.

4. The Today's English Version is a dynamic equivalent translation published by the United Bible Society. It attempts to translate the Bible in such a way that a modern English speaker can understand the meaning of the Greek text. Often, especially in the Gospels, it divides paragraphs by speaker rather than by subject, in the same way as the NIV. For the interpreter's purposes, this is not helpful. It is interesting to note that both the UBS[4] and TEV are published by the same entity, yet their paragraphing differs.

5. The Jerusalem Bible is a dynamic equivalent translation based on a French Catholic translation. It is very helpful in comparing the paragraphing from a European perspective.

The third principle is to read the Bible in different translations in order to grasp the widest possible range of meaning that biblical words or phrases have. Often a Greek phrase or word can be understood in several ways. These different translations bring out these options and help to identify and explain the Greek manuscript variations. These do not affect doctrine but they do help us to try to get back to the original text penned by an inspired ancient writer.

This commentary offers a quick way for the student to check his interpretations. It is not meant to be definitive, but rather informative and thought-provoking. Often, other possible interpretations help us not be so parochial, dogmatic, and denominational. Interpreters need to have a larger range of interpretive options to recognize how ambiguous the ancient text can be. It is shocking how little agreement there is among Christians who claim the Bible as their source of truth.

These principles have helped me to overcome much of my historical conditioning by forcing me to struggle with the ancient text. My hope is that it will be a blessing to you as well.

Bob Utley
East Texas Baptist University
June 27, 1996

A Word From the Editor

The Study Bible Commentary Series, inaugurated with this first volume, marks a very special time for students of the Bible everywhere. While English-language commentaries and study helps proliferate, many at reasonable cost, Bob Utley's commentaries are specially designed to help Bible students at all levels, from new Christians with limited knowledge of the Bible to mature scholars with extensive knowledge of the original languages. This series is truly unique in providing the Bible student with five parallel paragraph divisions preceding each chapter of commentary. These divisions attempt to show the author's flow of thought and argumentation in a way, not readily seen in one translation in isolation. While paragraph divisions and literary units are not inspired per se, they are essential interpretive keys for those wanting to discover the exciting truths the Bible has to offer.

Dr. Utley's call to make the Scriptures understandable has been balanced with his desire to see each person come to a real encounter with God's Word through the discipline of personal, systematic study. While the commentary may be used to assist preparation for sermons and Sunday School lessons, the intent behind the Study Guide Commentary's publication is to supplement engaging research and study of the Bible pursued by each student. Accordingly, the following section discussing the four reading cycles is highly recommended as one way the student may optimize his time spent in the Word. The discipline required for proper Bible study does not come naturally for most Christians, yet it is precisely that discipline which produces the best rewards.

Having had the privilege of knowing Dr. Utley for six years, it has been refreshing for me not only to encounter his insights in biblical interpretation, but to observe a life and ministry sincere in motivation, orthodox in belief, and dedicated in purpose. Dr. Utley actively pursues a closer relationship with God and exemplifies the Christlike spirit—an end for which a passionate love for the Bible is the means. As he has often declared with conviction, each of us should, "walk in the light that we have, be tolerant to those who do not have the same light, and always seek more light." This principle he preaches and practices consistently. So also it is my hope that the prayer and work Dr. Utley has invested through the years, culminating in this first volume in the Study Guide Commentary Series, will be a blessing to believers and students of

God's Word around the world.

William G. Wells
October 8, 1996

A Guide to Good Bible Reading:
A Personal Search For Verifiable Truth

Can we know truth? Where is it found? Can we logically verify it? Is there an ultimate authority? Are there absolutes which can guide our lives, our world? Is there meaning to life? Why are we here? Where are we going? These questions—questions that all rational people contemplate—have haunted the human intellect since the beginning of time (Eccl. 1:13-18; 3:9-11).

I can remember my personal search for an integrating center for my life. I became a believer in Christ at a young age, based primarily on the witness of significant others in my family. As I grew to adulthood, questions about myself and my world also grew. Simple cultural and religious clichés did not bring meaning to the experiences I read about or encountered. It was a time of confusion, searching, longing, and often a feeling of hopelessness in the face of the insensitive, hard world in which I lived.

Many claimed to have answers to these ultimate questions, but after research and reflection I found that their answers were based upon: (1) personal philosophies, (2) ancient myths, (3) personal experiences, or (4) psychological projections. I needed some degree of verification, some evidence, some rationality on which to base my worldview, my integrating center, my reason to live.

These I found in my study of the Bible. I began to search for evidence of its trustworthiness, which I found in: (1) the historical reliability of the Bible from archaeology, (2) the accuracy of the prophecies of the Old Testament, (3) the unity of the Bible message over the sixteen hundred years of its production, and (4) the personal testimonies of people whose lives had been permanently changed by contact with the Bible. Christianity, as a unified system of faith and belief, has the ability to deal with complex questions of human life. Not only did this provide a rational framework, but the experiential aspect of Biblical faith brought me emotional joy and stability.

I thought that I had found the integrating center for my life—the Bible. It was a heady experience, an emotional release. I can still remember the shock and pain when it began to dawn on me how many different interpretations of this book were advocated, sometimes even within the same churches and schools of thought. Affirming the inspiration and trustworthiness of the Bible was not the end, but only the beginning. How do I verify or reject the varied and conflicting interpretations of the many difficult passages in Scripture by those who were claiming its authority and trustworthiness?

This task became my life's goal and pilgrimage of faith. I knew that my faith in Christ had brought me great peace and joy. My mind longed for some absolutes in the midst of the relativity of my culture and the dogmatism of conflicting religious systems and denominational arrogance. In my search for valid approaches to the interpretation of ancient literature, I was surprised to discover my own historical, cultural, denominational and experiential biases. I had often read the Bible simply to reinforce my own views. I used it as a database to attack others while affirming my own insecurities and inadequacies. How painful this realization was to me!

Although I can never be totally objective, I can become a better reader of the Bible. I can limit my biases by identifying them and acknowledging their presence. I am not yet free of them, but I have confronted my own weaknesses. The interpreter is often the worst enemy of good Bible reading!

Therefore, let me list some of the presuppositions I bring to my study of the Bible so that you, the reader, may examine them along with me:

(1) I believe the Bible is the only inspired self-revelation of the one true God. Therefore, it must be interpreted in light of the intent of the original divine author through a human writer in a specific historical setting.

(2) I believe the Bible was written for the common man—for all men! God accommodated Himself to speak to us clearly within a historical and cultural context. God does not hide truth—He wants us to understand! Therefore, it must be interpreted in light of its day, not ours. The Bible cannot mean to us what it never meant to those who first read or heard it. It is understandable by the average human mind and uses normal human communication forms and techniques.

(3) I believe the Bible has a unified message and purpose. It does not contradict itself, though it does contain difficult and paradoxical passages. Therefore, the best interpreter of the Bible is the Bible itself.

(4) I believe that every passage (excluding prophesies) has one and only one meaning based on the intent of the original, inspired author. Although we can never be absolutely certain we know the original author's intent, many indicators point in its direction:

    (a) the genre (literary type) chosen to express the message

    (b) the historical setting and/or specific occasion that elicited the writing

    (c) the literary context of the entire book as well as each literary unit

    (d) the textual design (outline) of the literary units as they relate to the whole message

    (e) the specific grammatical features employed to communicate the message

    (f) the words chosen to present the message

The study of each of these areas becomes the object of our study of a passage. Before I explain my methodology for good Bible reading, let me delineate some of the inappropriate methods being used today that have caused so much diversity of interpretation, and that consequently should be avoided:

(1) Ignoring the literary context of the books of the Bible and using every sentence, clause, or even individual words as statements of truth unrelated to the author's intent or the larger context. This is often called "proof-texting."

(2) Ignoring the historical setting of the books of the Bible by substituting a supposed historical setting that has little or no support from the text itself.

(3) Ignoring the historical setting of the books of the Bible and reading it as the morning hometown newspaper written primarily to modern individual Christians.

(4) Ignoring the historical setting of the books of the Bible by allegorizing the text into a philosophical/theological message totally unrelated to the first hearers and the original author's intent.

(5) Ignoring the original message by substituting one's own system of theology, pet doctrine, or contemporary issue unrelated to the original author's purpose and stated message. This phenomenon often follows the initial reading of the Bible as a means of establishing a speaker's authority. This is often referred to as "reader response" ("what-the-text-means-to-me" interpretation).

At least three related components may be found in all written human communication:

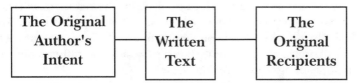

In the past, different reading techniques have focused on one of the three components. For those of us who affirm the unique inspiration of the Bible, a modified diagram is more appropriate:

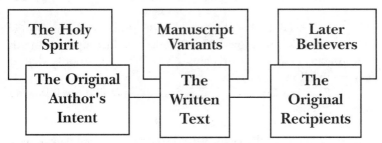

In truth all three components must be included in the interpretive process. For the purpose of verification, my interpretation focuses on the first two components: the original author and the text. I am probably reacting to the abuses I have observed: (1) allegorizing or spiritualizing texts and (2) "reader response" interpretation (what-it-means-to-me). Abuse may occur at each stage. We must always check our motives, biases, techniques, and applications. But how do we check them if there are no boundaries to interpretations, no limits, no criteria? This is where authorial intent and textual structure provide me with some criteria for limiting the scope of possible valid interpretations.

In light of these inappropriate reading techniques, what are some possible approaches to good Bible reading and interpretation which offer a degree of verification and consistency?

At this point I am not discussing the unique techniques of interpreting specific genres but general hermeneutical principles valid for all types of biblical texts. A good book for genre-specific approaches is *How To Read The Bible For All It Is Worth*, by Gordon Fee and Douglas Stuart, published by Zondervan.

My methodology focuses initially on the reader allowing

the Holy Spirit to illumine the Bible through four personal reading cycles. This makes the Spirit, the reader, and the text primary, not secondary. This also protects the reader from being unduly influenced by commentators. I have heard it said: "The Bible throws a lot of light on commentaries." This is not meant to be a depreciating comment about study aids, but rather a plea for an appropriate timing for their use.

We must be able from the text itself to support our interpretations. Five areas provide at least limited verification:

(1) historical setting   (4) contemporary word usage
(2) literary context   (5) relevant parallel passages
(3) grammatical structures (syntax)

We need to be able to provide the reasons and logic behind our interpretations. The Bible is our only source for faith and practice. Sadly, Christians often disagree about what it teaches or affirms.

Four reading cycles are designed to provide the following interpretive insights:

(1) The first reading cycle

    (a) Read the book during one sitting. Read it again in a different translation, hopefully from a different translation theory:

        (i) word-for-word (NKJV, NASB, NRSV)
        (ii) dynamic equivalent (TEV, JB)
        (iii) paraphrase (Living Bible, Amplified Bible)

    (b) Look for the central purpose of the entire writing. Identify its theme.

    (c) Isolate (if possible) a literary unit, a chapter, a paragraph or a sentence which clearly expresses this central purpose or theme.

    (d) Identify the predominant literary genre:

        (i) Old Testament

            1) Hebrew narrative
            2) Hebrew poetry (wisdom literature, psalm)
            3) Hebrew prophecy (prose, poetry)
            4) Law codes

        (ii) New Testament

            1) Narratives (Gospels, Acts)
            2) Letters/epistles
            3) Apocalyptic literature

(2) The second reading cycle
  (a) Read the entire book again, seeking to identify major topics or subjects.
  (b) Outline the major topics and briefly encapsulate their contents in a declarative statement.
  (c) Check your purpose statement and broad outline with study aids.
(3) The third reading cycle
  (a) Read the entire book again, seeking to identify the historical setting and specific occasion for the writing.
  (b) List the historical items:
      (i)   the author
      (ii) the date
      (iii) the recipients
      (iv) the specific reason for writing
      (v)   aspects of the cultural setting that relate to the purpose of the writing
  (c) Expand your outline to paragraph level for that part of the biblical book you are interpreting. Always identify and outline the literary unit. This may be several chapters or paragraphs. This enables you to follow the original author's logic and textual design.
  (d) Check your historical setting by using study aids.
(4) The fourth reading cycle
  (a) Read the specific literary unit again in several translations.
  (b) Look for literary or grammatical structures:
      (i)   repeated phrases
      (ii) repeated grammatical structures
      (iii) contrasting concepts
  (c) List the following items:
      (i)   significant terms
      (ii) unusual terms
      (iii) important grammatical structures
      (iv) particularly difficult words, clauses, and sentences
  (d) Look for relevant parallel passages:
      (i) look for the clearest teaching passage on your subject using:
          a) "systematic theology" books

        b) reference Bibles

        c) concordances

   (ii) look for a possible paradoxical pair within your subject; many biblical truths are presented in dialectical pairs; many denominational conflicts come from proof-texting half of a biblical tension. All of the Bible is inspired, and we must seek out its complete message in order to provide a Scriptural balance to our interpretation.

  (iii) look for parallels within the same book, same author or same genre; the Bible is its own best interpreter because it has one author, the Spirit.

(e) Use study aids to check your observations of historical setting and occasion

   (i) study Bibles

  (ii) Bible encyclopedias, handbooks and dictionaries

 (iii) Bible introductions

 (iv) Bible commentaries (At this point in your study, allow the believing community, past and present, to aid and correct your personal study.)

At this point we turn to application. You have paid the price to understand the text in its original setting; now it must be applied to your life, your culture. I define biblical authority as "understanding what the original biblical author was saying to his day and applying that truth to our day."

Application must follow interpretation of the original author's intent both in time and logic. One cannot apply a Bible passage to his own day until he knows what it was saying to its day! A Bible passage cannot mean what it never meant!

Your detailed outline, to paragraph level (reading cycle #3), will be your guide. Application should be made at paragraph level, not word level. Words only have meaning in context; clauses only have meaning in context; sentences only have meaning in context. The only inspired person involved in the interpretive process is the original author. We only follow his lead by the illumination of the Holy Spirit. But illumination is not inspiration. To say "thus saith the Lord," we must abide in the original author's intent. Application must relate specifically to the general intent of the whole writing, the specific literary unit and paragraph level thought development.

Do not let the issues of our day interpret the Bible; let the Bible speak! This may require us to principalize the text. This is valid if the text supports a principle. Unfortunately, many times our principles are just that, "our" principles—not the text's principles.

In applying the Bible, it is important to remember that (except in prophecy) one and only one meaning may be valid for a particular Bible text. That meaning is related to the intent of the original author as he addressed a crisis or need in his day. Many possible applications may be derived from this one meaning. The application will be based on the recipients' needs but must be related to the original author's meaning.

So far I have discussed the logical process involved in interpretation and application. Now let me discuss briefly the spiritual aspect of interpretation. The following checklist has been helpful for me:

(1) Pray for the Spirit's help (cf. I Cor. 1:26-2:16).
(2) Pray for personal forgiveness and cleansing from known sin (cf. I Jn. 1:9).
(3) Pray for a greater desire to know God (cf. Psa. 19:7-14; 42:1ff.; 119:1ff).
(4) Apply any new insight immediately to your own life.
(5) Remain humble and teachable.

It is so hard to keep the balance between the logical process and the spiritual leadership of the Holy Spirit. The following quotes have helped me balance the two:

(1) from James W. Sire, *Scripture Twisting*, IVP, p. 17-18:

> "The illumination comes to the minds of God's people—not just to the spiritual elite. There is no guru class in biblical Christianity, no illuminati, no people through whom all proper interpretation must come. And so, while the Holy Spirit gives special gifts of wisdom, knowledge and spiritual discernment, He does not assign these gifted Christians to be the only authoritative interpreters of his Word. It is up to each of His people to learn, to judge and to discern by reference to the Bible which stands as the authority even to those to whom God has given special abilities. To summarize, the assumption I am making throughout the entire

book is that the Bible is God's true revelation to all humanity, that it is our ultimate authority on all matters about which it speaks, that it is not a total mystery but can be adequately understood by ordinary people in every culture."

(2) on Kierkegaard, found in Bernard Ramm, *Protestant Biblical Interpretation*, (Grand Rapids, Mich.: Baker Book House, 1970), p. 75:

According to Kierkegaard the grammatical, lexical, and historical study of the Bible was necessary but preliminary to the true reading of the Bible. "To read the Bible as God's word one must read it with his heart in his mouth, on tip-toe, with eager expectancy, in conversation with God. To read the Bible thoughtlessly or carelessly or academically or professionally is not to read the Bible as God's Word. As one reads it as a love letter is read, then one reads it as the Word of God."

(3) H. H. Rowley in *The Relevance of the Bible*, p. 19:

"No merely intellectual understanding of the Bible, however complete, can possess all its treasures. It does not despise such understanding, for it is essential to a complete understanding. But it must lead to a spiritual understanding of the spiritual treasures of this book if it is to be complete. And for that spiritual understanding something more than intellectual alertness is necessary. Spiritual things are spiritually discerned, and the Bible student needs an attitude of spiritual receptivity, an eagerness to find God that he may yield himself to Him, if he is to pass beyond his scientific study unto the richer inheritance of this greatest of all books."

The Study Guide Commentary is designed to aid your interpretive procedures in the following ways:

1. A brief historical outline introduces each book. After you have done "reading cycle #3" check your information.
2. Contextual insights are found at the beginning of each chapter. This will help you see how the literary unit is structured.
3. Paragraph divisions and their descriptive captions are provided from several modern translations:
   a. The United Bible Society Greek text, fourth edition

revised (UBS[4])

   b. The New American Standard Bible, 1995 update (NASB)
   c. The New King James Version (NKJV)
   d. The New Revised Standard Version (NRSV)
   e. Today's English Version (TEV)
   f. The Jerusalem Bible (JB)

   Paragraph divisions are not inspired. They must be ascertained from the context. By comparing several modern translations from differing translation theories and theological perspectives, one is able to analyze the supposed structure of the original author's thought.

   Each paragraph has one major truth. This has been called "the topic sentence" or "the central idea of the text." This unifying thought is the key to proper historical, grammatical interpretation. One should never interpret, preach or teach on less than a paragraph! Also remember that each paragraph is related to its surrounding paragraphs. This is why a paragraph level outline of the entire book is so important. One must be able to follow the logical flow of the subject being addressed by the original inspired author.

4. The notes follow a verse-by-verse approach to interpretation. This forces us to follow the original author's thought. The notes provide information from several areas:
   a. literary context
   b. historical, cultural insights
   c. grammatical information
   d. word studies
   e. relevant parallel passages

5. At certain points in the commentary, the text of the New American Standard Version, updated, will be supplemented by the translations of several other modern versions:
   a. The New King James Version (NKJV), which follows the textual manuscripts of the "Textus Receptus."
   b. The New Revised Standard Version (NRSV), which is a word-for-word revision from the National Council of Churches of the Revised Standard Version.

    c. The Today's English Version (TEV), which is a
       dynamic equivalent translation from the American
       Bible Society.

    d. The Jerusalem Bible (JB), which is an English
       translation based on a French Catholic dynamic
       equivalent translation.

6. For those who do not read Greek fluently, comparing
  English translations helps in identifying problems in the
  text:

    a. manuscript variations
    b. alternate word meanings
    c. grammatically difficult texts and structure
    d. ambiguous texts

Although the English translations cannot solve these problems, they do target them as places for deeper and more
thorough study.

7. At the close of each chapter relevant discussion questions
  are provided which attempt to target the major interpretive issues of that chapter.

Paul's Letter
to the
Galatians

GALATIANS

INTRODUCTION TO GALATIANS

A. The book of Galatians is one of the clearest expressions of the radically new and free truth of salvation by grace alone, through faith alone. It is often called "The Magna Carta of Christian Liberty."

B. This letter stirred the fires of the Protestant Reformation.
   1. Martin Luther said "the little book of Galatians is my letter; I have betrothed myself to it; it is my wife."
   2. John Wesley found lasting peace from a sermon on Galatians.
   3. In his *Study Guide Commentary*, p. 11, Curtis Vaughan wrote "few books have more profoundly influenced the minds of men, have so significantly shaped the course of human history, or continued to speak with such relevance to the deepest needs of modern life."

C. This doctrinally oriented letter, possibly Paul's first, was a precursor to Romans and its development of the doctrine of justification by faith apart from Judaism's emphasis on keeping the Law:
   1. Salvation cannot be found in both Law and grace.
   2. Salvation must be found in either Law or grace.
   3. Christlikeness will follow a true conversion.
   4. Beware of Christian legalism.

D. This radically free salvation, by grace alone through faith alone, is desperately needed in our day because of the recurrent, subtle pull of our self-oriented, works-oriented religious consciousness. In every age the simple truth of God's initiating, self-giving, unconditional love mediated through human repentance and humble faith is challenged! It is not that the false teachers were rejecting Christ's central place in redemption, but they were adding to Him. It is not what we add, but that we add anything!

1

AUTHOR

Paul's authorship of this letter has never been seriously doubted, as it forms a significant pillar of the Pauline Corpus. Galatians is very autobiographical and personal. It is highly emotional yet precisely logical.

DATE AND RECIPIENTS

A. These two aspects of background material must be dealt with together because two opposing theories of the identities of the recipients affect the dating of the letter. Both theories have logical weight and limited biblical evidence.

B. The two theories are:
1. The traditional theory that was unanimous until the eighteenth century.
    a. It is called the "Northern Galatian Theory."
    b. It assumes that "Galatia" refers to the ethnic Galatians of the northern central plateau of Turkey (cf. I Pet. 1:1). These ethnic Galatians were Celts (Greek Keltoi or Latin Gall) who invaded this area in the third century B.C. They were called "Gallo-Graecians" to distinguish them from their western European brothers. They were defeated in 230 B.C. by Attalus I, the King of Pergamum. Their geographical influence was limited to northern central Asia Minor or modern Turkey.
    c. If this ethnic group is assumed, then the date would be the mid 50's during Paul's second or third missionary journey. Paul's traveling companions would be Silas and Timothy.
    d. Some have linked Paul's illness in Gal. 4:13 to malaria. They assert that Paul went north into the highlands to get away from the marshy, malaria-infested, coastal lowlands.
2. The second theory is championed by Sir Wm. M. Ramsay, *St. Paul the Traveller and Roman Citizen*, New York: G. P. Putnam's Sons, 1896.

a. As the traditional theory defined "Galatia" as ethnic, this theory defines it as administrative. It seems that Paul often used Roman provincial names (cf. I Cor. 16:19; II Cor. 1:1; 8:1, etc.)   The Roman province of "Galatia" included a larger area than ethnic "Galatia." These ethnic Celts supported Rome very early and were rewarded with more local autonomy and expanded territorial authority.   If this large area was known as "Galatia," then it is possible that Paul's first missionary journey to these southern cities of Antioch in Pisidia, Lystra, Derbe and Iconium, recorded in Acts 13-14, is the location of these churches.

b. If one assumes this "Southern Theory," the date would be very early—close to, but before, the "Jerusalem Council" of Acts 15, which addresses the same subject matter as the book of Galatians. The Council occurred in A.D. 48-49 and the letter was probably written during the same period. If this is true, Galatians is the first letter of Paul in our New Testament.

c. Some evidences for the southern Galatian theory:

> (1) There is no mention of Paul's traveling companions by name but Barnabas is mentioned three times (cf. 2:1,9,13). This fits the first missionary journey of Paul.
>
> (2) It is mentioned that Titus was not circumcised (cf. 2:1-5). This fits best before the Jerusalem Council of Acts 15.
>
> (3) The mention of Peter (cf. 2:11-14) and the problem of fellowship with Gentiles fits best before the Jerusalem Council.
>
> (4) When the money was taken to Jerusalem several companions of Paul from different areas (cf. Acts 20:4) were listed. None, however, were listed from northern Galatia cities, although we know these ethnic Galatian

churches participated (cf. I Cor. 16:1).

3. For the detailed presentation of the different arguments concerning these theories consult a technical commentary. They each have valid points but at this point in time there is no consensus, but the "Southern Theory" seems to fit all of the facts best.

C. Relationship of Galatians to Acts:

1. Paul made five visits to Jerusalem, recorded by Luke in the book of Acts:

a. 9:26-30, after his conversion

b. 11:30; 12:25, to bring famine relief from the Gentile churches

c. 15:1-30, the Jerusalem Council

d. 18:22, brief visit

e. 21:15ff., another explanation of Gentile work

2. There are two visits to Jerusalem recorded in Galatians:

a. 1:18, after three years

b. 2:1, after fourteen years

3. It seems most probable that Acts 9:26 is related to Gal. 1:18. Acts 11:30 & 15:1ff are the setting of unrecorded meetings which are mentioned in Gal. 2:1.

4. There are some differences between the Acts 15 and Gal. 2 accounts but this is probably due to:

a. different perspectives

b. different purposes of Luke and Paul

c. the fact that Gal. 2 may have occurred sometime before the meeting described in Acts 15 but in conjunction with it.

PURPOSE OF THE LETTER

A. Paul addressed three distinct areas of concern about the message of the false teachers. These heretics have been labelled "Judaizers" because they believed that one had to become a Jew before he could become a Christian (cf. 6:12). His concerns revolved around the charges of the Judaizers:

1. Paul was not truly an Apostle like the Twelve (cf. Acts

4

1:21-22); therefore, he was dependent on their authority or at least the authority of the Mother Church in Jerusalem.

2. Paul's message was different from theirs, and thus, false. This seems directly related to the concept of "justification by faith apart from the Law." The Apostles in Jerusalem were still very Jewish in their personal lives.

3. An element of libertinism was connected in some way with these churches (cf. 5:18-6:8). Exactly how this is to be explained is debated. Some have even seen two target groups in Paul's letter: Judaizers and gnostics (cf. 4:8-11). However, it seems best to relate these verses to pagan practices. The Jews were concerned about the lifestyle of Gentiles. How did Paul's radical free grace relate to pagan idolatry and excess?

B. Doctrinally, this letter is very similar to Paul's letter to the Romans. These two books contain Paul's major doctrines repeated and developed in different settings.

BRIEF OUTLINE

A. Prologue, 1:1-10
   1. general introduction to the book
   2. the occasion for writing the book

B. Paul defends his Apostleship, 1:11-2:14

C. Paul defends the doctrinal truths of his gospel, 2:15-4:20

D. Paul defends the practical implications of his gospel, 5:1-6:10

E. Personal summary and closing, 6:11-18

READING CYCLE ONE (see p. vi)

This is a study guide commentary which means that you are responsible for your own interpretation of the Bible. Each of us must walk in the light we have. You, the Bible and the Holy Spirit are priority in interpretation. You must not relinquish this to a commentator.

Therefore, read the entire biblical book at one sitting. State the central theme of the entire book in your own words.

1. Theme of entire book

2. Type of literature (genre)

READING CYCLE TWO (see pp. vi-vii.)

This is a study <u>guide</u> commentary which means that you are responsible for your own interpretation of the Bible. Each of us must walk in the light we have. You, the Bible and the Holy Spirit are priority in interpretation. You must not relinquish this to a commentator.

Therefore, read the entire biblical book a second time at one sitting. Outline the main subjects and express the subject in a single sentence.

1. Subject of first literary unit

2. Subject of second literary unit

3. Subject of third literary unit

4. Subject of fourth literary unit

5. Etc.

GALATIANS 1

PARAGRAPH DIVISIONS OF MODERN TRANSLATIONS*

UBS⁴	NKJV	NRSV	TEV	JB
Salutation	Greetings	The Salutation	Salutation	Address
1:1-5	1:1-5	1:1-5	1:1-2	1:1-5
			1:3	
			1:4-5	
There is No Other Gospel	The One Gospel	The Galatian Apostasy	Only One Gospel	A Warning
1:6-9	1:6-9	1:6-10	1:6-10	1:6-10
1:10	1:10			
How Paul Became An Apostle	Call to Apostleship	Paul's Vindication of his Apostleship	How Paul Became an Apostle	God's Call
1:11-12	1:11-17	1:11-12	1:11-12	1:11-24
1:13-17		1:13-17	1:13-14	
			1:15-19	
	Contacts at Jerusalem			
1:18-24	1:18-24	1:18-24		
			1:20	
			1:21-24	

READING CYCLE THREE (see p. vii)
FOLLOWING THE ORIGINAL AUTHOR'S INTENT AT THE PARA-GRAPH LEVEL

This is a study <u>guide</u> commentary which means that you are responsible for your own interpretation of the Bible. Each of us must walk in the light we have. You, the Bible and the Holy Spirit are priority in interpretation. You must not relinquish this to a commentator.

Read the chapter in one sitting. Identify the subjects. Compare your subject divisions with the five translations above.

---

*Although not inspired, paragraph divisions are the key in understanding and following the original author's intent. Each modern translation has divided and summarized chapter one. Obviously vv. 1-5, 6-10, 11-17, and 18-24 are units of thought (paragraphs). Every paragraph has one central topic, truth, or thought. Each version encapsulates that topic in its own distinct way. As you read the text, which translation fits your understanding of the subject and verse divisions?

Notice that TEV structures vv. 1-5 into three topics or subjects while the others have only one. Also notice how in vv. 6-10, that UBS⁴ and TEV make v. 10 a separate thought. The summary statements vary as well: UBS⁴, NKJV, and TEV characterize it as referring to "the gospel," but NRSV and JB understand the paragraph as a "warning" and relate it to the heresy.

In every chapter you must read the Bible first and try to identify its subjects (paragraphs). Then com - pare your understanding with the modern versions. Only when one understands the original author's intent by following his logic and presentation can one truly understand the Bible. Only the original author is inspired—readers have no right to change or modify the message. Bible readers do have the responsibility of applying the inspired truth to their day and their lives.

Note that all technical terms and abbreviations are explained fully in Appendices One, Two and Three.

Paragraphing is not inspired but it is the key to following the original author's intent which is the heart of interpretation. Every paragraph has one and only one subject.

1. First paragraph

2. Second paragraph

3. Third paragraph

4. Etc.

CONTEXTUAL INSIGHTS

A. Verses 1-5, basically the prologue to Galatians, form only one sentence in Greek.

B. Paul's usual note of thanksgiving is absent (cf. Rom., I and II Cor., Eph., Phil., Col., I and II Thes.) This reflects the tension between Paul and this group of churches.

C. Verses 6-10 establish the theological theme of the entire book. It could almost be said that these few verses contain all of the theological elements which are later developed.

D. Galatians 1:11-2:21 forms an autobiographical section where Paul defends his Apostleship and, by that, his gospel. This is very similar to II Corinthians 10-13.

E. Galatians 1:11-2:21 divides into the following areas:
   1. Paul was not dependent on the Apostles in Jerusalem, 1:11-24.
   2. Paul was recognized by the Church in Jerusalem, 2:1-10.
   3. An example of Paul's equality, 2:11-21.

F. The main body of this letter is contained in 1:11-6:10. It can be divided as follows:

1. Paul defends his Apostleship, 1:11-2:14.
2. Paul defends the doctrinal truths of his gospel, 2:15-4:20.
3. Paul defends the implication of his gospel, 5:1-6:10.

WORD AND PHRASE STUDY

> **NASB (UPDATED) TEXT: 1:1-5**
> **Paul, an apostle (not *sent* from men nor through the agency of man, but through Jesus Christ and God the Father, who raised Him from the dead), and all the brethren who are with me, to the churches of Galatia: Grace to you and peace from God our Father and the Lord Jesus Christ, who gave Himself for our sins so that He might rescue us from this present evil age, according to the will of our God and Father, to whom be the glory forevermore. Amen.**

1:1 "Paul," The Greek name *Paulos* meant "little." Several theories have been advanced about the origin of his Greek name: (1) the second century tradition that Paul was short, fat, bald, bow-legged, bushy eye-browed, and had protruding eyes is a possible source of the name, deriving from a non-canonical book from Thessalonica called *Paul and Thekla*; (2) passages where Paul calls himself the "the least of the saints" because he persecuted the Church as in Acts 9:1-2 (cf. I Cor. 15:9; Eph. 3:8; I Tim. 1:15). Some have seen this "leastness" as the origin of the self-chosen title. However, in a book like Galatians, where he emphasized his independence and equality with the Jerusalem Twelve, this is somewhat unlikely (cf. II Cor. 11:5; 12:11; 15:10).

❖ **"an apostle"** "Apostle" comes from the Greek word "to send." Jesus chose twelve of His disciples to be with Him in a special sense and called them "Apostles" (cf. Lk. 6:13). This term is often used of Jesus being sent from the Father (cf. Mt. 10:40; 15:24; Mk. 9:37; Lk. 9:48; Jn. 4:34; 5:24, 30, 36, 37, 38; 6:29, 38, 39, 40, 57; 7:29; 8:42; 10:36; 11:42; 17:3, 8, 18, 21, 23, 25; 20:21). In Jewish sources, an apostle was someone sent as an official representative of another, similar to "ambassador."

❖ **"sent"** As the Father sent Jesus, He sends us (cf. Jn. 17:18; 20:21). Because of its use in the synagogue to describe a rabbinical phrase that meant "one sent with official authority" it came to

NOTES

have this connotation. Paul asserted his apostleship in all of his letters except for Phil., I and II Thes. and Philem. This introductory paragraph was one of the strongest affirmations of his apostleship found in any of his letters, due to the situations in the churches where false teachers tried to refute his gospel by attacking him personally.

❖ NASB   "not *sent* from men, nor through the agency of man,"
    NKJV   "not from men nor through man,"
    NRSV   "sent neither by human commission nor from human authorities"
    TEV   "did not come from man or by means of man,"
    JB   "who does not owe his authority to men or his appointment to any human being"

This underscores one of Paul's major emphases, that his apostleship originated from a divine—not human—source. The false teachers may have alleged that Paul received his gospel from: (1) the Twelve in Jerusalem (cf. Acts 9:19-22); or (2) the Mother Church, but had subtly changed this gospel that he had been given. Paul defended himself in this regard because the gospel itself, not his credentials or reputation, was at stake (cf. II Cor. 10-13).

❖ **"but through Jesus Christ and God the Father"** Note Paul's bold assertion that he received his revelation and the content of the gospel from Jesus Himself (cf. 1:17). Although Paul did not fit the criteria of apostleship found in Acts 1:21-26, he believed he was called by the Lord to perform this specific task.

"Jesus" means YHWH saves (cf. Mt. 1:21). When this term is used alone in the NT, it emphasizes the humanity of Jesus. "Christ" is equivalent to the Hebrew term, *Messiah* or Anointed One, which emphasizes the OT promise of the uniquely called, divinely inspired, coming One to bring in the New Age of righteousness.

"Jesus Christ" and "God the Father" are linked by one preposition which is the NT author's way of asserting the full deity of Christ; this occurs both in v. 1 and v. 3.

God is Father, not in the sense of sexual generation or chronological precedence, but interpersonal relationship, as in a

Jewish home.

❖ **"who raised Him from the dead"** Paul emphasized that God the Father, who raised Jesus from the dead, is the one who gave him the gospel. Paul may have been saying he was called by the Risen Lord while the Twelve in Jerusalem were called by the still-human Lord, although this may be reading too much into the phrase. In most passages, it is God the Father who raised Jesus from the dead and thereby gives Him the divine stamp of approval on His ministry (cf. II Cor. 4:14; Acts 2:24; 3:15; 10:40; Rom. 6:4; I Pet. 1:21). In Rom. 8:17 it is the Spirit who raises Jesus from the dead. However, in Jn. 10:17-18, Jesus asserted that He laid down His own life, and took it up again. This shows the fluidity between the work of the persons of the Trinity.

1:2 "and all the brethren who are with me" It is unfortunate for modern Bible students that Paul did not name his companions, which would have confirmed one of the two theories concerning the recipients of the letter. The Northern Theory focuses on ethnic Galatia while the Southern Theory focuses on the Roman administrative province of Galatia. Paul did not mention whether it was Barnabas (first journey) or Timothy and Silas (second journey). The name "Barnabas" occurs three times in Galatians implying the first journey. Paul used "brethren" often in this letter (cf. 3:15; 4:12; 5:11; 6:18), possibly because his message to these churches was so pointed, stern, or even combative. Also, Paul often introduced new subjects by beginning with "brothers" which implies the first journey (referring to Timothy and Silas, not just one brother, Barnabas).

❖ **"to the churches of Galatia:"** Again, the exact location of these churches remains undetermined. Some assert that it is Northern Galatia (cf. I Pet. 1:1), and make the date of this epistle in the middle 50's AD. Acts 26:6 and 18:23 are interpreted as evidence that Paul preached in this area. Others interpret Galatia as the Roman province of Galatia, which encompassed a much larger area referred to in Acts 13 and 14—the first missionary journey of Paul and Barnabas. This would make the date in the late 40's AD, just before, but not identical with, the Jerusalem Council of Acts 15.

1:3 "Grace to you and peace" The normal Greek epistolary greeting was the word *charein*. Paul characteristically changed this to the similar sounding Christian term *charis*, or grace. Many have suggested Paul combined the Greek greeting of "grace" with the Hebrew greeting "peace" *[shalom]*. Although this is an attractive theory, it may be reading too much into this typically Pauline introductory phrase.

❖ **"the Lord"** The term "Lord" can be used in a general sense or in a developed theological sense. Alternative translations might include "Mister," "Sir," "Master," "Owner," "Husband," or "the full God-man." The OT usage of this term comes from the reluctance of the Jews to pronounce the covenant name for God, YHWH, which is the CAUSATIVE FORM of the Hebrew verb "to be" (cf. Ex. 3:14). They were afraid of breaking one of the Ten Commandments which said, "Thou shalt not take the name of the Lord Thy God in vain." Therefore, they thought if they did not pronounce it, they could not take it in vain. So, they substituted the Hebrew *adonai* [Lord] which has a similar meaning to the Greek *kurios* [Lord]. The NT authors used this term to describe the full deity of Christ. The phrase "Jesus is Lord" was the public confession of faith and baptismal formula of the early church (cf. Rom. 10:9-14).

1:4 This series of phrases illuminates three major aspects of Paul's gospel message. Paul expanded the introduction to show the centrality of the person and work of Jesus of Nazareth. The three aspects are: (1) His substitutionary death on our behalf (cf. Rom. 4:25; 5:6,8; I Cor. 15:3; II Cor. 5:14,21); (2) His introduction of the New Messianic Age—this is an AORIST MIDDLE VERBAL FORM which means "He, Himself, once and for all, plucked us out of this present evil age. "Wicked" is placed in an EMPHATIC POSITION which conveys the idea that "this is an evil, godless age" (cf. Jn. 12:31; II Cor. 4:4; Eph. 2:2-7). The concept of the two Jewish ages—a current evil age and the age to come which will be brought in by God's Messiah—can be seen in Mt. 12:32; 13:39; 28:20 and other passages in the NT. Although Jesus has ushered in the New Age, it has not yet been fully consummated; and (3) His mission was in obedience to the plan of God. He came to die (cf. Acts 2:22-23; 4:27-28; II Tim. 1:9; Mk. 10:45; Jn. 3:16; I Pet. 1:20 and Rev. 13:8).

1:5 "to whom *be* the glory forevermore. Amen" Typically Pauline,

NOTES

this doxology breaks into the context because of the majesty of the gospel. Often the pronouns in Paul's writings have ambiguous antecedents. Most of the time, in these occurrences, the MASCULINE SINGULAR PRONOUNS refer to God the Father.

NASB (UPDATED) TEXT: 1:6-10

I am amazed that you are so quickly deserting Him who called you by the grace of Christ, for a different gospel; which is *really* not another; only there are some who are disturbing you and want to distort the gospel of Christ. But even if we, or an angel from heaven, should preach to you a gospel contrary to what we have preached to you, he is to be accursed! As we have said before, so I say again now, if any man is preaching to you a gospel contrary to what you have received, he is to be accursed! For am I now seeking the favor of men, or of God? Or am I striving to please men? If I were still trying to please men, I would not be a bond-servant of Christ.

1:6 "I am amazed" Instead of a thanksgiving—so common in Pauline writings—Paul observed with astonishment that the Galatians had been too easily wooed away from the pure, simple, majestic gospel of justification by faith because of these false teachers.

❖ **"so quickly"** Two senses are possible: (1) so soon after they accepted the gospel that Paul preached, or (2) so soon after the false teachers came.

❖ **"deserting Him"** This verb is PRESENT TENSE, indicating the Galatians were in the process of turning away. "Turn away" is a military term for revolt. Note the emphasis is on the personal element of turning away from God Himself by rejecting Paul's gospel. "Turn away" can be a PRESENT PASSIVE VERBAL FORM but the larger context (cf. 3:1ff. and 5:7) implies a PRESENT MIDDLE FORM. This emphasizes that although the false teachers instigated the turning, the Galatians willingly participated in it.

❖ **"who called you by the grace of Christ"** The phrase "called you" usually refers to God the Father (cf. Rom. 8:30; 9:24; I Cor. 1:9). This is significant because of the textual problem with the addition of the phrase "of Christ." It is not found in the papyrus P[46],

15

but it is found in the papyrus P[51], and manuscripts ℵ, A, B, K and P. This may be an early addition to clarify that this Christian hymn refers to God the Father who calls us through Christ. It must be stated again: God always takes the initiative in our salvation (cf. Jn. 6:44,65).

❖ **"for a different gospel"** "Different" [*heteros*] is sometimes used in the sense of "another of a different kind," (cf. II Cor. 11:4). In verse 7 [*allos*] is also used; it can be translated "another of the same kind in a series." However, in Koine Greek these terms were becoming synonymous and a distinction should not be insisted upon too strongly. But, in context, Paul obviously used both for contrast.

1:7	NASB	"which is *really* not another;"
	NKJV	"which is not another;"
	NRSV	"not that there is another gospel,"
	TEV	"there is no 'other gospel,'"
	JB	"Not that there can be more than one Good News;"

There are not two gospels, though the one true gospel is often perverted. The KJV translation of 2:7 has been often interpreted as referring to two gospels, one for the pagans and one for the Jews. This is an unfortunate and untrue inference, although it may have been one of the charges of the false teachers.

❖	NASB	"only there are some who are disturbing you"
	NKJV	"but there are some who trouble you"
	NRSV	"but there are some who are confusing you"
	TEV	"there are some people who are upsetting you"
	JB	"it is merely that some troublemakers among you"

"Disturbing" refers to a purposeful action like a military revolt. "False teachers" is PLURAL in 5:12, but possibly only the leader of the false teachers is actually meant in 5:7 and twice in 5:10 because of the use of the SINGULAR. They are called "agitators" in 5:12. Many assume the Judaizers of Galatians are synonymous with the converted Pharisees or priests of Acts 15:1,5,24. They emphasized the necessity of becoming a Jew before one could become a Christian. The Judaizers' emphasis on the Jewish Law can be seen in: (1) the necessity of circumcision (cf. 2:3-4; 5:1; 6:12-15); (2) their keeping of special days (cf. 4:10); and (3) a possible inclusion of keeping the food laws which is implied in Paul's confrontation with Peter (cf. 2:11-14). This was probably the same group of false teachers mentioned in II Cor. 11:26 and II Thes. 2:14-16. Their problem was not that they depreciated the central place of Christ in salvation, but that they added to Christ's finished work.

❖	NASB	"and want to distort the gospel of Christ"
	NKJV, NRSV	"and want to pervert the gospel of Christ"
	TEV	"and trying to change the gospel of Christ"
	JB	"want to change the Good News of Christ"

"To distort" is an AORIST INFINITIVE meaning "to reverse," possibly another military term. Although the Christian life is a significant element of the gospel, it always follows salvation. It does not precede it as the Judaizers asserted (cf. Eph. 2:8-9 & 10). Paul's gospel was Christ, then Christlikeness; their gospel was works righteousness and then God's righteousness.

1:8 "but even if" This THIRD CLASS CONDITIONAL SENTENCE with an AORIST MIDDLE SUBJUNCTIVE shows a hypothetical situation (cf. II Cor. 11:3-4). Paul asserted that if he, or an angel from heaven, should preach a different gospel, they should be sent to Hell.

❖	NASB	"he is to be accursed!"
	NKJV	"let him be accursed"
	NRSV	"let that one be accursed"
	TEV	"may he be condemned to hell!"
	JB	"he is to be condemned."

"Curse" *[anathema]* (cf. Mt. 18:7; Rom. 9:3; I Cor. 12:3; 16:22) may reflect the Hebrew word *herem* which was employed in the sense of dedicating something to God. *Herem* developed a

NOTES

negative connotation from its use in the case of Jericho being dedicated to God for destruction (cf. Joshua 6-7). God's curse is a natural result of His people breaking a covenant (cf. Deut. 27:11-26). However, Paul specifically used this term to show the seriousness of the false teachers' gospel by consigning them to Hell.

Syntactically, verses 8 and 9 are a doublet. However, the THIRD CLASS CONDITION of verse 8 shows probable action while the FIRST CLASS CONDITION of verse 9 shows current, assumed action.

1:9 "a gospel contrary to that which you have received," The VERB "received" is a technical term in rabbinical writings connected with the Oral Tradition," indicating Paul was passing on a tradition (cf. I Cor. 15:3), but the context is emphatic that he did not receive his tradition from men.

It must be clarified that the central elements of Paul's gospel came from Jesus directly. He contemplated and developed them for several years before he went to visit the Mother Church and its leaders in Jerusalem (cf. Gal. 1:18; 2:1). But Paul also learned much about the words and actions of Jesus from those who knew Him in the flesh: (1) those he persecuted witnessed to him; (2) he saw and heard the defense of Stephen (cf. Acts 7:58); (3) Ananias witnessed to him (cf. Acts 9:10-19); (4) he visited with Peter for 15 days (cf. 1:18). Additionally, Paul also used many of the hymns of the early Church in his writings (cf. 1:4-5; I Cor. 15:3-4; Eph. 5:14; Phil. 2:6-11; Col. 1:15-20; Tit. 3:16); and mentioned Christian traditions several times (cf. I Cor. 11:2; II Thes. 3:6). Paul was speaking in very specific terms and in a guarded sense because of the accusations of the false teachers.

1:10 "For am I now seeking the favor of men, or of God?" This is a development and continuation of the theme which began in 1:1. Paul's strong words to the false teachers proved that he was not trying to please men which they had apparently alleged. Some see this text in light of Paul's statement that he became all things to all men (cf. I Cor. 9:19-23; Acts 21:17-26). This was being misinterpreted as: (1) compromising with pagan culture; and (2) his preaching two gospels, one for Jews and another easier one for pagans.

❖ **"If"** Verse 10 is a SECOND CLASS CONDITIONAL SENTENCE which expresses a statement "contrary to fact." Amplified,

19

the sentence would read: "If I were still trying to please men, which I am not, then I would not be a bond-servant of Christ, which I am."

❖ **"I were still trying to please men,"** There has been much discussion about the word "still." Some believe it means that he never appealed to men. Others believe it is a confession that he was a zealous Pharisee in his earlier days and that some of his actions were directed toward self-achievement.

❖ **"I would not be a bond-servant of Christ."** This is an allusion to Christ's teaching that one cannot serve two masters (cf. Mt. 6:24). "Slave" or "servant" when used by Paul may refer to: (1) Jesus as LORD and Paul as slave; or (2) an honorific title from the OT used of Moses, Joshua and David

---

NASB (UPDATED) TEXT: 1:11-17

For I would have you know, brethren, that the gospel which was preached by me is not according to man. For I neither received it from man, nor was I taught it, but *I received it* through a revelation of Jesus Christ. For you have heard of my former manner of life in Judaism, how I used to persecute the church of God beyond measure and tried to destroy it; and I was advancing in Judaism beyond many of my contemporaries among my countrymen, being more extremely zealous for my ancestral traditions. But when God, who had set me apart even from my mother's womb and called me through His grace, was pleased to reveal His Son in me so that I might preach Him among the Gentiles, I did not immediately consult with flesh and blood, nor did I go up to Jerusalem to those who were apostles before me; but I went away to Arabia, and returned once more to Damascus.

1:11	NASB	"For I would have you know, brethren"
	NKJV	"But I make known to you, brethren"
	NRSV	"For I want you to know, brothers and sisters"
	TEV	"Let me tell you, my brothers,"
	JB	"The fact is, brothers, and I want you to realize this,"

The KJV translates this as "I certify to you," a technical rendering of the phrase (cf. I Cor. 15:1).

1:11-12 "the gospel which was preached by me" This begins a phrase which repeats the twin disclaimers of 1:1. Paul claimed that his message does not have a human origin (cf. II Thes. 2:13; II Pet. 1:20-21). He further asserted that he did not receive it from any man, but that it was taught to him by a revelation from Jesus Christ (cf. Eph. 3:2-3). He stated this three times in verses 11-12!

1:12 "of Jesus Christ." This may be either SUBJECTIVE GENITIVE CASE (emphasizing Jesus as the agent of the revelation) or OBJECTIVE GENITIVE CASE (emphasizing Jesus as the content of the revelation).

1:13 "you have heard of my former manner of life in Judaism," It is not certain how these churches heard: (1) it was common knowledge; (2) Paul shared with them; or (3) the false teachers had alluded to his former conduct. "Judaism" seems to refer to Pharisaism. After the destruction of Jerusalem in A.D. 70 by the Roman general Titus, the Pharisaic party moved to the city of Jamnia. The Sadducean element was completely eliminated and Pharisaism developed into modern rabbinical Judaism. Paul mentioned something of his life as a zealous Pharisee in Phil. 3:4-6.

❖ | NASB | "how I used to persecute" |
NKJV	"how I persecuted"
NRSV	"I was violently persecuting"
TEV	"how I persecuted without mercy"
JB	"how much damage I did to it,"

This IMPERFECT TENSE verb is used in Acts 9:4, referring to his repeated activity described in Acts 8:1-3; 22:20; and 26:10. These are the same general contexts in which Paul shared his personal testimony three different times in the book of Acts.

❖ **"the church of God"** *Ekklesia is* from two Greek words, "out of" and "to call." This was used in Koine Greek to describe any kind of assembly, such as a town assembly (cf. Acts 19:32). The Church chose this term because it was used in the Septuagint, the Greek translation of the Old Testament, written as early as 250 B.C. for the library at Alexandria, Egypt. This term translated the Hebrew

NOTES

term *qahal* which was used of "the assembly of Israel" (cf. Num. 20:4). The NT writers asserted that they were the "divinely called out ones" who were to be the People of God in their day. They saw no radical break between the OT People of God and themselves, the NT People of God. We must assert that the Church of Jesus Christ is the true heir to the OT Scriptures, not modern rabbinical Judaism.

Note that Paul mentioned the local churches in 1:2 and the universal Church in 1:13. "Church" is used in three different ways in the NT: (1) house churches (cf. Rom. 16:5); (2) local or area churches (cf. 1:2; I Cor. 1:2); and (3) the whole body of Christ (1:13; Mt. 16:18).

❖ **"and tried to destroy it;"** This verb phrase is IMPERFECT TENSE, meaning repeated action in past time.

1:14 "I was advancing in Judaism beyond many of my contemporaries" This refers to Paul's fellow rabbinical students in Jerusalem. No one is more enthusiastic than a first-year theology student! The Jewish zeal for the Law (cf. Rom. 10:2ff.) is actually devotion and zeal without knowledge and truth.

❖ **"being more extremely zealous for my ancestral traditions"** Here is the use of the term "traditions" which was a technical term for "the Oral Tradition." The Jews believed that the Oral Tradition, like the written Old Testament, was given by God to Moses on Mt. Sinai. The Oral Tradition was meant to surround, protect, and interpret the written Old Testament. Later codified in the Babylonian and Palestinian Talmuds, it resulted in formalism and folklore instead of a vital faith relationship (cf. Isa. 29:13; Col. 2:16-23; II Tim. 3:1-5).

1:15	NASB	"But when God,"
	NKJV	"But when it pleased God,"
	NRSV	"But when God,"
	TEV	"But God,"
	JB	"Then God,"

Many reliable ancient manuscripts, instead of having the term "God," use the MASCULINE PRONOUN "he," (cf. manuscripts P[46] and B). *Theos* [God] does occur in manuscripts ℵ, A, and D. "He" was likely original and scribes later added *theos* to clarify

23

the ambiguous pronoun.

❖ **"who had set me apart** *even* **from my mother's womb and called me through His grace,"** Paul was alluding to the call of some OT prophets, particularly Jeremiah (cf. Jer. 1:4-5, or the Servant of YHWH, Isaiah 49:1,5). He asserted the divine aspect of his call to the ministry. This is another way of asserting that his authority and apostleship were not from men. The concept of being called by God is emphasized in Paul's personal testimony (cf. Acts 9:1-19; 22:1-16; and 26:9-18). Some of the strongest biblical passages on election can be found in Paul's writings (cf. Rom. 9 and Eph. 1:3-11).

1:16   **NASB, NKJV, JB**   **"to reveal His Son in me"**
          NRSV, TEV   **"to reveal his Son to me,"**
      "Unveil" *[apocalupsis]*, translated "revelation" in verse 12 typically means "a clear manifestation or unveiling." Apparently this occurred on the Damascus road.

      The phrase "in me" has been much debated. Some believe it means that God revealed Jesus to Paul while others think it means that God revealed Jesus through Paul. Both are true. The *Revised English Bible* translation combines both possibilities ("to reveal His Son in and through me").

❖ **"that I might preach about Him among the Gentiles,"** The phrase "in me" is paralleled by "in the Gentiles." God called Paul to call the heathen (cf. Acts 9:15; 22:15; 26:16-18; Gal. 2:9). We derive the English word "ethnic" from this Greek word for "Gentiles."

❖	NASB	"I did not immediately consult with flesh and blood,"
	NKJV	"I did not immediately confer with flesh and blood,"
	NRSV	"I did not confer with any human being,"
	TEV	"I did not go to anyone for advice,"
	JB	"I did not stop to discuss this with any human being,"

This seems to refer to Paul's private study time in Arabia (cf. verse 17). We are not sure how long he studied or how long he remained in Arabia. It was probably the Nabatean kingdom, which was very close to the city of Damascus, just to the southeast (cf. II Cor. 11:32). From verse 18 it seems that he could have stayed for as long as three years, but we are just not certain. Paul's basic purpose for mentioning this (it is omitted in the book of Acts) was to show that he did not receive his gospel from the Apostles in Jerusalem, nor was he officially sanctioned by the Church in Jerusalem, but <u>from</u> God and <u>by</u> God.

1:17 "to those who were apostles before me;" Paul certainly recognized the leadership of the original Twelve, but also asserted his equality to them.

NASB (UPDATED) TEXT: 1:18-24

Then three years later I went up to Jerusalem to become acquainted with Cephas, and stayed with him fifteen days. But I did not see any other of the apostles except James, the Lord's brother. (Now in what I am writing to you, I assure you before God that I am not lying.) Then I went into the regions of Syria and Cilicia. I was *still* unknown by sight to the churches of Judea which were in Christ; but only, they kept hearing, "He who once persecuted us is now preaching the faith which he once tried to destroy." And they were glorifying God because of me.

1:18 "Then three years later I went up to Jerusalem to become acquainted with Cephas," Paul freely admitted that he visited Jerusalem. The emphasis of this sentence is that Paul had no contact with Jerusalem or the Twelve until three years after his conversion. The book of Acts records five visits by Paul to Jerusalem, but Galatians only records two. It is very difficult to know which of the visits recorded in Acts are similarly recorded in the book of Galatians or if there were additional visits. Most people believe that this visit mentioned in verse 18 is equal to the visit recorded in Acts 9:26-30.

"Get acquainted with" is a Greek phrase from which we get our English word "history." Paul went for the specific purpose of learning from Peter the oral teachings of Jesus. Yet Paul did not stay with Peter the entire time (cf. Acts 9:28-30). He was preaching in the area and probably just spent the evenings and the Sabbath with him. This verse also emphasizes that he only stayed for fifteen days, which is much too short a stay for extended instruction.

NOTES

However, from I and II Pet., Peter may have learned more from Paul than Paul did from Peter.

1:19 "But I did not see any other of the apostles except James, the Lord's brother." This Greek sentence is very ambiguous. The context implies that James was an apostle, but this meaning is not certain. It could refer to Peter in verse 18. James seems to be an "apostle" in the same sense as Barnabas (cf. Acts 14:4, 14); Andronicus and Junius (cf. Rom. 16:7); Apollos (cf. II Cor. 4:9); Epaphroditus (Phil. 2:25); or Silvanas and Timothy (cf. I Thes. 2:6; Acts; 18:5). This James was identified as the Lord's half-brother (cf. Mt. 13:55; Mk. 6:3), in order to differentiate him from James the Apostle, part of the Inner Circle, who was killed very early (cf. Acts 12). For several generations the church in Jerusalem had a physical relative of Jesus as their leader. Several biblical passages (cf. Acts 12:17; 15:13; 21:18; I Cor. 15:7; and Jas. 1:1) indicate that James was a very important leader in the Church in Jerusalem.

1:20 "I assure you before God that I am not lying" Paul knew the seriousness of oath-taking and still felt that it was important to assert his truthfulness by God (cf. Rom. 9:1; I Tim. 2:7). Paul also employed God as a witness to his truthfulness elsewhere (cf. Rom. 1:9; II Cor. 1:23; 11:31; I Thes. 2:5, 10). Paul was certain of the divine origin and content of his message.

1:21 "Then I went into the regions of Syria and Cilicia." Syria and Cilicia were Roman provinces but the smaller province of Cilicia was not totally independent (cf. Acts 15:41). This may be the reason it was mentioned second, even though in chronology it is first, Paul's work was in Cilicia first, for it was the area in which Tarsus, his hometown, was located. This seems to be recorded in Acts 9:30. Paul's time in Syria is recorded in conjunction with Antioch which was located in the Roman province of Syria. This period is recorded in Acts 11:25-26.

1:22 "but I was *still* unknown by sight to the churches of Judea" The word "unknown" in Greek is reflected in the English cognate "agnostic." "Knowledge" [*gnosis*] in this case has the ALPHA PRIVITIVE which negates it. This is somewhat surprising because Paul was a famous persecutor of the Church; however, not all of the churches knew who he was, and he did not seek recognition from the churches of Palestine for his ministry.

1:23 Although Paul did not seek affirmation from these early Jewish Christian churches, they gave it to him when they heard about his ministry among the Gentiles. This is another point in his argument against the Jewish Christian false teachers who said that he did not have proper authority.

❖ **"the faith"** This term may have three distinct connotations: (1) its OT background means "trustworthiness;" therefore, it is used of our trusting in the trustworthiness of God; (2) in our accepting or receiving God's free offer of forgiveness in Christ; or (3) in the collective sense of the Christian faith or truth about Jesus (cf. Acts 6:7 and Jude 3 & 20). In several passages, such as II Thes. 3:2, determining which is meant is difficult.

DISCUSSION QUESTIONS FOR GALATIANS 1:1-24

This is a study guide commentary which means that you are responsible for your own interpretation of the Bible. Each of us must walk in the light we have. You, the Bible and the Holy Spirit are priority in interpretation. You must not relinquish this to a commentator.

These discussion questions are provided to help you think through the major issues of this section of the book. They are meant to be thought provoking, not definitive.

1. What is unique about Paul's opening remarks to the churches of Galatia?

2. List the three phrases which describe the person and work of Christ found in verse 4.

3. Why was Paul so appalled at the action of the Galatian churches?

4. Who were the false teachers and what was the basic content of their message?

5. What does the term "accursed" mean?

6. How does Paul prove that he is not a man-pleaser?

7. Why does Paul repeat the emphasis he made in 1:1 again in verses 11 and 12?

8. How were the false teachers using Paul's previous life against him?

9. Why did Paul go to Arabia?

10. Explain some of the possible charges that the false teachers were making against Paul and how he answered them in 1:10ff.

NOTES

GALATIANS 2

PARAGRAPH DIVISIONS OF MODERN TRANSLATIONS

UBS⁴	NKJV	NRSV	TEV	JB
Paul Accepted By Other Apostles	Defending the Gospel	Paul's Apostleship Recognized in Jerusalem	Paul's and the Other Apostles	The Meeting At Jerusalem
2:1-10	2:1-10	2:1-10	2:1-5 2:6-10	2:1-10
Paul Rebukes Peter at Antioch 2:11-21	No Return To the Law 2:11-21	Paul Rebukes Peter's Inconsistency at Antioch 2:11-14	Paul Argues with Peter 2:11-14	Peter and Paul at Antioch 2:11-13 2:14
		A Statement of Principle		The Good News As Proclaimed By Paul
		2:15-21	2:15-16 2:17-21	2:15-21

READING CYCLE THREE (see p. vii)
FOLLOWING THE ORIGINAL AUTHOR'S INTENT AT THE PARA-GRAPH LEVEL

This is a study <u>guide</u> commentary which means that you are responsible for your own interpretation of the Bible. Each of us must walk in the light we have. You, the Bible and the Holy Spirit are priority in interpretation. You must not relinquish this to a commentator.

Read the chapter in one sitting. Identify the subjects. Compare your subject divisions with the five translations above. Paragraphing is not inspired but it is the key to following the original author's intent which is the heart of interpretation. Every paragraph has one and only one subject.

1. First paragraph

2. Second paragraph

3. Third paragraph

4. Etc.

CONTEXTUAL INSIGHTS

A. This section continues the literary unit which began in
   1:10 and extends through 2:14.

B. In 2:15-21 a transition passage introduces the content of
   Paul's gospel, further elaborated in chapters 3 & 4. This is
   Paul's autobiographical defense of his apostleship and
   gospel as based on the revelatory will of God and not on
   any human tradition, even those traditions derived from
   the Twelve Apostles and the Jerusalem Church.

C. This passage is notoriously difficult to interpret for two
   reasons:
   1. The first section, verses 1-10, contains grammatical
      idiosyncrasies. Paul began a subject in verses 1 and 2,
      but in verses 3-10 he broke into this subject with a
      series of three parentheses and broken sentences.
      The subject of verses 1-2 resumes again in verses 6-10.
      Although this is difficult to graph grammatically, the
      overall meaning is clear.
   2. The next section, verses 11-21, is also difficult to
      interpret because the conclusion of Paul and Peter's
      discussion is uncertain. The NRSV, TEV, and JB
      restrict the quote to verse 14 while the NASB ends the
      quote at verse 21. Paul apparently concluded his
      address to Peter at verse 14 and a theological sum-
      mary relating to believing Jews and Judaizers' under-
      standing of the place of the Law begins in verse 15
      and goes through verse 21. Paul answered a series of
      questions, charges or misunderstandings about his
      gospel of God's free grace in verses 15-21. The ques-
      tions are not from Peter but from the Judaizers and
      their Pharisee backers. His response to these ques-
      tions will be expanded in chapters 3 and 4.

WORD AND PHRASE STUDY

NASB (UPDATED) TEXT: 2:1-10

Then after an interval of fourteen years I went up again to Jerusalem with Barnabas, taking Titus along also. It was because of a revelation that I went up; and I submitted to them the gospel which I preach among the Gentiles, but *I did so* in private to those who were of reputation, for fear that I might be running, or had run, in vain. But not even Titus, who was with me, though he was Greek, was compelled to be circumcised. But *it was* because of the false brethren secretly brought in, who had sneaked in to spy out our liberty which we have in Christ Jesus, in order to bring us into bondage. But we did not yield in subjection to them for even an hour, so that the truth of the gospel would remain with you. But from those who were of high reputation (what they were makes no difference; God shows no partiality)—well, those who were of reputation contributed nothing to me. But on the contrary, seeing that I had been entrusted with the gospel to the uncircumcised, just as Peter *had been* to the circumcised (for He who effectually worked for Peter in *his* apostleship to the circumcised effectually worked for me also to the Gentiles), and recognizing the grace that had been given to me, James and Cephas and John, who were reputed to be pillars, gave to me and Barnabas the right hand of fellowship, so that *we might go* to the Gentiles and they to the circumcised. *They* only *asked* us to remember the poor—the very thing I also was eager to do.

2:1 "after an interval of fourteen years" The fourteen year period has been the subject of much scholarly disagreement. This period of time may either relate to: (1) Paul's conversion (cf. 1:15-16); or (2) his first visit to Jerusalem (cf. 1:18). The time element is only significant to show how sporadic were his visits and contacts with the Apostles in Jerusalem.

❖ **"I went up again to Jerusalem"** "Again" implies the second or later visit of several. The exact time is uncertain, for in Acts five different visits by Paul to Jerusalem are recorded. The last two are too late to refer to this context, but which of the other three he meant is uncertain. I personally believe Galatians 2 relates to Acts 15 because in both cases Barnabas was present, the subject matter

NOTES

is the same, and Peter and James are both named. Beyond this author's speculation, other scholars such as the preeminent F.F. Bruce in the *New International Commentary Series* and Richard Longenecker in the *Word Biblical Commentary Series* believe that Gal. 2 relates to the famine visit recorded in Acts 11:30.

The phrase "went up to Jerusalem" is theological in nature. A converse reference occurs in Acts 11:27 when they went "down to Antioch." Jerusalem, because it is the holy city, is considered to be "up" from any direction.

❖ **"with Barnabas,"** Acts 4:6 provides the information that Barnabas was a Levite from Cyprus whose name was Joseph. The disciples nicknamed him Barnabas meaning "son of encouragement." He was the first one to accept Paul's conversion (cf. Acts 9:17). He was obviously a leader in the Jerusalem Church (cf. Acts 11:22) as was Silas (cf. Acts 15:22). He was the missionary companion of Paul on the first missionary journey (cf. I Cor. 9:6). He went to Tarsus and searched Saul out to get him to help with the work in Antioch (cf. Acts 11:19-27).

❖ **"taking Titus along also"** Titus was one of Paul's faithful helpers (cf. II Cor. 8:23). He used him in especially difficult places such as Corinth and Crete. He was a full Gentile, and not half-Gentile as Timothy. The Jerusalem church did not demand that Paul circumcise him (cf. Acts 15). Surprisingly, Titus is never mentioned by name in Acts. Sir William Ramsay and A.T. Robertson speculate that Titus was Luke's brother, explaining the absence of any specific mention of him, but this is unsubstantiated. Martin Luther speculated that Paul took Titus with him to Jerusalem as a test case. Others say that he took Titus along, but only later did he realize the significance of the Jerusalem Church's failure to demand that Titus be circumcised because he was a pure Greek (cf. v. 3).

2:2 "It was because of a revelation that I went up;" If one assumes that Acts 15 is the setting, Acts 15:2 produces a discrepancy. However, it has been supposed that the revelation came from one of the five prophets at Antioch who conveyed it to the church. Then the church at Antioch passed on the need to visit Jerusalem to Paul.

❖ **"and I submitted to them the gospel which I preach among the**

Gentiles" This is very significant in its relationship to verses 3-5. Why did Paul lay his gospel before the Apostles? (1) Did he want them to agree with him and affirm his gospel? (2) Or was he reacting to the presence of false teachers? The latter possibility best fits the parenthetical aside of verses 4 and 5.

❖ NASB   "but I *did* so in private to those who were of reputation,"
   NKJV   "but privately to those who were of reputation,"
   NRSV   "(though only in a private meeting with the acknowledged leaders)"
   TEV   "In a private meeting with the leaders,"
   JB   "and privately I laid before the leading men"

Reading Acts 15 to find a private meeting first poses a difficulty. However, Acts 15:2b and verse 6 could refer to a meeting of the top leadership. Paul may have met with the leadership first for the purpose of getting a better hearing instead of meeting with the whole congregation which may have been previously infiltrated with Judaizers (those who demanded that one had to be a Jew before one could be saved).

Some scholars have suggested in recent years, probably due to the overemphasis of the Tübingen theologians from Germany, that tension existed between Paul and the Apostles in Jerusalem. Some assert that Paul's three unusual phrases referring to the Jerusalem leaders found in 2:2, 6 (twice), and 9 are somewhat disparaging. These phrases may be viewed pejoratively with three points in mind. (1) They underscore the false teachers' overemphases made by the original Twelve Apostles in their attempt to depreciate Paul, not that Paul had any personal tension with the Twelve. (2) Possibly Paul was disappointed with some of the Apostles' actions as in Acts 8:1 where they did not really grasp the worldwide mission of the Church, or in Peter's tactless withdrawal from the fellowship table with Gentiles in Gal. 2:11-14. (3) These phrases may refer not to the Apostles but to other church leaders, or they refer to only some of the Apostles.

❖ NASB, TEV   "for fear that I might be running, or had run, in vain"

NKJV	"lest by any means I might run, or had run, in vain"
NRSV	"in order to make sure that I was not running, or had not run, in vain"
JB	"for fear the course I was adopting or had already adopted would not be allowed."

This obviously does not refer to Paul seeking theological affirmation from the Jerusalem leaders for this would go against the entire context. But here, the practicality of the mission effort among the Gentiles was at stake and Paul hoped and prayed for the consensus which he would subsequently receive. Paul expressed similar fears elsewhere (cf. I Cor. 15:58 and Phil. 2:16).

2:3 "But not even Titus who was with me, though he was a Greek, was compelled to be circumcised." Even with its straightforward meaning, questions arise regarding: (1) a manuscript variation in verse 5 where the word "not" is omitted in the western family of manuscripts, particularly manuscript D; and (2) the ambiguity of verse 4 which has caused some to say that Paul did circumcise Titus, not out of compulsion but to show his freedom. However, this undermines the entire structure of Paul's argument. Paul was already under attack, apparently for circumcising Timothy (cf. Acts 16:3), who was half-Jewish, but he would not, for a minute, yield to the circumcision of Titus. In reality the issue was not really circumcision (cf. Rom. 2:28-29 and Gal. 6:15), but how a man becomes right with God. In Galatians, Paul contrasted the works-oriented way of the Jews and Judaizers and the grace-oriented way of the gospel of Jesus.

2:4	NASB	"But *it was* because of the false brethren...who had sneaked in"
	NKJV	"but *this occurred* because of false brethren secretly brought in"
	NRSV	"But because of false believers secretly brought in"
	TEV	"had pretended to be brothers and joined the group,"
	JB	"The question came up only because some who do not really belong to the brotherhood have furtively crept in"

These false brothers are mentioned in other places (cf.

NOTES

Acts 15:1,5; II Cor. 11:13 and I Thes. 2:14-16). The verbal form is PASSIVE, implying that they were smuggled in by someone. The false brothers were possibly: (1) unbelieving Jews, (2) a sect of believing Jews called Judaizers, or (3) Satan himself. "False teachers" is also used in II Pet. 2:1. The term's usage in Koine Greek commonly designated traitors within a city who allowed the enemy to sneak into the city and survey its defenses. Another problem in interpretation concerns the locale of the treachery. Did the false brothers sneak into: (1) the Church at Jerusalem, (2) the Jerusalem Council, or (3) the Church at Antioch? On these minutiae of interpretation, certainty is impossible and, therefore, dogmatism is unwarranted.

❖ **"to spy out our liberty which we have in Christ Jesus, in order to bring us into bondage"** Paul's emphasis on freedom in Christ was paramount (cf. Acts 13:39; Gal. 5:1,13). In this context, freedom from Jewish rules and regulations is meant, a concept expanded in the following chapters. It is important to note that we are truly free in Christ, but our freedom is not intended as a license for sin (cf. Rom. 14 and I Cor. 8-10). This dialectical tension between freedom and responsibility, inherent in the gospel, is illustrated in Paul's emphases on responsibility to the church at Corinth and on freedom to the churches of Galatia. Both are true!

2:5 "But we did not yield in subjection to them for even an hour," "We" must refer to Paul and Barnabas. They were agreed in their opposition to the requirement that all Gentiles be circumcised after their conversion.

"Not" is present in manuscripts P⁴⁶, ℵ, B, C, D, and G. It is missing only in Codex D. The reason that Paul emphasizes submission to each other in Eph. 5:21 and yet staunchly stands against submission in this case is because he believes that these "false brothers" are not really Christian. Paul asserts his belief that those who base their right standing with God upon their own effort are not true Christians (cf. Gal. 1:8,9; 5:2-12; Rom. 10:2-5; and I Thes. 2:14-16). The question, then, is "on whom do they base their trust: themselves or Christ?"

❖ **"so that the truth of the gospel might remain with you"** No small matter, this argument was the basis for continuing the Gentile mission.

2:6	NASB	"But from those who were of high reputation"
	NKJV	"But from those who seemed to be something—whatever they were,"
	NRSV	"And from those who were supposed to be acknowledged leaders"
	TEV	"But those who seemed to be the leaders"
	JB	"these people who are acknowledged leaders"

This phrase can either refer to: (1) some of the Twelve; or (2) certain leaders in the Jerusalem church. Paul's point was that their opposition does not affect his God-given call, assignment and gospel. However, F.F. Bruce quotes Josephus in *War of the Jews*, 3:453; 4:141,159 to illustrate that "seemed" is not always used derogatorily.

❖ **"God shows no partiality"** This metaphor means literally "to lift the face" (cf. Acts 10:34). Paul was alluding to the contemporary practice of making judicial decisions based on favoritism, and repudiated this as a characteristic of divine justice. "God is no respecter of persons." Intended was either: (1) some of the original Twelve; or (2) the other leaders in the Jerusalem church who opposed Paul's divinely given gospel; or (3) Paul.

❖	NASB, NRSV	"contributed nothing to me."
	NKJV	"added nothing to me."
	TEV	"made no new suggestions to me."
	JB	"had nothing to add to the Good News as I preach it"

Here is Paul's central affirmation of independence, both for himself and for his gospel, from the authority of the Twelve or the Mother Church in Jerusalem. This is not a debasement of the Twelve or the leaders of the Jerusalem Church but an emphasis on the divine nature of Paul's call and revelation.

2:7 "But on the contrary, seeing that I had been entrusted with the gospel to the uncircumcised," A major Pauline point, he continued to build on the context begun in 1:10. When the Jerusalem leaders saw and heard Paul, they affirmed that God had called and chosen him. "Their" refers to the Apostles mentioned in verse 9. "I had been entrusted" is a PERFECT PASSIVE VERBAL FORM, emphasizing Paul's continuing role as a steward of the gospel by means of God's call and equipping through the Spirit (cf. I Cor. 9:17; I Thes. 2:4,17; I Tim. 1:11). Other passages further support Paul's call to be an Apostle to the Gentiles (cf. Acts 9:15; and Gal. 1:16).

❖ **"just as Peter"** The use of the term "Peter" in verses 7 and 8 is somewhat unusual in Galatians. In all of the other citations where Peter is named, he is called "Cephas," Aramaic for "rock," (cf. 1:18; 2:9,11,14). However, "Peter" does seem to be original here, and the two names are synonymous.

2:8 Another parenthesis inside the complex grammatical structure of verses 1-10, it may refer to either geography or an ethnic community.

2:9 "and recognizing the grace that had been given to me, James, Cephas, and John, who were reputed to be pillars, gave to me and Barnabas the right hand of fellowship," The "pillars" were the three leaders of the Christian church in Jerusalem. This title was used in connection with "the Apostles" by Clement of Rome and Ignatius. It is also used positively in Rev. 3:12. Possibly the phrase originated in the Jews' use of the term to describe Abraham and Moses. Paul again supported his claim that not only was he independent, but that at least some of the Apostles recognized his God-given authority and affirmed him with the right hand of fellowship. This "James" is not one of the Twelve but Jesus' half-brother and the leader of the Jerusalem church (cf. Acts 15).

2:10 "*They* only *asked* us to remember the poor" Paul was first introduced to the concept of a special offering for the poor in Jerusalem by the church at Antioch (cf. Acts 11:27-30). He developed this into a regular initial procedure with the Gentile churches (cf. I Cor. 16:1-2; II Cor. 8,9; and Rom. 15:25-27). If Gal. 2 parallels Acts 15, explaining why the other stipulations of Acts 15:23-29 are not mentioned becomes more difficult. Therefore many have seen this verse as an argument for making this visit contemporary with Acts 11:27-30.

NOTES

But when Cephas came to Antioch, I opposed him to his face, because he stood condemned. For prior to the coming of certain men from James, he used to eat with the Gentiles; but when they came, he *began* to withdraw and hold himself aloof, fearing the party of the circumcision. The rest of the Jews joined him in hypocrisy, with the result that even Barnabas was carried away by their hypocrisy. But when I saw that they were not straightforward about the truth of the gospel, I said to Cephas in the presence of all, "If you, being a Jew, live like the Gentiles and not like the Jews, how is it that you compel the Gentiles to live like Jews? We *are* Jews by nature and not sinners from among the Gentiles; nevertheless knowing that a man is not justified by the works of the Law but through faith in Christ Jesus, even we have believed in Christ Jesus, so that we may be justified by faith in Christ and not by the works of the Law; since by the works of the Law no flesh will be justified. But if, while seeking to be justified in Christ, we ourselves have also been found sinners, is Christ then a minister of sin? May it never be! For if I rebuild what I have *once* destroyed, I prove myself to be a transgressor. For through the Law I died to the Law, so that I might live to God. I have been crucified with Christ; and it is no longer I who live, but Christ lives in me; and the *life* which I now live in the flesh is by the Son of God, who loved me and gave Himself up for me. I do not nullify the grace of God, for if righteousness *comes* through the Law, then Christ died needlessly.

2:11 "But when Cephas came to Antioch" The time of Peter's visit to Antioch is unknown. Some place the visit immediately after the Jerusalem Council; some place it before. Apparently the mention of this visit is out of chronological order. It could have followed the Council meeting of Acts 15 highlighting the fact that all of the practical problems were not completely solved. However, it is difficult to imagine Peter acting like this after affirming Paul and his gospel at the Council (cf. 2:9; Acts 15:6-11), another argument for those who think it refers to the Acts 11 vision.

❖ **"I opposed him to his face"** Paul again asserted his independence from and equality with the Jerusalem Apostles.

❖   **NASB**   **"because he stood condemned."**

NKJV	"because he was to be blamed;"
NRSV	"because he stood self-condemned,"
TEV	"because he was clearly wrong."
JB	"since he was manifestly in the wrong."

This PARAPHRASTIC PLUPERFECT PASSIVE VERB speaks of something that had already happened, that had become a settled position and had been performed by the outside agent. This construction does not imply that Peter continued in this attitude. Also notice that the leader of the Apostolic group made a mistake. The Apostles were inspired to write trustworthy and eternal Scripture but this never implied that they did not have sin or did not make poor choices in other areas!

2:12 "For prior to the coming of certain men from James," The "certain men" were probably members of the Church in Jerusalem, but whether they had official authority or not is uncertain. Clearly they were not James' henchmen or spies, for James agreed completely with Paul's position concerning Gentile Christianity (cf. Acts 15:13-21). Perhaps they had exceeded their authority. They were possibly there to check on the implementations of the Council's stipulations (cf. Acts 15:20-21). They caught Peter, a believing Jew, in table fellowship with Gentile believers in direct contravention of Mosaic Law. Peter had answered these very charges earlier (cf. Acts 11:1-18). This issue was not minor even during Jesus' life (cf. Mt. 9:11; 11:19; Lk. 19:1-10; 15:2; Acts 15:28-29).

❖ **"he *began* to withdraw and hold himself aloof, fearing the party of the circumcision."** Three IMPERFECT TENSE verbs occur in verse 12. The first states that Peter ate regularly with the Gentile believers. The second and third stress that when the delegation from the Jerusalem Church arrived Peter began to reduce his social contact with the Gentile believers. This was not over the single issue of circumcision but rather the general relationship of the Mosaic Law to the new Gentile believers.

2:13 "The rest of the Jews joined him in hypocrisy, with the result that even Barnabas was carried away by their hypocrisy." The deadly tentacles of the Judaizers's corrupting influence reached even the most faithful. Paul was clearly disappointed by the actions of Barnabas. Barnabas had preached to Gentiles and stood up for the free gospel in Acts 15. The problem here was not the freedom of Gentile believers from the requirements of the Mosaic Law, but rather the implications of this freedom for the Jewish believers. Were Peter and Barnabas also free to reject the Mosaic Law?

2:14 "I said to Cephas in the presence of all," Usually church problems need to be dealt with privately, but the actions of Peter hit at the heart of the gospel. The conflict had affected the entire church at Antioch and had to be addressed publicly and decisively in order to resolve the church's disunity (cf. I Tim. 5:20).

❖ **"If you, being a Jew"** This FIRST CLASS CONDITIONAL SENTENCE (assumed to be true from the author's perspective or for his literary purposes) is the beginning of Paul's discussion with Peter. Gal. 2:15-21 is probably a theological summary and not necessarily Paul's exact words to Peter. Paul's public confrontation of Peter over his hypocrisy and inconsistency further proved Paul's independence.

2:15 "We *are* Jews by nature" Obviously, the Jews had some spiritual advantages (cf. Rom. 3:1,2; 9:4,5). But their advantages did not relate to salvation but to revelation and fellowship with God through the Old Covenant as the People of God. Thus, the heart of Paul's gospel to the Gentiles was the equality of Jews and Gentiles before God (cf. Eph. 2:11-3:13).

❖ **"and not sinners from among the Gentiles"** Paul was apparently using a derogatory phrase which was common in rabbinical Judaism and was possibly used by the false teachers.

2:16 "that a man is not justified by the works of the Law but through faith in Christ Jesus" This verse contains a threefold emphasis concerning the doctrine that justification by faith alone is for every human, beginning with the phrase "a man," then to "we" and concluding with "no man." This threefold repetition is overwhelming in its impact. The truth of justification by faith for all men is the essence of Paul's definitive statements in Rom. 1-8, summarized in Rom. 3:21-31. "Justification" was a legal term meaning "to be declared righteous."

"Righteous" denotes the OT concept of a measuring reed. YHWH used this metaphor for His own character and moral stan-

NOTES

dards. God is the standard of spiritual measurement (cf. Mt. 5:48). In the NT God gives us: (1) His own righteousness through the death of Christ (cf. II Cor. 5:21), and (2) repentance and faith on man's part (cf. Mk. 1:15 and Acts 20:21).

Justification by faith—presented in verses 16 and 17 as our position in Christ—is based entirely on God's initiating love and Christ's finished work. However, the emphasis on our Christlike living is fully stated in verse 21 where our position must result in living a Christlike life (cf. Rom. 8:29; Gal. 4:19). Paul did not deny that good works were significant. He just denied that they were the grounds of our acceptance. Eph. 2:8-10 shows Paul's gospel clearly—God's initiating grace, through man's faith response, unto good works. Gal. 2:20 emphasizes our sanctification, but in context, proves the validity and pervasiveness of the doctrine of the imputed righteousness of Jesus, totally apart from human merit or lifestyle.

❖	NASB, NKJV	**"even we have believed in Christ Jesus,"**
	NRSV	**"And we have come to believe in Christ Jesus,"**
	TEV	**"We, too, have believed in Christ Jesus"**
	JB	**"we had to become believers in Christ Jesus"**

The Greek term *pistis* may be translated in English as "trust," "believe," or "faith." This term conveys two distinct aspects of our relationship with God: (1) we put our trust in the trustworthiness of God's promises and Jesus' actions; and (2) we believe the message about God, man, sin, Christ, salvation, etc. Hence, it can refer to the message of the gospel or our trust in the gospel.

❖ **"the Law" (twice)** The NASB, NKJV, NRSV, TEV, and JB translations all have the DEFINITE ARTICLE twice. The DEFINITE ARTICLE does not appear in the Greek text but it is assumed because of Paul's continuing use of this phrase for the Mosaic Law. Although he had this primarily in mind, any other human effort serving as a supposed basis for our right standing with God could be implied here.

2:17 "if" "If" introduces a FIRST CLASS CONDITIONAL SENTENCE, assumed to be true from the author's perspective or for his literary purposes. Paul and his companions are assumed to be sinners.

❖ **"we ourselves have also been found sinners"** This phrase proves difficult to interpret. Several possible theories have been advanced: (1) most relate it to Rom. 3:23 and say "We, like the heathen, are all in need of God's righteousness because we all have sinned;" (2) some relate this phrase to the antinomian question of Rom. 6-8, that if one is saved apart from human effort, why does God judge us in relation to our sin?; (3) this phrase may set the stage for Paul's discussion of the Law in chap. 3 where to break it once, in any area, removes the possibility of being right with God through keeping the Law. The believing Jews, Peter, Paul, and Barnabas had broken the Law by eating forbidden food. This view would relate verse 17 to the immediate context denying an untrue conclusion which has been based on a valid premise; or (4) Paul was referring to Jews and Gentiles being one in Christ. If this is not God's will, this unity would make the Jewish believers sinners and Christ a party to their sin (cf. Eph. 2:11-3:6).

❖		
NASB	"is Christ then a minister of sin? May it never be!"	
NRSV	"is Christ then a servant of sin?"	
NKJV	"is Christ therefore a minister of sin? Certainly not!"	
TEV	"does this mean that Christ has served the interest of sin? By no means!"	
JB	"it would follow that Christ had induced us to sin, which would be absurd."	

Paul's argument continued, though difficult to follow. That he was responding to the charges or the teachings of the false teachers is obvious, but the exact issue to which this relates remains uncertain.

Paul's other usages of the phrase "may it never be" or "God forbid" are important in interpreting this passage (cf. Gal. 3:21; Rom. 6:2). Usually Paul used this rare OPTATIVE structure to deny an untrue conclusion based on a valid premise.

2:18 "For if I rebuild what I have once destroyed, I prove myself

to be a transgressor." Scholars are unsure of Paul's exact reference here. Was it his preaching of the gospel or his previous life in Judaism? This same ambiguity is found in Rom. 7. "Rebuild" and "destroy" may be rabbinical terms similar to "bind" and "loose" of Mt. 16:19.

2:19 "For through the Law I died to the Law," This significant statement is not so much mystical in its focus as it is legal. Somehow when Jesus died on our behalf, we died with Him (cf. II Cor. 5:14-15). Therefore, our mandatory relationship to the Law, as far as salvation is concerned, was broken. We are able to come to Christ freely. This is the focus in verses 20 and 21, similar to Paul's developed argument in Rom. 6:1-7:6.

❖ **"so that I may live to God."** Again, the twin theological aspects of our position in Christ and our lifestyle for Christ is made. This paradoxical truth can be stated in several ways: (1) the indicative and the imperative; (2) the objective and subjective; or (3) "we have won" but now "we must run." This is the dual nature of the gospel—salvation is absolutely free, but it costs us everything that we are and have! It must be reiterated that the free gift comes before the call to Christlikeness. We died to sin that we might serve God (cf. Rom. 6:10).

2:20 "I have been crucified with Christ;" In the Greek sentence, "with Christ" is placed first for emphasis. A PERFECT PASSIVE VERBAL FORM, the verb implies that something happened in the past with abiding results and was accomplished by an outside agent. It is the focus of Rom. 6:1-11 and 7:1-6.

Paul used the term "crucified" in Gal. 5:24 and 6:4, which relate to our relationship with this fallen world system. However, the emphasis here seemed to be our connection to the Law. It is important to remember that once we have died with Christ, we are alive to God (cf. v. 19; Rom. 6:10). This concept is emphasized over and over again as our responsibility to walk as He walked (cf. I Jn. 1:7), and that we ought to walk worthy of the calling wherewith we have been called (cf. Eph. 4:1; 5:2). Once we know Christ in free forgiveness it is important that we live a life of responsible servanthood (cf. Col. 2:12-14, 20; 3:1-4; and II Cor. 5:14-15).

❖ **"but Christ lives in me;"** Jesus is often said to indwell believers

NOTES

(cf. Mt. 28:20; Rom. 8:10; Col. 1:27). This is the ministry of "the other Jesus," the Holy Spirit. The work of the Spirit is to magnify and reproduce the Son in believers (cf. Jn. 16:7-15; Rom. 8:28-29; Gal. 4:19).

❖ **"I live by faith"** As we have seen earlier, the Greek term *pistis* can be translated "trust," "believe," or "faith," primarily emphasizing our trust in God's trustworthiness or our faith in God's faithfulness. This faith is our initial response to God's promises, followed by a continuing walk in those promises. "Faith" may be used in two senses: (1) personal trust; or (2) a reference to the body of Christian doctrine, such as in Jude 3 and 20.

❖ **"who loved me and delivered Himself up for me."** This is the heart of the substitutionary atonement (cf. Gal. 1:4; Mk. 10:45; Rom. 5:6,8,10; Isa. 53:4-6).

2:21 "if" This introduces another FIRST CLASS CONDITIONAL SENTENCE which is assumed to be true from the author's perspective or for his literary purposes. There is only one way to God—not through Law, but through faith in the finished work of Christ (cf. 3:21). If the Law could have brought salvation, then Christ did not need to die!

DISCUSSION QUESTIONS

This is a study guide commentary which means that you are responsible for your own interpretation of the Bible. Each of us must walk in the light we have. You, the Bible and the Holy Spirit are priority in interpretation. You must not relinquish this to a commentator.

These discussion questions are provided to help you think through the major issues of this section of the book. They are meant to be thought provoking, not definitive.

1. Why is it so difficult to interpret this chapter?

2. Does Paul speak disparagingly of the Jerusalem Apostles in verses 2, 6 and 9?

3. Why was the situation concerning Titus such an important issue in connection with the Jerusalem Council?

4. Who were the false teachers? What did they infiltrate? What was their purpose?

5. Why was Peter's refusal to eat with the Gentiles so condemning in light of Paul's understanding of the gospel?

6. Define the word "justification."

7. Define the word "faith."

8. How are verses 19 and 20 related to their context?

GALATIANS 3

PARAGRAPH DIVISIONS OF MODERN TRANSLATIONS

UBS⁴	NKJV	NRSV	TEV	JB
Law or Faith 3:1-6	Justification by Faith 3:1-9	An Appeal to Experience 3:1-5	Law or Faith 3:1-5	Justification by Faith 3:1-5
		An Appeal to Abraham's Experience in Scripture 3:6-9	3:6-9	3:6-9
3:7-14	The Law Brings a Curse 3:10-14	3:10-14	3:10-12 3:13-14	The Curse Brought by the Law 3:10-14
The Law and the Promise 3:15-20	The Changeless Promise 3:15-18	An Example from the Covenant with Abraham 3:15-18	The Law and the Promise 3:15-18	The Law did not Cancel the Promise 3:15-18
	Sons and Heirs	The True Purpose of the Mosaic Law 3:19-20	3:19-20	The Purpose of the Law 3:19-22
Slaves and Sons (3:21-4:7) 3:21-22 3:23-25		3:21-22 3:23-26	The Purpose of the Law (3:21-4:7) 3:21-22 3:23-25	The Coming of Faith 3:23-29
3:26-4:7	3:26-4:7	An Appeal to Baptismal Equality 3:27-29	3:26-29	

READING CYCLE THREE (see p. vii)
FOLLOWING THE ORIGINAL AUTHOR'S INTENT AT THE PARA-GRAPH LEVEL

This is a study <u>guide</u> commentary which means that you are responsible for your own interpretation of the Bible. Each of us must walk in the light we have. You, the Bible and the Holy Spirit are priority in interpretation. You must not relinquish this to a commentator.

Read the chapter in one sitting. Identify the subjects. Compare your subject divisions with the five translations above. Paragraphing is not inspired but it is the key to following the original author's intent which is the heart of interpretation. Every paragraph has one and only one subject.

53

1. First paragraph

2. Second paragraph

3. Third paragraph

4. Etc.

CONTEXTUAL INSIGHTS

A. Chapter 3 continues the literary unit begun in 2:15-21. In chapters 3 and 4 Paul developed the theological aspects of his gospel. Apparently, the Judaizers attacked him personally as a means of attacking his preaching.

B. The structure of chapter 3 is easily discernible.
   1. In verses 1-5 Paul appealed to the personal salvation experiences of the Galatians. He used his personal testimony as evidence of the truth of his gospel in 1:10-2:21, but then he used their experiences. He does this with four or five questions.
   2. In verses 6-18 Paul develops the Old Testament experience of Abraham as a paradigm for the experience of all men in the area of salvation. He particularly focuses on Abraham receiving justification by faith before and apart from the Mosaic Law.

C. Paul quoted the Old Testament five times in verses 6-18. The possible reasons for the extensive use of the OT was:
   1. Paul wanted the Judaizers and Galatians to see that his gospel was based on the OT also.
   2. The Judaizers used the OT in their argument, therefore, Paul did also.

D. Because of Paul's vehement attack on the misinterpretation and application of the Law by the Judaizers, he states the purpose of the Mosaic legislation (verses 19-29). He accomplished this with two questions (vv. 19 and 21). It must be asserted that Paul was using the term "law" here in a very specific manner. Paul was refuting the theology of the false teachers, i.e. that the Law is a means of salvation (cf. Rom. 4:14). One must balance this view of the Law with Jesus' use of the term in Matthew 5:17-21. The Law is good—the Law is from God! The Law is eternal (cf. Rom. 7:7,12-14).

E. The Mosaic Law is personified by four Greek terms (cf. 3:23-25; 4:1) used in the Greco-Roman world:
1. v. 23, "we were locked up under the law" - the law as jailor
2. v. 24, "the law has been our attendant" - the law as a child's custodian
3. v. 4:2, "guardians" - a child's custodian from birth through 14 years of age
4. v. 4:2, "trustee" - a child's custodian from age 14 to 25 years of age

WORD AND PHRASE STUDY

NASB (UPDATED) TEXT: 3:1-5

You foolish Galatians, who has bewitched you, before whose eyes Jesus Christ was publicly portrayed as crucified? This is the only thing I want to find out from you: did you receive the Spirit by the works of the Law, or by hearing with faith? Are you so foolish? Having begun by the Spirit, are you now being perfected by the flesh? Did you suffer so many things in vain—if indeed it was in vain? So then, does He who provides you with the Spirit and works miracles among you, do it by the works of the Law, or by hearing with faith?

3:1, 3 NASB, NKJV, NRSV, TEV   "You foolish Galatians,"
JB   "are you people in Galatia mad?"
"Mind" or "thought" [*nous or noema*] with the ALPHA PRIVITIVE is translated "senseless." Paul posited that they had not clearly thought through the implications of the Judaizers' false teachings.

❖ **"who has bewitched you,"** The use of the SINGULAR PRONOUN "who" may be a method of pointing out one primary false teacher to whom Paul was referring (cf. 5:7,10). But this may be reading too much into this context since the plural is used in 5:12.

NOTES

"Bewitched" is likely a metaphor for mental confusion, though others place it in an OT context as "the evil eye," (cf. Deut. 15:9; 28:54; Prov. 23:6; 28:22; Mt. 20:15; Mk. 7:22).

❖ **"before whose eyes Jesus Christ was portrayed"** The Egyptian Papyri have shown that "pictured" meant: (1) to "vividly portray," or (2) an official legal notice posted publicly. This metaphor was used of Paul's clear teaching and preaching of the person and work of Jesus Christ. Evidently, the Galatian churches were turning from Paul's teaching to Jewish legalism.

❖ **"as crucified"** "Crucified" is a PERFECT PASSIVE PARTICIPLE (cf. I Cor. 1:23; 2:2) implying that Jesus remains the crucified One. When we see Him, He will still have the marks of His crucifixion.

3:2 "did you receive the Spirit...?" Receiving the Spirit is not a secondary act of grace; it occurs when one becomes a Christian (cf. Rom. 3:14; 8:9). The Spirit here is seen as a sign of the New Age spoken of in Jeremiah 31:31-34. Beyond this point in Galatians, Paul mentioned the Holy Spirit sixteen times.

❖	NASB	"by the works of the Law, or by hearing with faith?"
	NKJV	"by the works of the law, or by the hearing of faith?"
	NRSV	"by doing the works of the law or by believing what you heard?"
	TEV	"by doing what the Law requires, or by hearing and believing the gospel?"
	JB	"was it because you practiced the Law that you received the Spirit, or because you believed what was preached to you?"

"Faith" [*pistis*] is used repeatedly in this chapter and may be interpreted or translated in English as "faith," "trust," or "believe." The concepts of believing and trusting are very similar (cf. 2:26; 3:2, 6, 7, 8, 9, 11, 12, 14, 22, and 26). In this context with the definite article, this term refers to the body of Christian truth (cf. 1:23 and 3:23-25; Jude 3 and 20).

3:3 "Are you so foolish?" This is the same term as in verse 1.

❖ NASB "Having begun by the Spirit, are you
now being perfected by the flesh?"

NKJV "Having begun in the Spirit, are you
now being made perfect by the
flesh?"

NRSV "Having started with the Spirit, are
you now ending with the flesh?"

TEV "You began by God's Spirit; do you
now want to finish by your own
power?"

JB "Are you foolish enough to end in
outward observances what you began
in the Spirit?"

This grammatical structure can be understood as: (1)
MIDDLE VOICE (NRSV, TEV, JB), or (2) PASSIVE VOICE
(NASB, NKJV). The MIDDLE VOICE emphasized the Galatians'
actions while the PASSIVE would emphasize an outside agent.
The middle voice fits the context best. The Galatians were trying
to complete their salvation by their own efforts at fulfilling the
Mosaic Law. Both our salvation and maturity are appropriated by
grace through faith! The two significant terms in this phrase are
also used together in Phil. 1:6. The rest of Paul's argument will
focus on the fact that we are complete and mature in Jesus Christ.

Paul's statement in verse 3 does not imply that believers do
not make choices about how they live. Salvation is a response to
God's initiating grace; so, too, is the Christian life a response to
the Spirit's guidance by repentance, faith and progressive
Christlikeness! (cf. 5:1-6:10).

3:4 NASB "Did you suffer so many things in
vain-"

NKJV "Have you suffered so many things
in vain-"

NRSV "Did you experience so much for
nothing?"

TEV "Did all your experience mean
nothing at all?"

JB "Have all the favours you received
been wasted?"

"Suffer" has two possible connotations. The most common is physical suffering and we do have some record of the

churches in southern Asia Minor experiencing Jewish persecution (cf. Acts 14:2, 5, 19, 22). However, in context, it seems to evoke the emotional upheaval in their conversion.

❖ **"if indeed it was in vain?"** There are two theories about this phrase: (1) it may relate to 1:16; or (2) it may relate to Paul's sustained argument about the spiritual futility of trusting in human performance of the Mosaic Law. If they are reverting to human effort then Christ's grace will not help them (cf. 4:11; 5:2-4; I Cor. 15:2).

3:5 "So then, does He who provides you with the Spirit" Provision of the Spirit is a reference to salvation (cf. 3:14; Rom. 8:9). The verb is PRESENT TENSE, also used of God's provision in II Cor. 9:10. Earlier uses of the word suggest it meant "to lavish upon" or "to grant freely."

❖ **"and works miracles among you,"** This PERFECT TENSE VERB may indicate the continuing effect of: (1) the miracle of their salvation; (2) the accompanying signs and miracles which confirmed the gospel; or (3) the spiritual gifts which were being manifested within the Galatian congregations. Translators disagree whether the phrase should read "in you," speaking of individuals, or "among you," speaking of "in your midst." Both translations are valid.

Did God graciously give all the blessings because you were performing the Law of Moses? No! They were God's confirmation of the gospel that you received by grace through faith.

NASB (UPDATED) TEXT: 3:6-9

Even so Abraham believed God, and it was reckoned to him as righteousness. Therefore, be sure that it is those who are of faith who are sons of Abraham. The Scripture, foreseeing that God would justify the Gentiles by faith, preached the gospel beforehand to Abraham, saying, "All the nations will be blessed in you." So then those who are of faith are blessed with Abraham, the believer.

3:6 "Even so Abraham" Verses 6-9 amplify the example of Abraham, the spiritual and racial father of the Jewish nation. The false teachers may have used Abraham as an example of someone who believed God and then later was circumcised. This explains

NOTES

why Paul's argument recorded in Rom. 4 is not developed here. Abraham is paradigmatic of how all men come to God (cf. Gen. 15:6).

❖ **"it was reckoned to him as righteousness."** "Reckoned," an AORIST PASSIVE verb, is a commercial term that meant "to make a deposit into another's account" (cf. Rom. 4:3, 99, 22). God's righteousness was given to Abraham because of God's love and Abraham's faith that God would give him an heir. The Gen. 15:6 quotation comes from the Septuagint. Paul quoted the Law of Moses several times to strengthen his argument. Since the false teachers used the Law to make their argument, Paul used the same technique to prove them wrong. The writings of Moses were the most authoritative section of the Hebrew canon for the Jews.

3:7 "be sure that it is those who are of faith who are sons of Abraham" This statement is the major thrust of this contextual unit. This declaration would have appalled the false teachers (cf. 3:14, 29; Rom. 2:28-29; 14:16-17). This same truth is alluded to in the message of John the Baptist (cf. Lk. 3:8) and specifically in the words of Jesus in Jn. 8:37-59. One can tell Abraham's sons by how they live, not by who their parents are!

3:8 "The Scripture, foreseeing that God" This Hebraic idiom affirms the full inspiration of the OT. In this verse the Scripture is personified twice.

❖ **"would justify the Gentiles by faith"** The salvation of all men has always been God's plan (cf. Gen. 3:15). There is only one God and all men are made in His image (Gen. 1:26; 5:1; 9:6); therefore, He loves all men (cf. Ezek. 18:32; Jn. 3:16; I Tim. 2:4; II Pet. 3:9). The universal love of God which includes the Gentiles is clearly seen in Isaiah, Jonah, Jn. 3:16, and Eph. 2:11-3:21.

❖ **"All the nations will be blessed in you."** Here Paul quoted God's promise to Abraham, recorded in Gen. 12:3; 18:18; 22:18; 26:4. The ambiguous Hebrew verb form may be: (1) a PASSIVE form, "will be blessed," (cf. Gen. 18:18; 28:14); or (2) a MIDDLE REFLEXIVE form, "will bless themselves," (cf. Gen. 22:16-18; 26:4). However, in the Septuagint and in Paul's quote, it is PASSIVE, not MIDDLE. In this text Paul combined Gen. 12:3 with

61

18:18 from the Septuagint.

3:9	NASB	"those who are of faith are blessed with Abraham, the believer"
	NKJV	"those who *are* of faith are blessed with believing Abraham."
	NRSV	"those who believe are blessed with Abraham who believed"
	TEV	"Abraham believed and was blessed; so all who believe are blessed as he was."
	JB	"Those therefore who rely on faith receive the same blessing as Abraham, the man of faith."

The preposition "with" [*syn*], meaning "joint participation with," shows the close identification between Abraham and all those who have faith in God. The description of Abraham as "faithful" or "believing" emphasizes that Abraham believed God by trusting in His promise. NT faith also means trusting in the trustworthiness of God and His promises.

NASB (UPDATED) TEXT: 3:10-14

For as many as are of the works of the Law are under a curse; for it is written, "Cursed is everyone who does not abide by all things written in the book of the law to perform them." Now that no one is justified by the Law before God is evident; for, "The righteous man shall live by faith." However, the Law is not of faith; on the contrary, "He who practices them shall live by them." Christ redeemed us from the curse of the Law, having become a curse for us—for it is written, "Cursed is everyone who hangs on a tree"—in order that in Christ Jesus the blessing of Abraham might come to the Gentiles, so that we would receive the promise of the Spirit through faith.

3:10	NASB	"For as many as are of the works of the Law are under a curse;"
	NKJV	"For as many as are of the works of the law are under a curse;"
	NRSV	"For all who rely on the works of the law are under a curse;"
	TEV	"Those who depend on obeying the

	Law live under a curse."
JB	"those who rely on the keeping of the Law are under a curse,"

In the next step in the argument, Paul moved from Abraham to the strict legal requirements of the Mosaic Law. The argument challenges the bad theology of the Judaizers. Trusting in adherence to the Law characterized the Pharisees of Jesus' day (cf. Rom. 10:2-5). Paul asserted that self-effort to obtain right standing is only a road to damnation (cf. 2:16). Paul knew this road well! Although Paul was primarily referring to the Mosaic Law, the referent is "law" in general or human effort by means of some external moral standard. Which standard is not important—the essential truth is that fallen man cannot claim that his moral accomplishment deserves acceptance from God. We call this approach self-righteous legalism. It is alive and well and thrives among religious people!

❖ "for it is written, 'Cursed is everyone who does not abide by all things written in the book of the law to perform them.'" This alludes to Deut. 27:26 and 28:58ff. Although the word "all" does not appear in Deut. 27:26, it does appear in 28:58. The curse of the Law is alluded to in Jn. 7:49. If one breaks the law in one way, even just once, he falls under the condemnation of the Law, (cf. Jas. 2:10; Gal. 5:3). The OT Law became a death sentence for all men (Col. 2:14). God said "the soul that sins, it will surely die." All of the children of Adam have sinned! The Law, as a means of right standing with God, is only applicable to the one who never commits sin. The problem with this is that all have sinned and have come short of the glory of God (cf. Rom. 3:9,11,22,23; 11:32).

3:11	NASB	"for, 'The righteous man shall live by faith.'"
	NKJV	"'The just shall live by faith.'"
	NRSV	"'The one who is righteous will live by faith'"
	TEV	"He who is put right with God through faith shall live."
	JB	"the righteous man finds life through faith."

Here Paul quoted Hab. 2:4, quoted again in Rom. 1:17 and Heb. 10:38. Rather an ambiguous verse, Hab. 2:4 has been understood in several different ways: (1) the Masoretic Text has

NOTES

"the righteous shall live by his faith/faithfulness;" (2) the Septuagint has "the righteous shall live on the basis of my (God's) faithfulness;" and (3) Paul's use favors faith-based righteousness through Christ versus works-based righteousness through the Mosaic Law. There may be an allusion to Gen. 15:6. Both Hab. 2:4 and Gen. 15:6 have the same two key terms: faith and righteousness.

3:12	NASB, NKJV	"the Law is not of faith;"
	NRSV	"the law does not rest on faith;"
	TEV	"the Law does not depend on faith."
	JB	"The Law is not even based on faith,"

Here is the basic assumption! In the matter of right standing with God, the choice is faith or law, not faith and law. The Judaizers had turned faith in God into rules for God. Even in the OT the individual Israelite was only right by personal faith in YHWH. Never were all Israelites right with God because of their descent from Abraham.

❖ **"on the contrary, 'He who practices them shall live by them'"** This quotation comes from Lev. 18:5, also quoted in Rom. 10:25, stressing the importance of performing the demands of God. However, the OT is a history of man's inability to perform the OT Law. Therefore, another way of salvation was introduced, which in reality, had always been God's means of salvation: not human effort, but faith. Salvation by grace through faith is the essence of the New Covenant (Jer. 31:31-34; Eph. 2:8-9).

3:13 "Christ redeemed us" Here Paul referred to the substitutionary atonement of Christ. He purchased for us that which we could not purchase for ourselves. The term "redeemed" or "ransomed" means "to buy someone back from slavery" or "capture" (cf. Acts 20:28; I Cor. 6:20; 7:23; I Pet. 1:18-19).

❖ **"from the curse of the Law, having become a curse for us"** This verse quotes Deut. 21:23 which was used to describe someone who had already been killed and was then publicly hanged or impaled as a sign of public shame and, thereby, was cursed by God (cf. Isa. 53:4, 10). Jesus' crucifixion as a sinless substitute meant that He took the curse of the Law on Himself for us (cf. II Cor. 5:21). This truth is overwhelming—He became the curse for us!

65

3:14 The two PURPOSE CLAUSES in verse 14 serve to describe the purpose of God in calling Abraham: (1) to bring the heathen into the blessing enjoyed by Israel through the promise to Abraham (cf. Gen. 12:3; Gal. 3:8-9); and (2) that by faith all might receive the Spirit which was the promised sign of the New Age. The experience of Pentecost was a sign to the Apostles that the New Age had dawned. Receiving the Spirit is a metaphor for salvation (cf. 3:1; Lk. 24:49; Acts 1:4; Rom. 8:9).

NASB (UPDATED) TEXT: 3:15-22

Brethren, I speak in terms of human relations: even though it is only a man's covenant, yet when it has been ratified, no one sets it aside or adds conditions to it. Now the promises were spoken to Abraham and to his seed. He does not say, "And to seeds," as referring to many, but rather to one, "And to your seed," that is, Christ. What I am saying is this: the Law, which came four hundred and thirty years later, does not invalidate a covenant previously ratified by God, so as to nullify the promise. For if the inheritance is based on law, it is no longer based on a promise; but God has granted it to Abraham by means of a promise. "Why the Law then? It was added because of transgressions, having been ordained through angels by the agency of a mediator, until the seed would come to whom the promise had been made. Now a mediator is not for one party only; whereas God is only one. Is the Law then contrary to the promises of God? May it never be! For if a law had been given which was able to impart life, then righteousness would indeed have been based on law. But the Scripture has shut up everyone under sin, so that the promise by faith in Jesus Christ might be given to those who believe

---

3:15-17	NASB, NKJV	"a man's covenant"
	NRSV	"a person's will"
	TEV	"that covenant"
	JB	"If a will"

Paul proceeded with his argument by means of a common human illustration. He used a term in Koine Greek which may be translated as "will" or "testament," in connection with one's inheritance. In Classical Greek it is translated "covenant." In the Septuagint this term is always used of a covenant between God and man. Due to this ambiguity, Paul used this legal metaphor as an example for God's covenanting or contracting with Abraham and his descendants. This contract cannot be changed! The same type of argumentation using the concept of a last will and testament is found in Heb. 9:15-20.

3:15	NASB	"yet when it has been ratified, no one sets it aside or adds conditions to it"
	NKJV	"yet if it is confirmed, no one annuls or adds to it."
	NRSV	"once a person's will has been ratified, no one adds to it or annuls it."
	TEV	"when two men agree on a matter and sign a covenant, no one can break that covenant or add anything to it."
	JB	"has been drawn up in due form, no one is allowed to disregard it or add to it."

Paul responded to one objection of the Judaizers that the Mosaic Law superseded the Abrahamic promise. The promise to Abraham in Gen. 15 was ratified by both God's promise and a sacrifice in which Abraham had no covenant responsibilities but faith (cf. Gen. 15:12-21).

3:16 "the promises" "Promises" is plural because of the number of times God repeats His promise to Abraham (cf. Gen. 12:1-3; 13:14-18; 15:1-5, 12-18; 17:1-14; 22:9-19).

❖ **"his seed"** The use of "seed" is a word play on a common idiom for descendant. Although singular in form, it can be singular or plural in meaning. In this case, Paul used it as a reference to Jesus, not Isaac—thus, God's promise was not linked to the Mosaic Covenant. "Seed" could be used in the corporate sense of God's children by faith, like Abraham.

3:17 "the Law, which came four hundred and thirty years later," Paul explained another reason for the superiority of the Abrahamic promise was that it preceded the Mosaic Law. There has been much discussion about the number four hundred and thirty years, which appears inaccurate when compared with the reference of Ex. 12:40 to the Egyptian captivity's duration as 430 years. Some use the Septuagint translation and the Samaritan

NOTES

Pentateuch of Ex. 12:40 which adds "and in the land of Canaan." Genesis 15:13 and Acts 7:6 record that Israel was in captivity in Egypt for 400 years. Others assert, however, that the aforementioned promise is not to Abraham, but is repeated to all of the Patriarchs, and simply refers to the time from the last repeated promise to the patriarchs to the time of Moses' receiving the Law. In context, Paul's explanation concerned not the exact amount of time, but the long interval between the promise to Abraham and the Law to Moses.

3:18	**NASB**	"but God has granted it to Abraham by means of a promise."
	NKJV	"but God gave *it* to Abraham by promise"
	NRSV	"but God granted it to Abraham through the promise."
	TEV	"However, it was because God had promised it that he gave it to Abraham"
	JB	"and it was precisely in the form of a promise that God made his gift to Abraham"

This PERFECT MIDDLE VERB emphasizes what God Himself has done in the past with results that abide into the present. The basic root of "gracious" is "gift" or "grace." It emphasizes the free nature of God's acts, solely on the grounds of His character through the work of the Messiah.

3:19	**NASB, NRSV**	"Why the Law then?"
	NKJV	"What purpose then *does* the law serve?"
	TEV	"What was the purpose of the Law, then?"
	JB	"What then was the purpose of adding the Law?"

Paul returned to his rhetorical style of verses 1-5. He began with two questions through which he tries to explain the purpose of the Mosaic Law in the plan of God (cf. v. 19 and 21). He engaged in this contrasting approach because he had so devastated the purpose of the Law in his previous argument that some would think he was advocating antinomianism.

❖ **"It was added because of transgressions, having been ordained through angels by the agency of a mediator, until the seed would come to whom the promise had been made."** Four elements regarding the Law's inferiority to the promise may be discerned here: (1) it was added later; (2) it increased transgressions; (3) it was only until the Messiah, the seed, came; and (4) it was given through an intermediary.

The phrase "increased transgressions" can be interpreted "limit transgressions." This translation is possible syntactically. However, according to Paul's full exposition in the early chapters of Romans (cf. Rom. 3:20; 4:15; 5:20; 7:1), the Law was given to clearly show us our sins.

Phil. 3:6 and Rom. 7:7-11 pose a paradox. Paul felt that he had fulfilled the requirements of the Law in his life. However, covetousness, which was later made obvious, showed him that he was a sinner and in need of spiritual salvation.

The view of angels as agents in the mediation of the Law can be seen in the rabbinical interpretation of Deut. 33:2 (in the Septuagint). The angel(s) who are related to the giving of the Law are also discussed in Acts 7:38,53 and Heb. 2:2; Josephus' *Antiquities of the Jews*, 15:5:3; and the non-canonical *Book of Jubilees*, 1:27-29. Paul may have had in mind the Angel of the Lord who continued with the people when YHWH did not (cf. Ex. 23:20-33; 32:34; 33:2).

3:20	NASB	"Now a mediator is not for one *party* only; whereas God is *only* one."
	NKJV	"Now a mediator does not *mediate* for one *only*, but God is one."
	NRSV	"Now a mediator involves more than one party; but God is one."
	TEV	"But a go-between is not needed when there is only one person; and God is one."
	JB	"Now there can only be an intermediary between two parties, yet God is one."

This verse presents the interpreter with many different possibilities. In context, an obvious reading would be that the order of the Law's transmission was from God, through angels, to Moses, to the people. Therefore, the promise is superior because it was given face-to-face between only two persons, God and

Abraham, while the Mosaic covenant involved four parties. The promise required no mediation. It could also refer to God's unconditional promise to Abraham in Gen. 15:12-21. Only God participated in its ratification. Now, although God's initial contact with Abraham was conditional (cf. Gen. 12:1), Paul is using the Gen. 15 passage to make his point. The Mosaic covenant was conditional for God and man. The problem was that since the Fall (cf. Gen. 3) man was incapable of performing his part of the covenant. The promise, therefore, is superior!

3:21 "Is the law then contrary to the promises of God?" The Greek text does not have the ARTICLE with the term "law" which would have implied the Mosaic Law. The use of "law" with no ARTICLE occurs three times in verse 21 and 4:5. Often "law" in Galatians does not have the ARTICLE in which case it refers to man's attempt to earn God's favor by means of the performance of religious guidelines or cultural norms. The key is not which guidelines but the belief that man cannot earn standing with a holy God (cf. Eph. 2:9). Here is where a careful reading of Romans 7 is crucial.

❖ **"For if a law had been given"** This SECOND CLASS CONDITIONAL SENTENCE expresses a concept "contrary to fact." An amplified translation would read: "if a law had been given that was able to impart life (which there never was), then right standing would have come through law (which it does not)." The Law was never the way to be right with God. A true revelation from God (Rom. 7:12), the Law is inspired revelation and valuable but not in the area of right standing or salvation.

3:22	NASB	"But the Scripture has shut up everyone under sin,"
	NKJV	"But the Scripture has confined all under sin,"
	NRSV	"But the scripture has imprisoned all things under the power of sin,"
	TEV	"But the Scripture has said that the whole world is under the power of sin,"
	JB	"Scripture makes no exceptions when it says that sin is master everywhere."

71

NOTES

To which OT text Paul was alluding is uncertain, though one possibility is Deut. 27:26, referred to in Gal. 2:16; 3:10. The fall of man and the estrangement of all creation is the first point of Paul's gospel (cf. Rom. 3:9, 23; 11:32).

Literally this is "all things," not "all men." Some see here the cosmic significance of Christ's redemption (cf. Rom. 8:18-25; Eph. 1:22 and the entire book of Colossians whose theme is cosmological redemption in Christ). However, in this context, it refers to all mankind, including Jews, Judaizers and Gentiles.

❖ "that the promise by faith in Jesus Christ might be given to those who believe" This is a summary of the entire discussion that God's grace and favor comes through His promise to Abraham and his Seed, not through human merit or performance! Notice the repetition of the term, *pistis*, translated as "faith," "trust," and "believe."

NASB (UPDATED) TEXT: 3:23-29

But before faith came, we were kept in custody under the law, being shut up to the faith which was later to be revealed. Therefore the Law has become our tutor *to lead us* to Christ, so that we may be justified by faith. But now that faith has come, we are no longer under a tutor. For you are all sons of God through faith in Christ Jesus. For all of you who were baptized into Christ have clothed yourselves with Christ. There is neither Jew nor Greek, there is neither slave nor free man, there is neither male nor female; for you are all one in Christ Jesus. And if you belong to Christ, then you are Abraham's descendants, heirs according to promise.

3:23 "But before this faith came," The DEFINITE ARTICLE used in tandem with "faith" implies the body of Christian truth (cf. Jude vv. 3,20). However, in this context, it means the gospel age.

| ❖ NASB | "we were kept in custody under the law, being shut up to the faith which was later to be revealed." |
| NKJV | "we were kept under guard by the law, kept for the faith which would afterward be revealed" |

NRSV	"we were imprisoned and guarded under the law until faith would be revealed."
TEV	"the Law kept us all locked up as prisoners, until this coming faith should be revealed."
JB	"we were allowed no freedom by the Law; we were being looked after till faith was revealed."

The law was first depicted as a jailor as in verse 22. We were put in protective custody until the Messiah came (cf. Phil. 4:7; I Pet. 1:5). The second metaphor used to describe the law is in verse 24 where it is called our custodian. In Greek and Roman society, this term referred to caretakers of young boys. The guardian was in charge of their protection, food, transportation, and tutoring, so "custodian" had a dual connotation: protector and disciplinarian. Paul distinguished the two intentional purposes of the law in the plan of God: (1) to show us our sinfulness; and (2) to keep us as a guardian until the free offer of grace in Christ came (cf. Jn. 1:12; 3:16; Rom. 1:16; 10:9-13).

3:24	NASB	"the Law has become our tutor to *lead us* to Christ,"
	NKJV	"the law was our tutor to bring us to Christ"
	NRSV	"the law was our disciplinarian until Christ came"
	TEV	"So the Law was in charge of us until Christ came,"
	JB	"The Law was to be our guardian until the Christ came"

Two varying interpretations of the PREPOSITIONAL PHRASE "to Christ" are possible: (1) to bring us to Christ, as in the NASB, NKJV, and NIV; or (2) until Christ came, as in NRSV, TEV, and the JB.

❖ **"that we may be justified by faith"** "Justified by faith" was the famous slogan of the Reformation. The Law has a part to play in God's free gift in Christ. It provides a necessary pre-condition to the gospel—our need! The saving "faith" always has a: (1) cognitive, (2) volitional, and (3) relational element.

3:25 "But now that this faith has come, we are no longer under a tutor." We are no longer underage children, but we have become full sons, full heirs! All of this occurs through God's grace, Christ's finished work, and our repentant faith response.

3:26 "you are all sons of God through faith in Christ Jesus." The phrase "are all sons of God" refers to those who have accepted Christ by faith (cf. Rom. 8:14-17). This verse does not advocate universalism; nor does Rom. 11:32, but it does speak of the universal offer of salvation. "All" appears first in the Greek sentence for emphasis.

3:27 "For all of you who were baptized into Christ" This is not an emphasis on baptism as a means to salvation, for that is exactly the argument the Judaizers were using in connection with circumcision. Christian baptism is a sign of the work of the Spirit which is mentioned earlier in verses 2,3,5,14 (cf. I Cor. 12:13). To be baptized in/by/with the Spirit was a biblical metaphor for becoming a Christian. Baptism was simply the opportunity for a public confession of faith in Christ and an accompanying symbol of an inner change. To make water baptism a precondition for salvation is to become a neo-Judaizer!

❖ **"have clothed yourselves with Christ."** This is an AORIST MIDDLE which emphasizes a purposeful action on our part. This involves the idea of our "putting on" (as a garment) the family characteristics of God. This clothing metaphor was used often by Paul (cf. Rom. 13:14; Eph. 4:24; Col. 3:10, 12). It is possible that it refers to the Roman rite of passage when a boy traded his childhood toga for his adult toga, thereby becoming a full citizen. This then would symbolize our becoming of full age and, thereby, a full heir.

3:28 The distinctions which the Judaizers emphasized are now totally removed in Christ. There are no barriers for anyone to become a Christian. The Jewish arrogance against Gentiles, slaves, and women has been totally removed. Distinctions are not made for salvation (cf. Rom. 3:22; I Cor. 12:13; and Col. 3:11), yet this does not mean that we are no longer male or female, slave or free, Jew or Greek. Those distinctions remain and there are passages that speak to those distinctions, but in the area of becoming a Christian there are no barriers. Every barrier raised by men Christ

NOTES

has knocked down once and for all. Hallelujah!

❖ **"for you are all one in Christ Jesus."** As we are all one in Adam (Rom. 5:12ff.), we are all potentially one in Christ. The only barrier is personal repentance and faith in Christ (Mk. 1:15; Acts 3:16; 19:20-21).

This collective emphasis is very similar to the concept of corporate Israel. We are now one new collective unit, the Church (cf. Jn. 17; Rom. 12:4,5; I Cor. 12:12ff.).

3:29 "if" Here, "if" introduces a FIRST CLASS CONDITIONAL SENTENCE, assumed to be true from the author's perspective or for his literary purposes.

❖ **"if you belong to Christ, then you are Abraham's descendants, heirs according to promise."** (cf. vv. 7, 14, 16; Rom. 8:17; Eph. 3:6). Not all national or racial Israel was truly spiritual Israel (cf. Rom. 9:6), but all who are the true Israel are so by faith. Therefore, no more distinction was made between Jew and Gentile; only between those who have faith in the Messiah and those who do not. There is no favoritism with God. God's one-time, universal gracious plan for the redemption of mankind is repentance and faith in His crucified Son. Those who respond by faith are made sons and heirs of God!

DISCUSSION QUESTIONS

This is a study guide commentary which means that you are responsible for your own interpretation of the Bible. Each of us must walk in the light we have. You, the Bible and the Holy Spirit are priority in interpretation. You must not relinquish this to a commentator.

These discussion questions are provided to help you think through the major issues of this section of the book. They are meant to be thought provoking, not definitive.

1. What does it mean "to receive the Spirit?"

2. Why did Paul use Abraham as the focus for his argument?

3. How does the term "curse" apply to us, to the Judaizers, and to all men?

4. Did Paul record an error in chronology in verse 17? Why or why not?

5. Give the four aspects of why the Law is inferior to the promises listed in verse 19.

6. List the two reasons for God's purpose for the Law in verses 23-24.

7. Explain the implications of verse 28 in the Church today.

GALATIANS 4

PARAGRAPH DIVISIONS OF MODERN TRANSLATIONS

UBS⁴	NKJV	NRSV	TEV	JB
Slaves and Son (3:21-4:7) 3:26-4:7	Sons and Heirs (3:26-4:7) 3:26-4:7	Enslavement under the Law; Freedom for God's Children 4:1-7 4:6-7	The Purpose of the Law (3:21-4:7) 4:1-5	Sons of God 4:1-7
Paul's Concern for the Galatians 4:8-11	Fears for the Church 4:8-20	4:8-11	Paul's Concern for the Galatians 4:8-11	4:8-11
4:12-20		An Appeal to the Galatians in their Relationship to Paul 4:12-20	4:12-16 4:17-20	A Personal Appeal 4:12-20
The Allegory of Hagar & Sarah 4:21-5:1	Two covenants 4:21-31	A Final Proof 4:21-5:1	The Example of Sarah & Hagar 4:21-27 4:28-31	The Two Covenants: Hagar/Sarah 4:21-31

READING CYCLE THREE (see p. vii)
FOLLOWING THE ORIGINAL AUTHOR'S INTENT AT THE PARA-GRAPH LEVEL

This is a study <u>guide</u> commentary which means that you are responsible for your own interpretation of the Bible. Each of us must walk in the light we have. You, the Bible and the Holy Spirit are priority in interpretation. You must not relinquish this to a commentator.

Read the chapter in one sitting. Identify the subjects. Compare your subject divisions with the five translations above. Paragraphing is not inspired but it is the key to following the original author's intent which is the heart of interpretation. Every paragraph has one and only one subject.

1. First paragraph

2. Second paragraph

3. Third paragraph

4. Etc.

CONTEXTUAL INSIGHTS

A. This chapter divides into three distinct sections:
    1. Verses 1-11 (or 1-7) continue discussing Gentiles as full heirs of God by faith (like Abraham) and not slaves to the world's crude notions. Verses 1-11 are very similar to the emphasis of Romans 8:1-17.
    2. Verses 12-20 (or 8-20) contain Paul's appeal to personal experience.
    3. Verses 21-31 contain an Old Testament allegory based on the first two sons of Abraham.

B. Paul used two cultural metaphors to emphasize the purpose of the Old Testament Law and its relationship to New Testament believers:
    1. Roman law concerning children and their guardians.
    2. Rabbinical typology concerning Abraham's life.

C. This chapter also further explains the relationship between Jesus and the Holy Spirit:
    1. Jesus asks the Father and He sends the Spirit
        a. Jesus sends the Spirit in 15:26; 16:7
        b. Jesus spoke out of His unity with the Father, so the Spirit speaks out of His unity with both of them
    2. "Another of the same kind." The best name for the Spirit is "the other Jesus:"
        a. both "sent" from the Father
            1) Son - Gal. 4:4
            2) Spirit - Gal. 4:6
        b. both called "truth"
            1) Son - John 14:6
            2) Spirit - John 14:17; 15:26; 16:13
        c. both called "paraclete"
            1) Son - I Jn. 2:1
            2) Spirit - Jn. 14:16, 26; 15:26; 16:7
        d. Spirit called by Jesus' name (ASB)

1) Acts 16:7 - "The Spirit of Jesus"
2) Rom. 8:9 - "Spirit of God...Spirit of Christ"
3) II Cor. 3:17 - "The Lord is Spirit...the Spirit of the Lord"
4) II Cor. 3:18 - "The Lord, the Spirit"
5) Gal. 4:6 - "The Spirit of His Son"
6) Phil. 1:19 - "The Spirit of Jesus Christ"
7) I Pet. 1:11 - "The Spirit of Christ"

e. both indwell believers
1) Son - Mt. 28:20; Jn. 14:20, 23; 15:4; 17:23; Rom. 8:10; II Cor. 13:5; Gal. 2:20; Eph. 3:17; Col. 1:27
2) Spirit - Jn. 14:16-17; Rom. 8:11; I Pet. 1:11
3) Father - Jn. 14:23; 17:23; II Cor. 6:16

f. both described as "holy"
1) Spirit - Lk. 1:35
2) Son - Lk. 1:35; 14:26

3. Possible definitions of "helper," "paraclete," Jn. 14:16, 26; 15:26; 16:7; I Jn. 2:1
a. defense advocate
b. prosecutor
c. comforter
d. Father gives comfort in II Cor. 1:3-7, from the same root word.

4. Throughout the NT the Spirit is often identified in terms linking Him to the ministry of the Son (cf. Acts 16:7; Rom. 8:9; II Cor. 3:17-18 and Phil. 1:19).

D. Definitions of Allegory and Typology (4:21-31)
1. Allegory seeks a hidden, deeper level of meaning in every text. It imports meaning into the text that has no relation at all to the intended meaning of the original author or his day or even the thrust of Scripture as a whole.
2. Typology seeks to focus on the unity of the Bible, based on one divine Author and one divine Plan. Similarities in the OT pre-figure NT truths. These similarities rise naturally out of a reading of the entire Bible (cf. I Cor. 10:6, 11).

WORD AND PHRASE STUDY

NOTES

4:1	NASB, NKJV	"Now I say,"
	NRSV	"My point is this:"
	TEV	"But to continue:"
	JB	"Let me put this another way:"

Paul used this standard technique to introduce an expansion of a previous subject (cf. 3:17; 5:16).

❖ **"the heir"** The great truth that we are heirs of God in Christ is the focus of Gal. 3:7,16,24-26. This same emphasis is continued in Gal. 4:1, 5, 6, 7, 28-31. The real descendants of Abraham are not ethnic, but spiritual (cf. Rom. 2:28-29).

❖ **"is a child,"** This was the Greek term for infant, used in the sense of: (1) spiritual babies; or (2) legal minors. In ancient Mediterranean cultures, the rite of passage from boyhood to manhood occurred at different ages and was a major cultural/religious event: (a) in Jewish culture, it was age 13; (b) in Greek culture, it was age 18; and (c) in Roman culture, it was usually at age 14.

4:2 "but he is under guardians and managers" Gal. 3:22-25 says we were "under the Law," described as: (1) a jailor which kept us in protective custody (cf. 3:22-23); or (2) an adolescent custodian (cf. 3:24-25). However, in chapter 4, the metaphor changes to "guardian" and "trustee." In Roman law, boys from birth to 14 years of age were in the charge of a legal guardian (cf. 3:23-25). From age 14 to 25, their property was administered by trustees (cf.

4:2). Paul was alluding to this Roman custom by using these precise terms.

❖ **"until the date set by the father."** This phrase gives further evidence that a Roman father had some discretion in setting the time of his son's transition from boyhood to manhood. This is a unique feature of Roman law. It also shows that God the Father chose the time that His Son would bring in our maturity (cf. v. 4).

4:3 "while we were children," The PRONOUN "we" could refer to: (1) the Jews who were under the guardianship of the Mosaic Law; (2) Jews and Gentiles who were part of the old age before the gospel; or (3) the Gentiles' paganism with all its rules and rites. In the context of Galatians 3 and 4, #1 fits best.

❖	NASB	"were held in bondage under the elemental things of the world"
	NKJV	"were in bondage under the elemental things of the world."
	NRSV	"we were enslaved to the elemental spirits of the world."
	TEV	"were slaves of the ruling spirits of the universe,"
	JB	"we were as good as slaves to the elemental principles of this world,"

This phrase is PERIPHRASTIC PLUPERFECT PASSIVE. This construction emphasizes our fixed status as slaves. "Elemental" [*stoicheia*] originally meant "to stand side by side in a row." It had a wide range of meanings in the Greco-Roman world of Paul's day: (1) the ABC's of a child's training or the elemental teachings of any subject (cf. Heb. 5:12; 6:1); (2) the basic components of the physical universe—air, water, fire, earth (cf. II Pet. 3:10,12), which were often deified by the Greeks; (3) the heavenly bodies (cf. I Enoch 52:8-9); and this is how the early church fathers interpreted its use in Col. 2:8,20.

Closely identified with #3 was the indirect meaning that behind heavenly bodies were spiritual powers, a common usage which would influence the interpretation of Gal. 4:3,8-10 (cf. the angels of Col. 2:18-20 and Gal. 3:19). However, in his new book *Christ and the Powers*, published by Herald Press, Henrik Berkhof states that these powers are impersonal structures (such as politics, democracy, social class, public mores, sports, philosophy, etc.) in our natural, fallen world which tend to unify mankind apart from God (cf. p. 32). This interpretation fits the biblical examples the best. Paul was making a parallel between the Law as adolescent custodian (cf. 3:22-4:7) and *stoicheia* as slave master (cf. 4:3).

4:4 "But when the fullness of the time came," This implies that God is in control of history and that Christ came in God's timing (cf. Mk. 1:15; Eph. 1:10; I Tim. 2:6; Tit. 1:3). Many commentators have seen the phrases related to: (1) Roman peace; (2) Roman highways, shipping; (3) a common language in the entire area; and (4) the religious and moral searching of the Mediterranean world. This statement relates to verse 2, "until the time fixed by the Father." The New Age was inaugurated by the Christ event, the New Covenant had come, the Old Covenant had passed away in Christ.

❖ **"God sent forth His Son,"** "Sent" is the Greek term *apostello* from which we derive "apostle." This same phrase occurs in verse 6, where God the Father sends the Holy Spirit. Notice that the three persons of the Trinity are mentioned in verses 4-6. Although the term "Trinity" does not appear in the Bible, the concept does over and over again (cf. Mt. 28:19; I Cor. 12:4-6; II Cor. 1:21-22; 13:14; Eph. 1:3-14; 4:4-6 and I Pet. 1:2).

The fact that He sent His Son implies the pre-existence of the Son in heaven and, thereby, the deity of the Son (cf. Jn. 1:1-3, 14, 18; I Cor. 8:6; Phil. 2:6; Col. 1:15-17; Heb. 1:2). The Messiah's coming inaugurated the New Messianic Age.

❖ **"born of a woman,"** Paul emphasized the full humanity of Jesus Christ possibly due to the tendency of the docetic Gnostics (Eph., Col., the Pastoral Epistles and I Jn.) to affirm the deity of Jesus but to deny His humanity. However, there is scant evidence that this heresy influenced the writing of Galatians (cf. v. 3).

The phrase "born of a woman" would certainly remind the Judaizers of Gen. 3:15 and Isa. 7:14. The author of the book of Hebrews makes this a cardinal point in his theology (cf. Heb. 2:14, 17). A very similar phrase which emphasizes the true humanity of Jesus but without a sin nature, is found in Rom. 8:3; Phil. 2:7. That Jesus was fully God and fully man is a major truth of the gospel of the first century Church (cf. I Jn. 4:1-6).

NOTES

Surprisingly, the virgin birth of Jesus is not emphasized or even mentioned outside of the passages on Jesus' birth in Matthew and Luke. Possibly it was too easily misunderstood and connected to the mythical activities of the Mt. Olympus gods.

❖ **"born under the Law,"** This shows that Jesus was born within the Jewish tradition under Jewish Law (cf. Rom. 1:3). There is no ARTICLE with the term "law," but the context shows it must refer to the Law of Moses, which was the *stoicheia* to which Jesus was subject. Jesus was also subject to Roman law. This phrase could also relate to "the curse of the Law" on mankind which He voluntarily shared (cf. 3:10-13).

4:5 "so that He might redeem those who were under the Law," "Redeem" is used in 3:13 to speak of God's buying back either: (1) all men from the slavery of sin; or (2) the Jews from the Mosaic Law and the Gentiles from the *stoicheia*, through the life, death and resurrection of Christ. This shows man's helplessness and God's gracious provision (cf. Mk. 10:45). It is difficult in this context to know if Paul was speaking of Mosaic Law, 3:19, or law in the general sense of human merit (cf. 3:21).

❖	NASB, NKJV	"that we might receive the adoption as sons"
	NRSV	"that we might receive adoption as children"
	TEV	"so that we might become God's sons"
	JB	"to enable us to be adopted as sons"

Paul continued his discussion of the privileges that believers receive as full heirs of Abraham through Christ. Paul used the familial metaphor "adoption" of our salvation while John used the familial term "born again." The adoption metaphor was used primarily in two contexts in Roman culture. In Roman law, adoption was very difficult. A long, involved and expensive legal procedure, once enacted adoption afforded several special rights and privileges: (1) all debts were cancelled; (2) all criminal charges were dropped; (3) they could not be legally put to death by their new father; and (4) they could not be disinherited by their new father. In legal terms, they were a completely new person. Paul was alluding to the believers' security in Christ by using

87

this Roman legal procedure (cf. Rom. 8:15, 23). Also, the metaphor was used in the official ceremony of a boy becoming a man, held on 17 March each year. When a father publicly adopted a son, he officially and permanently became his heir.

4:6 "Because you are sons, God has sent the Spirit of His Son into our hearts," Similar to Rom. 8:14-17, Paul reiterated God's gracious act in sending His Son and His Spirit. The exact meaning of the Greek phrase is unclear. Is the Spirit the evidence or the result of sonship? "Through His Son we become sons" is the motto of Gal. 2:15-4:31. It is interesting to note that the Spirit was mentioned so frequently in chapter 3 in reference to our becoming Christians (cf. v. 2,5&14). He is now called "the Spirit of His Son." This shows two works of the Spirit: (1) wooing to Christ; and (2) forming Christ in us (cf. Jn. 16:7-15). The ministry of the Son and the Spirit has always been closely identified.

Throughout the New Testament the Spirit is often identified in terms which link Him to the ministry of the Son (cf. Acts 16:7; Rom. 8:9; II Cor. 3:17-18 and Phil. 1:19). Also notice that the three persons of the Trinity are mentioned in this verse. Although the term "Trinity" does not appear in the Bible the concept does over and over (cf. Mt. 28:19; I Cor. 12:4-6; II Cor. 1:21-22; 13:14; Eph. 1:3-14; 4:4-6; and I Pet. 1:2).

❖ **"crying, 'Abba'! Father!'"** This phrase contains both the Greek and Aramaic terms for father. The term *Abba* was the Aramaic word for the intimate family relationship between a child and his father (cf. Mk. 14:36; Rom. 8:15), very similar to our use of "Daddy." Familial expressions such as this highlight the intimate relationship between Jesus and the Father. Because of our response to God's offer in Christ, we have this same intimate access to the Father (cf. Rom. 8:26-27). Truly, we are sons!

4:7 "Therefore you are no longer a slave, but a son; and if a son, then an heir through God" The Spirit removes our slavery and bondage and establishes our sonship (cf. Rom. 8:12-17). This assures our inheritance (cf. I Pet. 1:4-5).

❖ **"through God"** The KJV reads "through Christ." Older Greek manuscripts have "through God." This emphasizes God as the originator and initiator of grace (cf. Jn. 6:44,65 and Gal. 4:9).

Several manuscripts have variations but manuscripts P⁴⁶, ℵ, A, B, and C* have "through God." Of all the many variants, this one seems to be the most unusual and probably the source of all the others.

NASB (UPDATED) TEXT: 4:8-11

However at that time, when you did not know God, you were slaves to those which by nature are no gods. But now that you have come to know God, or rather to be known by God, how is it that you turn back again to the weak and worthless elemental things, to which you desire to be enslaved all over again? You observe days and months and seasons and years. I fear for you, that perhaps I have labored over you in vain.

4:8 "However at that time, when you did not know God," This is a PERFECT TENSE VERB which emphasizes a settled state. Although some modern commentators have tried to identify this with a Jewish background, it fits much better with the concept of the Gentiles who were estranged from God (cf. Eph. 2:12-13; Col. 1:21). It is true that all men have the potential of knowing God both from creation (Ps. 19:1-5 and Rom. 1:19-20) and also an inner moral witness (cf. Rom. 2:14-15). This knowledge is called natural revelation, but the Bible asserts that all of us, Jews and Gentiles, have rejected this knowledge (cf. Rom. 3:23). "Know" is used both in its Hebrew sense of interpersonal, intimate, family relationships and its Greek sense of cognitive content but the focus is on the Greek sense as verse 9 is on the Hebrew sense.

❖ **"you were slaves to those which by nature are no gods"** Idol worship is vain and futile (cf. Acts 17:29 and I Cor. 8:4-5). However, Paul asserted that behind the vanity of idol worship is demonic activity (cf. I Cor. 10:20; Rev. 9:20). Man's slavery to the demonic is also implied in the verb of I Cor. 12:2. Paul may have been referring to one of several possible things: (1) the *stoicheia* of verses 3 and 9; (2) pagan idols; (3) demons behind pagan idols; and (4) the Jewish Law, which in its legalism and ritualism had replaced YHWH.

4:9 "But now that you have come to know God, or rather to be known by God," The time element in verse 8 is contrasted in verse 9. In verse 9 Paul used another powerful, rhetorical question as

NOTES

he did in 3:1-5, 19,21, and 4:15. "Know" in verse 9 is a different, more relational Greek word choice than the term used in verse 8. This term carries the Hebrew connotation of knowledge as an interpersonal relationship (cf. Gen. 4:1; Jer. 1:5). Their new relationship was not based on facts about God but God's initiating a new covenant through Christ with those who had been estranged (cf. Eph. 2:11-3:13).

❖ NASB   "how is it that you turn back again to the weak and worthless elemental things"

NKJV   "how is it that you turn again to the weak and beggarly elements,"

NRSV   "how can you turn back again to the weak and beggarly elemental spirits?"

TEV   "how is it that you want to turn back to those weak and pitiful ruling spirits?"

JB   "how can you want to go back to elemental things like these, that can do nothing and give nothing,"

This is PRESENT TENSE. This verse contains the word *stoicheia* as in 4:3. They were trading the slavery of paganism for the slavery of Judaism as a means of salvation. Both Judaism and paganism were subject to the *stoicheia*! These fallen world structures are completely inadequate to bring salvation.

4:10 "You observe days and months and seasons and years." This is a PRESENT MIDDLE INDICATIVE VERB representing continuing action, in this case, a personal, scrupulous religious observance—a reference to the Jewish religious calendar (cf. Col. 2:16). These Galatians were exchanging one religious calendar (pagan) for another (Jewish). Paul's understanding of the gospel allowed him to apply the truth to different situations. The situation in the Galatian churches required Paul to oppose legalism and works righteousness. However, in Romans 14, Paul encouraged strong believers not to judge weaker believers who respected certain days (cf. 14:5-6). In the first it was a matter of the proper understanding of the gospel, in the latter it was concerning Christian fellowship.

4:11	NASB	"I fear for you, that perhaps I have labored over you in vain."
	NKJV	"I am afraid for you, lest I have labored for you in vain."
	NRSV	"I am afraid that my work for you may have been wasted."
	TEV	"I am afraid for you! Can it be that all my work for you has been for nothing?"
	JB	"You make me feel I have wasted my time with you."

Several modern versions translate this verse in reference to Paul's labor among the Galatian churches (cf. JB and Revised English Bible). However, this verse could be related to Paul's concern for the Galatian believers themselves (cf. TEV). There are two possibilities: (1) Paul was not doubting their salvation but rather their usefulness in spreading, living and enjoying the radically free Gospel; or (2) Paul was fearful they were rejecting grace for human performance (cf. 3:4; 5:2-4).

NASB (UPDATED) TEXT: 4:12-20

I beg of you, brethren, become as I *am*, for I also *have become* as you *are*. You have done me no wrong; but you know that it was because of a bodily illness that I preached the gospel to you the first time; and that which was a trial to you in my bodily condition you did not despise or loathe, but you received me as an angel of God, as Christ Jesus *Himself*. Where then is that sense of blessing you had? For I bear you witness that, if possible, you would have plucked out your eyes and given them to me. So have I become your enemy by telling you the truth? They eagerly seek you, not commendably, but they wish to shut you out so that you will seek them. But it is good always to be eagerly sought in a commendable manner, and not only when I am present with you. My children, with whom I am again in labor until Christ is formed in you—but I could wish to be present with you now and to change my tone, for I am perplexed about you.

4:12 "I beg of you, brethren, become as I *am*, for I also *have become* as you *are*" This verb phrase is a PRESENT MIDDLE IMPERATIVE. "Brothers" indicates Paul's transition to a new topic. Also, calling them "brothers" lessened the blow of his hard hitting criticisms (cf. v. 19; 1:11; 3:15). This verse has been variously interpreted: (1) The Williams translation reads "take my point of view," Paul asked them to accept his view of justification by faith because he once had accepted their current tendency of justification by works (Judaism); or (2) some say that "for I also have become as you are" is an allusion to I Cor. 9:20-22 where Paul asserted that he became all things to all men in order that he might win some. When he was with Jews, he lived like the Jews. When he was with Gentiles, he lived like the Gentiles. Yet in truth he had abandoned the Law as a way of salvation. He was flexible on the method but not on the message.

❖ **"You have done me no wrong;"** Some think this phrase expresses a negative statement, "in the past you did me no harm but now you do." But others read it as a positive expression of his appreciation of the Galatians and their original acceptance of him and his message. This phrase should be read with verses 13-15.

4:13 "it was because of a bodily illness that I preached the gospel to you the first time;" The mention of a "first time" implies a second time before the letter was written. However, the phrase may idiomatically mean "formally" as in I Tim. 1:13. Paul went to the churches of Galatia: (1) for a time of recuperation from some illness, or (2) because of an illness he had to stop and stay a while. Because of: (1) verses 14-15; (2) in tandem with 6:11; and (3) II Cor. 12:1-10, I personally believe Paul was alluding to his "thorn in the flesh," a physical ailment. With the combination of these verses it seems to me that it was some type of eye problem which possibly began with his Damascus Road experience and was made worse by the diseases of the first century. Paul's partial blindness may have been caused by the repulsive eye disorder ophthalmia.

4:14	NASB	"and that which was a trial to you in my bodily condition you did not despise or loathe,"
	NKJV	"And my trial which was in my flesh you did not despise or reject,"
	NRSV	"though my condition put you to the test, you did not scorn or despise me,"
	TEV	"But you did not despise or reject

93

NOTES

JB	me, even though my physical condition was a great trial to you" "you never showed the least sign of being revolted or disgusted by my disease that was such a trial to you;"

Many Jews and Gentiles would have seen Paul's illness as a judgment from God. The fact that Paul was in God's will, and sick, forces us to rethink the link between sin and sickness (cf. Jn. 9).

These two verbs invoke strong images. The first means "to count as good for nothing." The second means "to spit out." The use of the second verb is the reason that some relate Paul's illness to the superstition in the ancient Near East about "the evil eye" (cf. 3:1). The magical remedy was "to spit" and thereby protect yourself from its spell, possibly referring to: (1) an unusual-looking eye; or (2) a wild-eyed look (epilepsy).

❖ **"you received me as an angel of God, as Christ Jesus Himself"** A strong statement, Paul implied that they genuinely received the message of God through him, accompanied with great respect for the servant who brought it.

4:15	NASB	"Where then is that sense of blessing you had?"
	NKJV	"What then was the blessing you *enjoyed?*"
	NRSV	"What has become of the goodwill you felt?"
	TEV	"You were so happy! What has happened?"
	JB	"What has become of this enthusiasm you had?"

In this rhetorical question, Paul wanted to know where the original, positive feelings the Galatians held for him had gone. The Phillips translation reads, "What has happened to that fine spirit of yours?"

❖ **"that, if possible, you would have plucked out your eyes and given them to me."** This SECOND CLASS CONDITIONAL SENTENCE should be understood as, "If you had plucked out your eyes which you did not, you would have given them to me which you did not." This reading supports the theory that Paul's thorn in

95

the flesh was eye disease.

4:16 "So have I therefore become your enemy by telling you the truth?" Paul contrasted their radical change of heart toward him with their change of heart toward the gospel.

4:17-18 Two difficulties arise in interpreting verses 17 and 18: (1) the phrase "eagerly seek;" and (2) the ambiguity of the subject in verse 18. Some say that it refers: (1) to Paul; or (2) to the churches of Galatia. With this kind of ambiguity, a dogmatic interpretation is inappropriate but the general sense of the passage is not affected. The Judaizers wanted the Galatians to follow them exclusively and appreciate them the way they did Paul.

4:17	NASB	"They eagerly seek you,"
	NKJV	"They zealously court you,"
	NRSV	"They make much of you,"
	TEV	"Those other people show a deep concern for you,"
	JB	"The blame lies in the way they have tried to win you over:"

Literally, this reads "they are zealous of you." This must be a reference to the false teachers, especially in context with the next phrase, "but not sincerely." "Zealous," from the root "to burn," had two connotations in Koine Greek: (1) the affection of young lovers; and (2) envy of another. These strong emotions characterized the activity of the sweet-talking false teachers toward the Galatian churches, but their activity derived from selfish motivation.

❖	NASB	"but they wish to shut you out so that you will seek them."
	NKJV	"they want to exclude you, that you may be zealous for them."
	NRSV	"they want to exclude you, so that you may make much of them."
	TEV	"All they want is to separate you from me, so that you will have the same concern for them as they have for you."
	JB	"by separating you from me, they want to win you over to themselves."

The false teachers were jealous of the affection that the Galatian churches had shown Paul (cf. vv. 13-15). They wanted to alienate Paul so they could take his place! This may explain verse 18.

4:18 Paul was shocked that those who had been so kind and caring toward him had so dramatically become hostile (cf. v. 16). In the context of verses 13-20, this interpretation fits best.

4:19 "My children, with whom I am again in labor" Paul often used familial metaphors because of their warmth. He called himself a father in I Cor. 4:15 and I Thes. 2:11 and here, a mother (cf. I Thes. 2:7). Paul may have been making the point that he was the true spiritual parent of the Galatians, not the Judaizers.

❖ **"until Christ is formed in you-"** "Formed" [Gk. root *morphe*] was used in a medical sense for fetal development. *Morphe* could refer to the abiding character of something. This text refers to their maturity in Christ (cf. Eph. 4:13), or in other words, their Christlikeness (cf. II Cor. 3:18). This does not necessarily mean two different experiences of the Christian life—salvation and maturity—and yet we all know that maturity is a developmental experience.

Paul showed that his motives in teaching and preaching to the Galatian churches were totally different from those of the self-seeking false teachers.

4:20 "but I could wish to be present with you now and to change my tone," Paul wished they could sense the paternal care he felt for them. His heart was on fire for them, though the printed page seemed cold.

❖	NASB, NRSV	"for I am perplexed about you."
	NKJV	"for I have doubts about you."
	TEV	"I am so worried about you!"
	JB	"I have no idea what to do for the best."

The Greek word for "way" with the ALPHA PRIVITIVE may be translated in at least two ways: (1) the Living Bible reads "I frankly don't know what to do;" (2) the Phillips translation reads "I honestly don't know how to deal with you." These different

NOTES

idiomatic translations express the frustration of Paul in his dealings with these Galatian churches.

NASB (UPDATED) TEXT: 4:21-5:1

Tell me, you who want to be under law, do you not listen to the law? For it is written that Abraham had two sons, one by the bondwoman and one by the free woman. But the son by the bondwoman was born according to the flesh, and the son by the free woman through the promise. This is allegorically speaking, for these *women* are two covenants: one *proceeding* from Mount Sinai bearing children who are to be slaves; she is Hagar. Now this Hagar is Mount Sinai in Arabia and corresponds to the present Jerusalem, for she is in slavery with her children. But the Jerusalem above is free; she is our mother. For it is written,

"REJOICE, BARREN WOMAN WHO DOES NOT BEAR;
BREAK FORTH AND SHOUT, YOU ARE NOT IN LABOR;
FOR MORE NUMEROUS ARE THE CHILDREN OF THE DESOLATE
THAN OF THE ONE WHO HAS A HUSBAND."

And you brethren, like Isaac, are children of promise. But as at that time he who was born according to the flesh persecuted him who was born according to the Spirit, so it is now also. But what does the Scripture say?

"CAST OUT THE BONDWOMAN AND HER SON,
FOR THE SON OF THE BONDWOMAN SHALL NOT BE AN HEIR
WITH THE SON OF THE FREE WOMAN."

So then, brethren, we are not children of a bondwoman, but of the free woman. It was for freedom that Christ set us free; therefore keep standing firm and do not be subject again to a yoke of slavery.

4:21-31 Philo and the early church's use of allegory and Paul's use of the same technique differed significantly. The former totally ignored the historical setting, developing teachings entirely foreign to the original author's intent. Paul's approach was better characterized as typology. Paul assumed the historical setting of Genesis and the unity of the Old and New Covenants, thus he was able to build on the similarities between them because they have one author—God. In this particular context, Paul compared the Abrahamic Covenant and the Mosaic Covenant and drew application to the New Covenant of Jer. 31:31-34 and the NT.

Four connections in 4:21-31 may be drawn: (1) the two mothers stand for two families; one formed by natural means, the other by supernatural promise; (2) there was tension between these two mothers and their children as there was tension between the Judaizer's message and Paul's gospel; (3) both groups claimed to be descendants of Abraham, but one was in bondage to the Mosaic Law and the other was free in Christ's finished work; (4) two mountains were connected to these different covenants, Mt. Sinai with Moses and Mt. Zion with Abraham. Mt. Zion or Mt. Moriah was where Abraham offered Isaac as a sacrifice (cf. Gen. 22), which later became Jerusalem. Abraham was looking for a heavenly city (Heb. 11:10; 12:22; 13:14, New Jerusalem, Isa. 40-66) not an earthly Jerusalem.

Paul may have used this typology because: (1) the false teachers had used this same approach to their advantage claiming to be the true seed of Abraham; (2) the false teachers may have used an allegory from Moses' writings to push their Jewish covenant theology so Paul uses the father of the Jewish faith, Abraham; (3) Paul may have used it because of Gen. 21:9-10, which is quoted in verse 30 and says, "drive off" the natural son; in Paul's analogy this would refer to the Judaizers; (4) Paul may have used it because of the exclusivism of the Jewish false teachers, particularly in their contempt for the Gentiles; in Paul's typology the Gentiles are accepted and the racially confident ones are rejected by God (cf. Mt. 8:11-12); or (5) Paul may have used this typology because he has been emphasizing "sonship" and "heirship" in chapters 3 & 4. This was the heart of his argument: our adoption into the family of God by faith through Christ alone, not natural descent.

4:21 "Tell me, you who want to be under law, do you not listen to law?" Paul used the writing of Moses to combat errors based on Moses. This verse resumes the thought of verse 7. Verses 8-20 are another personal, emotional appeal by Paul. The concepts of "sonship" and "heir" in 4:7 and "seed" in 3:15-18 are the antecedents to this typology.

4:22 "Abraham had two sons," Abraham had more than two sons, but the ones spoken of here are contrasted: his first son, Ishmael, as is recorded in Gen. 16, and his second son, Isaac, recorded in Gen. 21. The whole point of the typology is that one was born by natural means by a servant girl and one was born by supernatural means according to the promise of God by a free woman, his wife. The emphasis throughout this context has been, as in verse 23, on the promise of God versus human effort.

4:24 The Jews would have agreed with Paul's typology until verse 23, where he said that in the sense of human effort, the Jews were really the descendants of Ishmael, while the Church was the true descendant of Sarah because of the promise.

❖ **"allegorically"** This was not "allegory" as used by Philo, Clement or Origen, but rather typology. Paul saw the current situation as analogous to the two children of Abraham; one by social custom, one by divine promise. One corresponds to works righteousness, the other to free grace! For Paul, the Law could not save but had become a death sentence on sinful mankind. Only in Christ could true salvation be found. The essence of OT faith was not in Moses but Abraham.

4:25 "Hagar is Mount Sinai in Arabia" There have been two ways of interpreting "is" here: (1) "it represents;" or (2) there is some kind of popular etymological connection between Hagar and Mount Sinai. Hagar is much like the Hebrew term for "rock" (metonymy for mountain). Most commentators choose option #1. Hagar stands for the Mosaic Law given on Mt. Sinai and, thereby, Judaism.

❖ **"corresponds to the present Jerusalem, for she is in slavery with her children."** The metaphor here is between the current system of Judaism centered in Jerusalem and the coming, eschatological city, New Jerusalem. This city, not made with hands, exists eternally in the heavens (cf. Heb. 11:10; 12:22; 13:14 and Rev. 21:2, 10). Notice that Paul made the Jerusalem above apply to the Church.

4:27 This is a quote from Isaiah 54:1. In context it refers to the restoration of the city of Jerusalem after the Babylonian exile. The New Jerusalem is mentioned specifically in chapters 65 and 66. Paul projected this eschatological understanding into his typology.

4:29 Paul associated all true followers of Jesus with the true

NOTES

descendants of Isaac through God's promise. Although the OT does not specifically mention persecution it does mention Hagar's haughty attitude toward childless Sarah (cf. Gen. 16:4-5), but also Sarah's mistreatment of Hagar (cf. Gen. 16:6). The rabbis interpreted Gen. 21:9 as Ishmael mocking Sarah and her child. The Hebrew text itself reads "playing" or "laughing." Possibly Paul was referring to the later animosity between Jews and Arabs (Gentiles.)

4:30 "But what does the Scripture say? 'Cast out the bondwoman and her son'" This is a quotation from Gen. 21:9, 10; the verb is AORIST ACTIVE IMPERATIVE meaning to "drive off the slave girl" and in the context of Galatians would mean "kick the Judaizers out!"

4:31 "So then, brethren, we are not children of a bondwoman, but of the free woman." This was the summary of the argument. We who trust in Jesus Christ are full heirs of the Abrahamic promise and not simply those who are of racial, or natural Israel. This same truth is expressed in Rom. 9-11.

DISCUSSION QUESTIONS

This is a study guide commentary which means that you are responsible for your own interpretation of the Bible. Each of us must walk in the light we have. You, the Bible and the Holy Spirit are priority in interpretation. You must not relinquish this to a commentator.

These discussion questions are provided to help you think through the major issues of this section of the book. They are meant to be thought provoking, not definitive.

1. Why did Paul continue to emphasize our sonship in Christ?

2. What is the threefold emphasis of verse 4 in connection with the person of Jesus?

3. What is the relationship between verses 8 and 9 as far as our knowing God or our being known by God?

4. What is the meaning of the phrase "the world's crude notion" or "*stoicheia?*" Explain.

5. What was Paul's thorn in the flesh which is apparently referred to in verses 14-15?

6. Why must we be careful of allegorical interpretations? If Jesus and Paul used it, why can't we?

7. Explain in your own words how verse 9 is related to verses 6 and 7.

8. If circumcision was not the emphasis of verse 15, why did Paul make such an issue of it?

9. What are the implications of the Church being called the true Israel of God in verse 16?

GALATIANS 5

PARAGRAPH DIVISIONS OF MODERN TRANSLATIONS

UBS⁴	NKJV	NRSV	TEV	JB
		A Final Proof (4:21-5:1)		
Christian Freedom	Christian Liberty	The Nature of Christian Liberty	Preserve your Freedom	Christian Liberty
5:2-6	5:1-6		5:1	5:1-6
	Love fulfills the Law	5:2-6	5:2-6	
5:7-12	5:7-15	5:7-12	5:7-10	5:7-12
			5:11-12	Liberty and Charity
5:13-15		5:13-15	5:13-15	5:13-15
The Fruit of the Spirit & the Works of the Flesh	Walking in the Spirit			The Spirit and Human Nature
5:16-21	5:16-26	5:16-21	5:16-18	5:16-24
5:22-26		5:22-26	5:19-26	5:25-26

READING CYCLE THREE (see p. vii)
FOLLOWING THE ORIGINAL AUTHOR'S INTENT AT THE PARA-GRAPH LEVEL

This is a study <u>guide</u> commentary which means that you are responsible for your own interpretation of the Bible. Each of us must walk in the light we have. You, the Bible and the Holy Spirit are priority in interpretation. You must not relinquish this to a commentator.

Read the chapter in one sitting. Identify the subjects. Compare your subject divisions with the five translations above. Paragraphing is not inspired but it is the key to following the original author's intent which is the heart of interpretation. Every paragraph has one and only one subject.

1. First paragraph

2. Second paragraph

3. Third paragraph

4. Etc.

CONTEXTUAL INSIGHTS

A. Chapter 5 articulates a crucial part of Paul's argument.
The Judaizers were concerned that the Gentile Christians would not conform to their conceptions of Mosaic godliness, therefore, they tried to force the OT regulations upon them. However, Paul was equally concerned with godliness, but he said that it is not a result of rules but of a changed heart. It is correct to say that the Judaizers had all of the elements of true salvation but they had them in a reverse order. They felt that man's performance led to an acceptable place with God. However, the gospel of the crucified Christ shows that it is a relationship with Christ which leads to godliness. Paul was also concerned with the children of God living a moral, upright, service-oriented life. Chapter 5 addresses this moral imperative.

B. The theme of freedom is expressed in chapter 5 in relation to two different perversions:
  1. Verses 1-12 deal with the legalistic perversion of freedom
  2. Verses 13-15 deal with the antinomian perversion of freedom (cf. Rom. 14; I Cor. 8; 10:23-33)

C. This book could be called a book of radical, free grace.
Paul uniquely understood the problems of self-effort. His gospel was a radical call to freedom, but not a freedom that leads to licensed excess but one that leads to loving service. In our day we need to see the balance that man is truly free in Christ, but by being free from the Law he is now free to respond appropriately to God's freely given love. Romans 14 is a great example of the biblical balance between freedom and responsibility. He gives us the power to live godly lives.

D. Verses 16-26 show us the supernatural source of Christian freedom which is the Holy Spirit. As salvation is a free act of God's love so also is the Christian life. As we must yield in repentance and faith to salvation, we must yield in

106

repentance and faith to the ongoing leadership of the Holy Spirit in our lives.

WORD AND PHRASE STUDY

5:1 "It was for freedom" Several textual variants appear at this point. The first phrase of 5:1 should probably go with 4:21-31 or start a new paragraph. This may be a play on "freewoman," 4:30,31; "freedom," 5:1, and "free," 5:1. The purpose of the gospel is to free people from the curse of the Mosaic Law so that they might willingly and appropriately respond to God in the likeness of the promise to Abraham. Therefore, believers are free not to sin and free to live for God (cf. 2:4 & Rom. 6, especially v. 11).

❖ **"that Christ set us free"** Christians are truly free in Christ (cf. Jn. 8:32,36; II Cor. 3:17). As Martin Luther said so well, "A Christian man is the most free lord of all, subject to none. A Christian man is the most dutiful servant of all, subject to all."

❖		
	NASB	**"therefore keep standing firm and do not be subject again to a yoke of slavery."**
	NKJV	**"Stand fast therefore in the liberty by which Christ has made us free, and do not be entangled again with a yoke of bondage."**
	TEV	**"Stand, then, as free men, and do not allow yourselves to become slaves again."**
	NRSV, JB	**"Stand firm therefore, and refuse to submit again to the yoke of slavery."**

Paul issued two admonitions in light of our true freedom in Christ: (1) that we persevere (cf. Rom 5:2 and I Cor. 16:13); and (2) that we stop turning back to different forms of legalism or self-effort. Both of these are PRESENT IMPERATIVES; however, the second has the NEGATIVE PARTICLE which means to stop an act which is already in process.

A good parallel for the yoke of slavery can be found in Acts 15:10. Jesus also has a yoke but His is easy (cf. Matt. 11:29-30). The rabbis used the yoke as a metaphor for the stipulations of the Law.

107

NOTES

The "law of Christ" is completely different from the law of man (cf. Jas 1:25 and 2:8, 12).

NASB (UPDATED) TEXT: 5:2-12

Behold I, Paul, say to you that if you receive circumcision, Christ will be of no benefit to you. And I testify again to every man who receives circumcision, that he is under obligation to keep the whole Law. You have been severed from Christ, you who are seeking to be justified by law; you have fallen from grace. For we through the Spirit, by faith, are waiting for the hope of righteousness. For in Christ Jesus neither circumcision nor uncircumcision means anything, but faith working through love. You were running well; who hindered you from obeying the truth? This persuasion *did* not *come* from Him who calls you. A little leaven leavens the whole lump *of dough.* I have confidence in you in the Lord that you will adopt no other view; but the one who is disturbing you will bear his judgment, whoever he is. But I, brethren, if I still preach circumcision, why am I still persecuted? Then the stumbling block of the cross has been abolished. I wish that those who are troubling you would even mutilate themselves.

5:2   NASB   "Behold I, Paul, say to you"
      NKJV   "Indeed I, Paul, say to you"
      NRSV   "Listen! I, Paul, am telling you"
      TEV   "Listen! I, Paul, tell you this:"
      JB   "It is I, Paul, who tells you this:"

This is the IMPERATIVE FORM of "behold" with the strong, PERSONAL PRONOUN. "I, Paul" shows the authoritative emphasis of Paul's remarks.

❖   NASB   "that if you receive circumcision,"
     NKJV   "that if you become circumcised,"
     NRSV   "that if you let yourselves be
                    circumcised,"
     TEV, JB   "if you allow yourselves to be
                    circumcised,"

This is a THIRD CLASS CONDITIONAL SENTENCE meaning potential, even probable, action. This would suggest that the Galatian Christians had not yet been circumcised but were

109

tending to submit to the new guidelines for obtaining salvation given by the Judaizers. Yet circumcision was not the fundamental issue (cf. v. 6; I Cor. 7:18-19). Circumcision was only one aspect of the entire Jewish system of works righteousness. Paul circumcised Timothy in Acts 16:3 in order that he might minister to Jews. But Paul reiterated that true circumcision is of the heart, not the body (cf. Rom. 2:28-29). The issue was not circumcision but how a man is brought into right standing with God (cf. v. 4).

❖ **"Christ will be of no benefit to you."** Paul was contrasting two ways of being right with God: (1) human effort; and (2) free grace. The theme of the entire paragraph is that these two ways are mutually exclusive: to choose human effort is to negate free grace; to choose free grace is to exclude human effort. One cannot mix them as Gal. 3:1-5 clearly shows.

5:3 "he is under obligation to keep the whole Law." If we choose the way of human effort, then we must adhere perfectly to the Law from birth to death (cf. Deut. 27:26; Gal. 3:10; Jas 2:10). The Bible asserts that since no one has ever done this, everyone is in the category of sinners (cf. Rom. 3:23; 6:23; 5:8 and 11:32).

5:4 "who are seeking to be justified by law;" The theological theme of chapters 3 and 4 is that our acceptance by God is based solely on His character and the work of the Messiah. This is the essence of Paul's radical, new gospel of justification by faith alone (cf. Rom. 1-8).

❖	NASB	"You have been severed from Christ,"
	NKJV	"You have become estranged from Christ,"
	NRSV	"You...have cut yourselves off from Christ;"
	TEV	"have cut yourselves off from Christ."
	JB	"you have separated yourselves from Christ,"

This Greek verb is translated in many ways. It was used by Paul more than twenty times. One can see some of its flavor from Gal. 3:17 and 5:11. If one tries to be right with God through human effort, he cuts himself off from grace righteousness as a means of salvation (cf. 5:12).

❖   **NASB, NKJV, JB**   **"you have fallen from grace."**
        NRSV   **"you have fallen away from grace."**
        TEV   **"You are outside God's grace."**

Those who seek God through human performance have lost the free grace approach which is found in the crucified Messiah. This context does not deal primarily with the theological question about the possibility of those who had salvation and have now lost it, but how man finds salvation (cf. 4:11).

5:5 "For we through the Spirit, by faith," This phrase shows the two necessary qualifications involved in our salvation: (1) man's response (cf. Mk. 1:15; Acts 3:16, 19; 20:21); and (2) the action of the Holy Spirit (cf. Jn. 6:44, 65; 16:7-13). These phrases are placed first in the Greek sentence for emphasis.

❖ **"are waiting for the hope of righteousness."** "Hope" is often used in the NT for the Second Coming. The Second Coming is the time when believers will be completely saved. The NT describes our salvation as: (1) a completed act; (2) a state of being; (3) a process; and (4) as a future consummation. These four attributes of salvation are complimentary not mutually exclusive. We are saved, have been saved, are being saved, and shall be saved. The future aspect of salvation entails the believers' glorification at the Second Coming (cf. I Jn. 3:2). Other passages describing the future event of salvation include Rom. 8:23; Phil. 3:21 and Col. 3:3, 4.

5:6 This statement encapsulates the theme of the book of Galatians: we are right with God by faith, not by human rituals or performance—including circumcision, the food laws, and moral living.

The concluding phrase has been understood in either a PASSIVE or MIDDLE sense. Roman Catholicism has mostly interpreted it as PASSIVE which means that love is the source of faith. However, most Protestants have understood it in a MIDDLE sense which means that love issues out of faith. This term is used regularly in the NT as MIDDLE (cf. Rom. 7:5, II Cor. 1:6; Eph. 3:20; I Thes. 2:13, and II Thes. 2:7). Faith is primary.

NOTES

This was Paul's answer to the false teachers concerning the lifestyle of pagans who are accepted freely in Christ. It is Spirit-motivated love that for believers sets the standard of conduct and gives the ability to obey. It is the new covenant, a new heart (cf. Jer. 31:31-34)!

5:7 "who" The SINGULAR PRONOUN used of a false teacher is also found in verse 7 and twice in verse 10. However, the PLURAL FORM occurs in verse 12. Some view this as a collective use of the SINGULAR. But because of 3:1, the use of the singular may imply: (1) a local ring-leader who was converted to the Judaizer's point of view and was now pulling the church in that direction; or (2) a persuasive leader of the Judaizers.

❖	NASB	"You were running well; who hindered you from obeying the truth?"
	NKJV	"You ran well. Who hindered you from obeying the truth?"
	NRSV	"You were running well; who prevented you from obeying the truth?"
	TEV	"You were doing so well! Who made you stop obeying the truth?"
	JB	"You began your race well: who made you less anxious to obey the truth?"

The verb "hindered" or "prevented" commonly had military and athletic connotations. In the military sense, the word meant the act of destroying a road in the face of an oncoming enemy. In the athletic sense, it meant the act of one runner cutting in front of another (here the Galatians), thereby causing them to lose the race.

Paul was engaging in a word play between "obeying the truth" in verse 2, and "persuasion" in verse 8. This does not imply that the Galatians were not responsible but that they had been influenced.

5:8 "Him who calls you." Often the pronoun antecedents are ambiguous. As in Gal. 1:6, this phrase is always used of the electing choice of God the Father.

5:9 "a little leaven" Yeast was a common NT metaphor (cf. Matt. 16:6; I Cor. 5:6). In the Bible, yeast is often used in a negative sense, though not always (cf. Matt. 13:33). Here the metaphor may be underscoring the pervasive power of the doctrine of works righteousness.

5:10 "that you will adopt no other view;" See note at 4:12 above.

❖	**NASB**	**"but the one who is disturbing you shall bear his judgment, whoever he is."**
	NKJV	**"but he who troubles you shall bear his judgment, whoever he is."**
	NRSV	**"But whoever it is that is confusing you will pay the penalty."**
	TEV	**"and that the man who is upsetting you, whoever he is, will be punished by God."**
	JB	**"and anybody who troubles you in the future will be condemned, no matter who he is"**

We are responsible before God. The severity of punishment for those who lead God's new believers astray can be seen in Matt. 18:6-7.

5:11 "if I still preach circumcision, why?" This is a FIRST CLASS CONDITIONAL SENTENCE which is assumed to be true from the author's perspective or for his literary purposes. Paul was using a rather unusual grammatical construction to say "since they are still accusing me of preaching circumcision" which may be a reference to: (1) his circumcision of Timothy (cf. Acts 16:3); and his unwillingness to circumcise Titus (cf. 2:2-5); or (2) Paul's statement in I Cor. 7:18-19. Whatever the background, Paul was declaring the Judaizers to be inconsistent, because if he preached circumcision they should have enthusiastically accepted him, but because they were persecuting him, it was good evidence that he was not advocating circumcision for Gentiles.

❖ **"then the stumbling-block of the cross has been abolished"** "Stumbling-block" or "hindrance" [*skandalon*] meant "a baited trap-stick used to capture animals" (cf. Rom. 9:33; I Cor. 1:23).

The cross was an offense to the Judaizers because it gave freely that which they were working so hard to achieve (cf. Rom. 10:2-5).

5:12	NASB	"I wish that those who are troubling you would even mutilate themselves"
	NKJV	"I could wish that those who trouble you would even cut themselves off!"
	NRSV	"I wish those who unsettle you would castrate themselves"
	TEV	"I wish that the people who are upsetting you would go all the way; let them go on and castrate themselves!"
	JB	"Tell those who are disturbing you I would like to see the knife slip"

This is used in the sense of "castration." It is known that the cult of Cybele was present in the province of Galatia and that all of their priests were eunuchs. Paul was making a sarcastic hyperbole of circumcision (cf. Phil. 3:2).

NASB (UPDATED) TEXT: 5:13-15

For you were called to freedom, brethren; only do not turn your freedom into an opportunity for the flesh, but through love serve one another. For the whole Law is fulfilled in one word, in the statement, "You shall love your neighbor as yourself." But if you bite and devour one another, take care that you are not consumed by one another.

5:13 "For you were called to freedom, brethren;" This begins a new stage of the argument. The term "brethren" usually marks a change of subject. As verses 1-12 have dealt with the perversion of legalism, verses 13-15 deal with the perversion of antinomianism. We must not use our freedom as a license for indulging the sinful passions of fallen human nature.

❖	NASB	"only do not turn your freedom into an opportunity for the flesh,"
	NKJV	"only do not use liberty as an opportunity for the flesh,"
	NRSV	"only do not use your freedom as an opportunity for self-indulgence,"

NOTES

TEV	**"But do not let this freedom become an excuse for letting your physical desires rule you."**
JB	**"but be careful, or this liberty will provide an opening for self-indulgence."**

"Opportunity" is a military term for an assault staging area (cf. Rom. 6:1-14). Several English translations identify "flesh" with the phrase "lower nature." This latter rendering agrees with Paul's use of "flesh" in this context as the natural propensities of mankind which have been twisted toward the self since Gen. 3. The same polarization between the Adamic nature and the Spirit-led life is expressed in Rom. 8:1-11.

❖ **"but through love serve one another."** This verb is PRESENT ACTIVE IMPERATIVE. Previously Paul asserted that they should not be slaves to legalism, but he now balances this with the admonition to be slaves to one another in love (cf. v. 6; Eph. 5:21; Phil. 2:3-4).

5:14	NASB	**"For the whole Law is fulfilled in one word,"**
	NKJV	**"For all the law is fulfilled in one word,"**
	NRSV	**"For the whole law is summed up in a single commandment,"**
	TEV	**"For the whole Law is summed up in one commandment:"**
	JB	**"since the whole of the Law is summarized in a single command:"**

This same truth is expressed in Rom. 13:8. This is the "law" as God's revealed will, not a works righteousness system of salvation. There is still a proper function for the OT in Christianity! This was a quote of Lev. 19:18 from the Septuagint. It may have functioned as a rabbinical summary regarding the purpose of the Law. It was also used by Jesus in a very similar way in Matt. 5:43-48; 22:39 and in Mk. 12:29-31; Lk. 10:25-28. This is a PERFECT TENSE VERB which emphasizes a continuing state or condition. It can be understood as: (1) a summary of the law; or (2) a fulfillment of the law.

5:15 This is a FIRST CLASS CONDITIONAL SENTENCE,

assumed to be true from the author's perspective or for his literary purposes. This verse uses violent imagery in descriptions of wild animals devouring each other, the terrible reality the false teachers had caused in the Galatian churches. This interpretation is reinforced by the equally strong statement in verse 26.

NASB (UPDATED) TEXT: 5:16-24

But I say, walk by the Spirit, and you will not carry out the desire of the flesh. For the flesh sets its desire against the Spirit, and the Spirit against the flesh; for these are in opposition to one another, so that you may not do the things that you please. But if you are led by the Spirit, you are not under the Law. Now the deeds of the flesh are evident, which are: immorality, impurity, sensuality, idolatry, sorcery, enmities, strife, jealousy, outbursts of anger, disputes, dissensions, factions, envying, drunkenness, carousing, and things like these, of which I forewarn you, just as I have forewarned you, that those who practice such things will not inherit the kingdom of God. But the fruit of the Spirit is love, joy, peace, patience, kindness, goodness, faithfulness, gentleness, self-control; against such things there is no law. Now those who belong to Christ Jesus have crucified the flesh with its passions and desires.

5:16 "walk by the Spirit," A PRESENT IMPERATIVE, Paul urged the Galatians to live a life supernaturally and continuously controlled by the Spirit of God (cf. Eph. 4:1; 5:2). A primary idea in Galatians was that the Spirit is that which brings initial salvation. Thus, this verse meant "that which was begun in the Spirit" (cf. 3:1), is also "that which is perfected in the Spirit" (cf. Rom. 5:16-25). The related term "law of the Spirit," Rom. 8:1 and implied in verse 18, is exactly the same as the "law of Christ" in I Cor. 9:21 & Jas. 1:25; 2:8,12. The law of love primarily serves others instead of self.

❖ **"and you will not carry out the desires of the flesh."** The strongest negation possible in Koine Greek utilizes the DOUBLE NEGATIVE with an AORIST SUBJUNCTIVE which means "never under any circumstances." This is found in this verse, followed by a very strong Greek word for "gratify." The Christian life and eternal salvation are of supernatural origin. We were not only called to

118

be saved—we were called to be disciples! The contrast between "flesh" and "spirit" is common in Paul. "Flesh" [*sarx*] is used in two senses by Paul: (1) the physical body; and (2) man's fallen, sinful, Adamic nature.

5:17 This contrast between the two ways of life is also found in Rom. 8:1-11. Paul presented the two supposed ways of being saved: (1) human effort; and (2) God's free grace in Christ. There are then two ways to live a godly life: (1) human effort; and (2) God's free power in the Spirit. The Judaizers were asserting human effort in both salvation and the Christian life, but Paul asserted God's supernatural provision in both.

5:18 "But if you are led by the Spirit," This is a FIRST CLASS CONDITIONAL SENTENCE, assumed true from the author's perspective or for his literary purposes. Those who are led by the Spirit are not subject to the law (cf. Rom. 6:14; 7:4,6). This does not imply that Christians will not sin (cf. Rom. 7 and I Jn. 2:1), but rather that their lives are not characterized by rebellion (cf. I Jn. 3:6,9).

❖ **"you are not under the Law."** No ARTICLE precedes "law" in the original Greek, so the word has a wider connotation than just the Jewish law. Here, the law has the sense of a way of life used to approach God. Here again is the contrast between the two ways of being saved, self-effort and God's free grace.

5:19 "Now the deeds of the flesh are evident," Many commentators see several distinct categories in this list of sins. However, there is a unity here based primarily on pagan worship excesses. People reveal their true selves in their actions and motives (cf. Matt. 7:20).

The KJV adds the term "adultery" to this list. It is only supported by the Greek manuscript D, Codex Bezea, which is from the sixth century A.D.

❖
NASB	"immorality, impurity,"
NKJV	"fornication, uncleanness,"
NRSV	"fornication, impurity,"
TEV	"immoral, filthy,"
JB	"fornication, gross indecency,"

NOTES

This first Greek term [*porneia*] originally meant "harlot," but it came to be used for sexual immorality in general (cf. I Cor. 6:9). We get the English term "pornography" from this Greek word. The second term [*akatharsia*], "impurity," is also a general term for sexual immorality, though originally used in the OT in the sense of ceremonial uncleanliness or moral uncleanliness. Paul intended the latter meaning.

❖   **NASB**   **"sensuality,"**
         NKJV,   NRSV   **"licentiousness,"**
         TEV   **"and indecent actions;"**
         JB   **"sexual irresponsibility;"**

This implied a public flaunting of sexual desires (cf. II Cor. 12:21). This kind of sexual activity knew no bounds or social inhibitions. Pagan worship was characterized by sexual activity.

5:20 "idolatry," This refers to the worship of anything in place of God. It especially related to acts of worship to statues or inanimate objects.

❖ **"sorcery,"** This was the Greek term *pharmakia* from which the English word "pharmacy" is derived. Sorcery may have referred to the practice of using drugs to induce a religious experience. It was later used for magical practices of any kind.

❖   **NASB**   **"enmities, strife, jealousy, outbursts of anger, disputes, dissensions, factions,"**
         NKJV   **"hatred, contentions, jealousies, outbursts of wrath, selfish ambitions, dissensions, heresies,"**
         NRSV   **"enmities, strife, jealousy, anger, quarrels, dissentions, factions,"**
         TEV   **"People become enemies and they fight, they become jealous, angry, and ambitious."**
         JB   **"feuds and wranglings, jealousy, bad temper and quarrels; disagreements, factions,"**

This litany describes the attitudes and actions of angry, fallen, selfish man.

❖ **"enmities"** This word described the condition of being characteristically hostile toward people.

❖ **"strife"** This meant "fighting for prizes."

❖ **"jealousy"** This word can have positive or negative connotations, but in this context it meant "self-centeredness."

❖ **"outbursts of anger"** This Greek term meant "a sudden, uncontrollable outburst of rage."

❖ **"disputes"** This implied conflicts based on self-seeking or ambition which knows no bounds.

❖ **"dissensions, factions"** These two terms go together. They describe a factious dogmatic division within a larger group, something akin to political parties (cf. Tim. 5:15 and 26). It is used to describe churches, like the Corinthian Church (cf. I Cor. 1:10-13; 11:19; II Cor. 12:20).

5:21 "envyings" A common Stoic proverb of the day said "envy is to grieve at another's good."

Some older Greek manuscripts add the word "murders" after the word "envy." It is included in manuscripts A, C, D, G, K and P, yet it is excluded in P⁴⁶, ℵ, and B. It is also excluded in the writings of Marcion, Irenaeus, Clement, Origen, Chrysostom, Jerome, and Augustine.

❖ **"drunkenness, carousing,"** These last two words describe the drunken orgies associated with pagan worship (cf. I Cor. 19:21).

❖ **"and things like these,"** This phrase indicates that this list is not exhaustive but representative (cf. I Cor. 6:9-10; Eph. 5:5). As a warning, it may have reminded the Galatians of Paul's preaching on a previous occasion. This verse, in tandem with I Jn. 5:16, is the source of the Roman Catholic distinction between mortal and venial sins. However, this interpretation is very dubious, in light of the overlapping definitions of the terms, as well as the fact that these sins are even committed by Christians. These verses warn that though Christians could sin in these areas and still be saved, if their lives are characterized or dominated by these sins, they have not really become new creatures in Christ (I Jn. 3:6,9).

❖ **"of which I forewarn you, just as I have forewarned you, that those who practice such things shall not inherit the kingdom of God."** The "kingdom of God" is the subject of Jesus' first and last sermons and most of His parables. The reign of God in men's hearts now will someday be consummated over all the earth (cf. Mt. 6:10; I Cor. 6:9-10; Eph. 5:5).

5:22 "But the fruit of the Spirit is" Paul described human effort as works of the flesh, but he described the Christian life as the "fruit" or product of the Spirit. He thereby distinguished human-focused religion and supernatural-focused religion. Obviously, the fruit of the Spirit and the gifts of the Spirit are different. While spiritual gifts are given to every believer at salvation (cf. I Cor. 12:7,11), the fruit is another metaphor to describe the motives, attitudes and lifestyle of Jesus Christ. As the gifts are the distribution of the different ministries of Christ among the body of Christ, the fruit is the collective attitude of Christ in performing those gifts. It is possible to have an effective gift and not have a Christlike attitude. Therefore, Christlike maturity, which the fruit of the Spirit brings, gives ultimate glory to God through the various gifts of the Spirit.

It is also interesting to note that fruit is SINGULAR in this verse. The use of the SINGULAR can be understood in two ways: (1) Love is the fruit of the Spirit, described by the varying terms that follow; or (2) it is a collective singular like "seed."

❖ **"love"** (cf. I Cor. 13:13). *Agape* was used by the early church of God's self-giving love. This noun was not used often in classical Greek. The church infused it with new meaning to describe God's special love. Love here is theologically analogous to *hesed*, God's covenant loyalty and love, in the OT.

❖ **"joy"** Joy is an attitude of life that rejoices in who we are in Christ regardless of circumstances (cf. Rom. 14:17; I Thes. 1:6; Jude 24).

❖ **"peace"** Peace may mean: (1) our sense of well-being because of our relationship to Christ; (2) our new worldview based on the

NOTES

revelation of God that does not depend on circumstances; or (3) tranquility in our relationship with other people, especially believers (cf. Jn. 14:27; Rom. 5:1; Phil 4:7).

❖ **"patience"** Longsuffering was proper in the face of provocation. This was a characteristic of God the Father (cf. Rom. 2:4; 9:22; I Tim. 1:18; I Pet. 3:20). As God has been patient with us, we are to be patient with other people, especially believers.

❖ **"kindness, goodness"** "Kindness" describes not only the life of Jesus, but His yoke (cf. Mt. 11:30). Together the two terms describe a positive, open and accepting attitude toward others, especially believers.

❖ **"faithfulness"** *Pistis* is used in its Old Testament sense of loyalty and trustworthiness. It was usually used of God (cf. Rom. 3:3). Here it describes the believer's new relationship with people, especially believers.

5:23 "gentleness" Sometimes translated as "meekness," *praotes* is characterized by a submissive spirit. It was a metaphor taken from domesticated animals. Gentleness was not included in the Greek or Stoic lists of virtues, because it was seen as a weakness. It is uniquely Christian. It was used of both Moses (cf. Num. 12:3) and Jesus (cf. Mt. 5:5).

❖ **"self-control"** The capstone of the list, self-control characterizes Christlike maturity (cf. Acts 24:25; II Pet. 1:6). This term was used in I Cor. 7:9 for the control of our sexual drive and may be alluded to here because of the sexual abuses of pagan worship. Compare Acts 24:25 and II Pet. 1:6.

❖ **"against such things there is no law"** There is a new inner law in the life of a believer which shows its presence by living in godliness. This is exactly the goal of the new covenant (cf. Jer. 31:31-34 and Ezek. 36:22-32). Christlikeness is the goal of God for every Christian (cf. Gal. 4:19; Rom. 8:29).

5:24 "those who belong to Christ Jesus have crucified the flesh" This is AORIST INDICATIVE which speaks of completed action in past time. This passage, and others which imply mystical union, can be interpreted within theological categories. Throughout the book of Galatians, particularly 2:20, "crucify" is used to characterize our relationship to the Law. Once we accept God's free offer of grace in Christ as our only means of salvation, we decisively cut ourselves off from the evil of our fallen nature and the fallen world system. This personal decision of cutting ourselves off is the biblical metaphor of "crucifixion" as seen in Gal. 2:20; 5:24 and 6:14.

❖ **"with its passions and desires"** The Greeks identified the body as the source of sinfulness because they did not have supernatural revelation about Creation and the fall of man. Therefore, they blamed the morally neutral physical body as the source of evil. We understand from Paul that the body is morally neutral (cf. Rom. 4:1; 9:3; I Cor. 10:18). Jesus had a real human body (cf. Jn. 1:14; Rom. 1:3; 9:5). Its goodness or wickedness depends on how we use it, for God or for evil. Once we become believers, we must yield our fallen, self-centered tendencies to the power of the Holy Spirit (cf. Rom. 7 and I Jn. 2:1).

NASB (UPDATED) TEXT: 5:25-26

If we live by the Spirit, let us also walk by the Spirit. Let us not become boastful, challenging one another, envying one another.

5:25 "If we live by the Spirit, let us also walk by the Spirit." This is a FIRST CLASS CONDITIONAL SENTENCE, assumed to be true from the author's perspective or for his literary purposes. It summarizes the entire section (cf. v. 16; Rom. 8:1-11). Since we have been given free grace, we ought to live appropriately.

5:26 This is parallel to verse 15 and shows the terrible consequences of the false teachings of the Judaizers among the churches of Galatia and the absence of the Spirit's control in the attitudes of their congregations.

DISCUSSION QUESTIONS

This is a study guide commentary which means that you are responsible for your own interpretation of the Bible. Each of us must walk in the light we have. You, the Bible and the Holy

126

Spirit are priority in interpretation. You must not relinquish this to a commentator.

These discussion questions are provided to help you think through the major issues of this section of the book. They are meant to be thought provoking, not definitive.

1. Outline chapter 5 in its relationship to the rest of Galatians.

2. Explain freedom and what it means in the Christian life.

3. Explain the contextual meaning of the concluding phrase of verse 4.

4. How does a gospel which is freely offered to us control our lifestyle?

5. What are the implications of verses 15 and 26 for the Church today?

6. Do verses 19-21 describe the churches of Galatia or the tendency of pagan worship?

7. How are the gifts of the Spirit related to the fruit of the Spirit?

NOTES

GALATIANS 6

PARAGRAPH DIVISIONS OF MODERN TRANSLATIONS

UBS¹	NKJV	NRSV	TEV	JB
Bear One Another's burdens 6:1-10	Bear and Share Burdens 6:1-5	Specifics in the Use of Christian Liberty 6:1-5	Bear One Another's Burdens 6:1-5	On Kindness & Perseverance 6:1-5
	Be Generous and Do Good 6:6-10	6:6 6:7-10	6:6 6:7-10	6:6 6:7-10
Final Warnings & Benedictions 6:11-16	Glory Only in the Cross 6:11-15 Blessing and a Plea 6:16-18	Paul's Autograph Postscript 6:11-16	Final Warning and Greeting 6:11-16	Epilogue 6:11-16
6:17		6:17	6:17	6:17-18
6:18		6:18	6:18	

READING CYCLE THREE (see p. vii)
FOLLOWING THE ORIGINAL AUTHOR'S INTENT AT THE PARA-GRAPH LEVEL

This is a study <u>guide</u> commentary which means that you are responsible for your own interpretation of the Bible. Each of us must walk in the light we have. You, the Bible and the Holy Spirit are priority in interpretation. You must not relinquish this to a commentator.

Read the chapter in one sitting. Identify the subjects. Compare your subject divisions with the five translations above. Paragraphing is not inspired but it is the key to following the original author's intent which is the heart of interpretation. Every paragraph has one and only one subject.

1. First paragraph

2. Second paragraph

3. Third paragraph

4. Etc.

CONTEXTUAL INSIGHTS

A. Galatians 5:1-6:10 is the practical aspect of Paul's radical free gospel of Christ, made available to us through the love and grace of God and our repentant faith response.
   1. Chapter 6:1-5 gives us specific guidelines on how to deal with a sinning Christian brother.
   2. Chapter 6:6-10 has two of the most memorable quotes in the NT. Some see it as a series of unrelated truths. Others see it as a literary unit relating to believers' use of money.

B. Galatians 6:12-16 is a brief summary of the entire letter.

C. Paul's brief close of 6:17-18 is reminiscent of his cyclical letter, Ephesians, where closing greetings are notably absent.

WORD AND PHRASE STUDY

> **NASB (UPDATED) TEXT: 6:1-5**
>
> Brethren, even if anyone is caught in any trespass, you who are spiritual, restore such a one in a spirit of gentleness; *each one* looking to yourself, so that you too will not be tempted. Bear one another's burdens, and thereby fulfill the law of Christ. For if anyone thinks he is something when he is nothing, he deceives himself. But each one must examine his own work, and then he will have *reason* for boasting in regard to himself alone, and not in regard to another. For each one will bear his own load.

6:1 "if" This introduces a THIRD CLASS CONDITIONAL SENTENCE meaning potential, even probable action.

❖ **"if anyone is caught"** Literally "surprised," the phrase points out our responsibility for our sin but also of sin's subtle temptations and traps. These people did not premeditatively violate God's grace; they were duped.

130

❖   **NASB, NKJV**   **"in any trespass,"**
          NRSV   **"in a transgression"**
          TEV   **"in any kind of wrongdoing,"**
          JB   **"misbehaves"**

At least three sins may be referred to here: (1) in light of the false teachers, this may refer to those who had succumbed to the temptation of being circumcised and were trying to gain perfection through the Mosaic legislation; (2) because of the strong terms used in 5:15,26, it may refer to the destructive tendencies which were present in the Galatian churches; or (3) this might be related to the pagan worship excesses described in 5:19-21. The guidelines which follow are extremely helpful to show the church how we are to restore a fallen brother to fellowship.

❖   **NASB, TEV**   **"you who are spiritual,"**
          NKJV   **"you who *are* spiritual,"**
          NRSV   **"you who have received the Spirit"**
          JB   **"the more spiritual of you"**

This should not be misconstrued to mean "you who are sinless." Spiritual maturity has already been discussed in 5:16-18 & 22-25. Spiritual maturity is: (1) having the mind of Christ; (2) living out the fruit of the Spirit; (3) having a servant's heart; and (4) serving fellow Christians.

❖ **"restore such a one"** "Restore" is a PRESENT ACTIVE IMPERATIVE, often used of setting a broken bone or fixing fishing nets (cf. I Cor. 1:10). It is crucial for those who are mature in Christ to help all others in the church to attain that stature (cf. Eph. 4:13). This is an ongoing command from Paul.

Forgiveness and being non-judgmental are biblical signs of a mature Christian (cf. Mt. 5:7; 6:14-15; 18:35; Lk. 6:36-37; Jas. 2:13; 5:9). Church discipline must always be redemptive not vindictive (cf. II Cor. 2:7; II Thes. 3:15; Jas. 5:19-20).

❖ **"looking to yourself, so that you too will not be tempted."** "Tempt" [*peirazo*] in this context connotes "to tempt with a view toward destruction." The same word is used of the evil one tempting Jesus in Mt. 4. Another word for "tempt" [*dokimazo*] is used twice in verse 4, but this word connotes "to test with a view toward approval." Satan will test and tempt believers in order to destroy

NOTES

them. Believers must be on guard, without and within (cf. I Cor. 10:12; II Cor. 13:5).

6:2 "Bear one another's burdens," This is a PRESENT ACTIVE IMPERATIVE. "One another" is placed in an emphatic position in the Greek sentence. As a way of life mature Christians are to carry their weaker, less mature brothers (cf. Rom. 14:1; 15:1). "Burden" was used of a crushing weight put on a domestic pack animal (cf. Mt. 23:4). In context it was used metaphorically for the oral traditions of the Judaizers. It is a different term than "burden" in verse 5, a soldier's backpack.

❖ **"and thereby fulfill the law of Christ."** The Law of Christ is also mentioned in I Cor. 9:21 and "the law of the Spirit of life in Jesus Christ" in Rom. 8:2. The Law of Christ is also characterized in different ways in James: (1) 1:25, "the flawless law that makes men free"; (2) 2:8, "the royal law" and (3) 2:12, "the law of liberty." As the yoke of the law had become a pressing burden to the Jews, the yoke of Christ is easy and light (cf. Mt. 11:29-30). However, a yoke it is, and this yoke is our responsibility to love and serve one another as brothers and sisters in Christ.

6:3 "if anyone thinks he is something when he is nothing," This is a FIRST CLASS CONDITIONAL SENTENCE, assumed true from the author's perspective or for the author's literary purposes. Christians should judge themselves so that they can appropriately relate to each other and can avoid overestimating themselves. This does not mean that Christians do not have sin, but that sin does not dominate their lives (cf. I Jn. 3:6, 9). Therefore, they can help and pray for those whose lives are dominated by sin (cf. I Cor. 3:18).

6:4 "he deceives himself." This word occurs only once in the entire NT, meaning to seduce oneself into error. Self-deception is the worst kind of blindness.

❖ **"But each one must examine his own work,"** This is the term for "test" or "tempt" [*dokimazo*] with the connotation of "to test with a view toward approval."

❖ **"and then he will have *reason* for boasting in regard to himself**

alone, and not in regard to another" Believers must be careful not to compare themselves with one another (cf. II Cor. 10:12), especially those who have been surprised and overtaken by sin (cf. v. 1).

6:5 "For each one will bear his own load." This may refer to the judgment seat of Christ in an eschatological/endtime setting (cf. II Cor. 5:10). At first glance, verses 2 and 5 seemingly contradict each other until a closer lexical study shows that the two words translated respectively as "burden" and "load" had different usages. The former word in verse 2 means a "crushing weight" while the latter word in verse 5 means a "soldier's backpack filled with his needed equipment." Mature Christians must carry the load of responsibility for themselves and sometimes, for others. An example of this might be II Cor. 8:13-14. The same term was used of Jesus' guidelines for Christians in Matt. 11:30.

NASB (UPDATED) TEXT: 6:6-10

The one who is taught the word is to share all good things with the one who teaches *him*. Do not be deceived, God is not mocked; for whatever a man sows, this he will also reap. For the one who sows to his own flesh will from the flesh reap corruption, but the one who sows to the Spirit will from the Spirit reap eternal life. Let us not lose heart in doing good, for in due time we will reap if we do not grow weary. So then, while we have opportunity, let us do good to all people, and especially to those who are of the household of the faith.

6:6 Verse 6 either relates to: (1) verses 1-5 which call on the mature to help weaker Christians; or (2) verses 7-10 which describes the law of spiritual sowing and reaping. Those who are taught are under the spiritual responsibility to share in the ministry of those who teach them (cf. Lk. 10:7; Rom. 15:27; I Cor. 9:9-14). This is a general principle, and although Paul did not personally take advantage of remuneration, he advocated it for other ministers. The English word "catechism" is derived from the Greek [*katecheo*] translated as "taught" and "teaches" which are found in this verse.

The teacher either refers to: (1) the gift of teaching as in Acts 13:1 and I Cor. 12:28, or the gift of pastoring/teaching as is found in Eph. 4:11; (2) a teacher in the local congregation who trained new believers and children; or (3) one who taught the entire congregation the implications of the teachings of the Apostles as they applied to their daily lives. This last option would be similar to the OT task of the local Levites and, later, professional scribes.

"Good things" is purposefully ambiguous, referring to the physical needs, spiritual needs or both. The obvious truth is that those who are being taught should be grateful and responsive. Exactly how this verse related to the false teachers is uncertain. Paul could have been referring to himself and the Gentile contribution for Jerusalem.

6:7 "Do not be deceived," This is a PRESENT IMPERATIVE with a NEGATIVE PARTICLE which means to stop an act which was already in process. They were already deceived.

❖ **"God is not mocked;"** This verb means "to turn one's nose up at" something or someone. This may refer to those who are called to minister as God's representatives, that is, the teachers of verse 6. To scoff at Christian ministers is, in a sense, to scoff at God. Jesus, in Mt. 10:42 and 25:40, mentioned that when we help others in His name we are helping Him. This is the same truth but from the opposite direction. However, how these verses relate to one another is uncertain. This may be a general proverb connected with "sowing and reaping" applied in a figurative sense.

This verse may relate to verses 8-10, but does not relate to verse 6 at all. We do not so much break God's law as much as we break ourselves on God's law. Be it known, believer or unbeliever, we reap what we sow. Sin always runs its course, even in the life of believers. Wild oats are very, very expensive—so, too, is self-centered sowing!

6:8 "For the one who sows to his own flesh will from the flesh reap corruption," This refers to the two basic approaches of being right with God (cf. 5:13, 16-17), human effort and free grace.

❖ **"eternal life."** The concept of eternal life which is found in verse 8 is from the word *zoe*. It is used particularly by John to refer to resurrection life. It has the same implication here. Verses 8-10 show the consequences of our sowing and reaping.

NOTES

6:9 "Let us not lose heart in doing good" This is literally "to despair" or "to lose heart" (cf. Lk. 18:1; II Thes. 3:13; II Cor. 4:1, 16). Often Christians grow weary of the very things that they have been called to do.

❖ **"for in due time we will reap if we do not grow weary."** Notice the CONDITIONAL element. It is conditioned on our continued faith response. Also, note the element of God's sovereign timing in our lives. We do not understand why things happen as they do, but because we believe in the sovereignty of God and the specific demands of the free gospel, we direct our lives to certain ways of service and giving.

"Give up" literally means "to loosen one's clothes," though it is often used as a metaphor for physical activity. It is similar to the idiom, "girding up the loins," which meant to pull the robe between the legs and tuck it tightly in the belt in front. This came to be used metaphorically for active mental alertness in spiritual areas.

6:10 "So then, while we have opportunity," This is a PRESENT MIDDLE SUBJUNCTIVE. Believers must continue to watch for opportunities to live out their faith in Christ.

❖ **"let us do good"** Paul stated with conviction that our standing with God does not come by human effort, but he was equally emphatic that once we know God we should live a life of strenuous service. These twin truths are found in Eph. 2:8-9, 10. We are not saved by good works, but we are most definitely saved unto good works.

❖ **"to all people, and especially to those who are of the household of the faith."** Notice that our love is meant for all men for there is always a view toward evangelism in all of our actions (cf. I Cor. 9:19-23). However, our primary focus is on members of the family of God. This is not denominationally focused for we are to take a man at his word that he has trusted in our Christ. Once he has made that confession we are to serve him as Christ served us.

NASB (UPDATED) TEXT: 6:11-16

See with what large letters I am writing to you with my own hand. Those who desire to make a good showing in the flesh

137

> try to compel you to be circumcised, simply so that they will not be persecuted for the cross of Christ. For those who are circumcised do not even keep the Law themselves, but they desire to have you circumcised so that they may boast in your flesh. But may it never be that I would boast, except in the cross of our Lord Jesus Christ, through which the world has been crucified to me, and I to the world. For neither is circumcision anything, nor uncircumcision, but a new creation. And those who will walk by this rule, peace and mercy be upon them, and upon the Israel of God.

6:11 "See with what large letters I am writing to you with my own hand." Paul dictated his letters to a scribe (cf. Rom. 16:22). Some see these final words in Paul's own handwriting as Paul's way of verifying his true letters, in light of II Thes. 2:2. We know from several of Paul's letters that he wrote the concluding sentences in his own hand (cf. I Cor. 16:21; Col. 4:18; II Thes. 3:17 & Philemon v. 19). Since I believe that Paul's thorn in the flesh was oriental ophthalmia, this is an added evidence of his need to write, not in the small, concise writing of a scribe, but with the scrawling hand of a man who was partially blind.

6:12	NASB	"Those who desire to make a good showing in the flesh"
	NKJV	"As many as desire to make a good showing in the flesh,"
	NRSV	"It is those who want to make a good showing in the flesh"
	TEV	"Those who want to show off and brag about external matters"
	JB	"It is only self-interest"

The Judaizers were more concerned with the outer aspects of religion; they wanted a religious show! Convincing the Galatians to be circumcised would be a "feather in their caps" (cf. v. 13c). The false teachers wanted self-affirmation and the absence of persecution at the expense of the Galatian believers.

❖ **"try to compel you to be circumcised,"** Verses 12-16 are a summary of the entire letter which focuses on the inappropriate emphasis of the false teachers on human effort as a means of being saved or of being fully matured. This is a recurrent danger in the modern church as we add service, enthusiasm, ritual, attendance, Bible knowledge, prayer, or any of the good discipleship techniques as a means of being complete in Christ. Paul's great truth was that we are complete in our standing with God when we have trusted Jesus Christ by faith. In light of this new, full acceptance, we will yield ourselves in gratitude and service to others.

❖ **"simply so that they will not be persecuted for the cross of Christ."** This may refer to: (1) Jewish persecution (cf. Acts 13:45,50; 14:2,5,19); the Judaizers by their insistence on the Law of Moses would not be rejected as strenuously as Paul's teaching of free grace in Christ alone; or (2) Roman persecution because Christianity was not a legal, recognized religion as was Judaism. We are not certain when the synagogue instituted its curse formula, which was a way of driving the Christians out (cf. Jn. 9:22,35; 12:42 & 16:2).

6:13 "For those who are circumcised do not even keep the Law themselves," The subject of this sentence is ambiguous, which could be: (1) the false teachers; or (2) aggressive converts within the churches of Galatia. The men who argued circumcision was a means of being right with God could not even keep the whole Law themselves (cf. Rom. 2:17-29). If you break the Law one time in one way, then Jas. 2:10 is a truth to be reckoned with!

6:14 "But may it never be that I would boast, except in the cross of our Lord Jesus Christ," Paul, of all people, knew what it was to be redeemed out of an undeserving life, zealous though it may be (cf. Phil. 3:2-16). Human boasting is excluded when human merit is excluded (cf. Jer. 9:23-26; Rom. 3:27-28; I Cor. 1:26-31).

❖ **"through which the world has been crucified to me, and I to the world."** This is the continuing metaphor throughout Galatians which speaks of our death to the Law and our being alive to God in Christ. This is a PERFECT PASSIVE INDICATIVE which emphasizes a continuing state accomplished by another agent, here the Spirit. This metaphor has been used in 2:20, 5:24, and here expressing how all things become new when we identify with Christ's death on the cross. We are now free from the Law in order to live for God (cf. Rom. 6:10-11, 12-23).

6:15 "For neither is circumcision anything, nor uncircumcision,

NOTES

but a new creation." Paul has already mentioned that circumcision is not the issue (cf. Gal. 5:6; Rom. 2:28-29; I Cor. 7:18-19). The truth is that if we try to make ourselves acceptable to God by human effort, either pagan or Jew, we are totally cut off from the absolutely free gift of God in Jesus Christ. Two mutually exclusive ways of being right with God are available: (1) the freeness of Christ's offer through repentance and faith and (2) human effort. Paul restated that circumcision is not really the issue, nor were the food laws (cf. I Cor. 8; 10:23-26), but how one pursues right standing with God.

❖ **"but a new creation"** This is the upshot; that we are brand new people in Jesus Christ. All old things have passed away and everything is new (cf. Rom. 6:4; II Cor. 5:17; Eph. 2:15; 4:24; Col. 3:10).

6:16 "And those who will walk by this rule, peace and mercy be upon them," This may be a loose quotation from Psa. 124:5 and 127:6. From the Greek word "rule" [*kanoni*] the English word "canon" is derived. This was a construction term used for a measuring reed. It is used here to refer to the gospel. Notice we are to walk in it, not just affirm it.

❖ **"the Israel of God."** Significantly Paul calls the Church "the true Israel of God." Throughout Galatians he has emphasized that Abraham's true seed is not by racial descent but by faith descent (cf. Gal. 3:29; Rom. 9:6; Phil. 3:3).

NASB (UPDATED) TEXT: 6:17

From now on let no one cause trouble for me, for I bear on my body the brand-marks of Jesus.

6:17 "From now on let no one cause trouble for me," To whom this is addressed or why is not known. Paul appealed to his service of Christ as the reason that this should not happen again. It possibly refers to the personal attacks that the false teachers used to alienate the Galatian believers from the gospel. The believers allowed this to happen!

❖ **"for I bear on my body the brand-marks of Jesus."** As the false teachers were emphasizing circumcision as a mark of God's covenant, Paul asserted that he also had an outward sign. They were the signs of his physical persecution for preaching the good news of Christ (cf. II Cor. 4:7-12; 6:4-6; 11:23-28).

NASB (UPDATED) TEXT: 6:18

The grace of our Lord Jesus Christ be with your spirit, brethren. Amen.

6:18 This is an example of a brief blessing in a cyclical letter. Note that the term "be with your spirit" is a good example of the small "s" (spirit) which is used of man's spirit, not the Holy Spirit. However, in many instances in the New Testament, it refers to man's spirit which is energized by the Holy Spirit. This is probably the implication here.

DISCUSSION QUESTIONS

This is a study <u>guide</u> commentary which means that you are responsible for your own interpretation of the Bible. Each of us must walk in the light we have. You, the Bible and the Holy Spirit are priority in interpretation. You must not relinquish this to a commentator.

These discussion questions are provided to help you think through the major issues of this section of the book. They are meant to be thought provoking, not definitive.

1. What are the biblical guidelines for restoring a fallen brother?

2. Are verses 2 and 5 contradictory?

3. What does verse 6 say about Christians supporting Christian ministries?

4. Describe in your own words the biblical law of sowing and reaping.

5. Describe in your own words the biblical idea of two ways to salvation that are brought out in such clarity in the book of Galatians.

6. Explain in your own words how verse 9 is related to verses 6 and 7.

7. If circumcision was not the issue of verse 15, why did Paul make such an issue of it?

8. What are the implications of the Church being called the true Israel of God in verse 16?

NOTES

PAUL'S EPISTLES
TO THE
THESSALONIANS

I THESSALONIANS
and
II THESSALONIANS

INTRODUCTION TO THE THESSALONIAN LETTERS

A. Brief Summary
 1. The Thessalonian letters provide tremendous insight into Paul as both missionary and pastor. We find him establishing a church in a brief time and continuing to pray and be concerned about its growth, development, and ministry.
 2. We see him faithfully proclaiming the Gospel of God, concerned for the converts, scolding them, praising them, guiding them, exhorting them, teaching them, loving them, even giving of himself to them. He was thrilled with their progress to that point, but was disappointed with the rate at which they matured.
 3. In these Epistles we meet a zealous, loving servant of Christ and a zealous, small, but growing new church. Both were faithful, both were used by God, and both served each other in a Christlike manner seldom found among God's people.

B. The City of Thessalonica
 1. Brief History of Thessalonica
  a. Thessalonica was located at the head of the Thermaic Gulf. Thessalonica was a coastal town on a major Roman road, the Ignatian Road, running eastward from Rome. A seaport, it was also very close to a rich, well-watered, coastal plain. These three advantages made Thessalonica the largest, most important commercial and political center in Macedonia.
  b. Thessalonica was originally named Therma, derived from the hot springs located in the area. An early historian, Pliny the Elder,

refers to Therma and Thessalonica existing together. If this is the case, Thessalonica simply surrounded Therma and annexed it (Leon Morris, *The First and Second Epistles to the Thessalonians*, Grand Rapids: Wm. B. Eerdmans Publishing Company, 1991, p. 11). Yet most historians believe Cassander, one of Alexander the Great's generals, renamed Therma in 315 B.C. after Philip of Macedonia's daughter and his wife, Thessalonica. Sometime during the early years of the spread of Christianity, Thessalonica was nicknamed "the orthodox city" because of its Christian character (Dean Farrar, *The Life and Work of St. Paul*, New York: Cassell and Company, Limited, 1904, p. 364). Today Thessalonica is known as Salonika and it still is an important city in Greece.

c. Thessalonica was a cosmopolitan metropolis similar to Corinth, inhabited by peoples from all over the known world.

   (1) Barbaric Germanic peoples from the north were living there, bringing with them their pagan religion and culture.

   (2) Greeks lived there, coming from Achaia to the south and from the islands of the Aegean Sea, in turn bringing their refinement and philosophy.

   (3) Romans from the west also settled there. They were mostly retired soldiers and they brought their strength of will, wealth and political power.

   (4) Finally, Jews came in large numbers from the east; by the tenth century, one third of the population was Jewish. They brought with them their ethical monotheistic faith and their national prejudices.

d. Thessalonica, with a population of about 100,000, was truly a cosmopolitan city (J. W. Shepard, *The Life and Letters of Paul*, Grand

148

Rapids: Wm. B. Eerdmans Publishing Company, 1950, p. 164). It was a resort and health center because of the hot springs. It was a commercial center because of its seaport, fertile plains and the proximity of the Ignatian Way.

e. As the capital and largest city, Thessalonica was also the central political headquarters of Macedonia (Morris, p. 11). Being a Roman provincial capital and home of many Roman citizens (mostly retired soldiers), it became a free city. Thessalonica paid no tribute and was governed by Roman law, since most Thessalonians were Roman citizens. Thus the Thessalonian rulers were called "politarchs." This title appears nowhere else in literature but it is preserved by an inscription over the triumphal arch at Thessalonica known as the Vardar Gate (Farrar, p. 371n.).

2. Events Leading to Paul's Coming to Thessalonica

a. Many events led Paul to Thessalonica, yet behind all the physical circumstances is the direct, definite call of God. Paul had not originally planned to enter the European continent. But his desire on this second missionary journey was to revisit the churches in Asia Minor that he had established on his first journey and then to turn eastward. Yet, just as the moment arrived to turn northeastward, God started closing the doors. The culmination of this was Paul's Macedonian vision (cf. Acts 16:6-10). This caused two things to happen: first, the continent of Europe was evangelized and second, Paul, because of circumstances in Macedonia, began writing his Epistles (Thomas Carter, *Life and Letters of Paul,* Nashville: Cokesbury Press, 1921, p. 112).

b. After noting the above spiritual direction, examine the physical setting that led Paul to Thessalonica:

(1) Paul went to Philippi, a small town with no synagogue. His work there was

149

thwarted by the owner of a prophetic, demonic slave girl and the town council. Paul was beaten and humiliated yet a church was formed even in the midst of all this. Because of the opposition and physical punishment, Paul was forced to leave, possibly sooner than he had wished.

(2) Where would he go from there? He passed through Amphipolis and Apollonia.

(3) He came to the largest city in the area, Thessalonica, which did have a synagogue. Paul had made it a pattern to go to the local Jews first. He did this because:

    (a) of their knowledge of the Old Testament;

    (b) of the opportunity for teaching and preaching that the synagogue presented;

    (c) of their position as the chosen people, God's covenant people (cf. Mt. 10:6; 15:24; Rom. 1:16-17; 9-11);

    (d) Jesus had offered Himself first to them, then to the world—so, too, Paul would follow Christ's example. (cf. Mt. 10:6; 15:24; Rom. 1:16-17; 9-11)

3. Paul's Companions

  a. Paul was accompanied by Silas and Timothy in Thessalonica. Luke was with Paul at Philippi but he remained there. We learn this by the "we" and "they" passages of Acts 16 and 17. Luke speaks of "we" at Philippi, but of "they" as traveling to Thessalonica.

  b. Silas, or Silvanus, was the man Paul chose to go with him on the second missionary journey after Barnabas and John Mark went back to Cyprus:

    (1) He is first mentioned in the Bible in

Acts 15:22 where he is called a chief man among the brethren of the Jerusalem Church.

(2) He was also a prophet (cf. Acts 15:32).

(3) He was a Roman citizen like Paul (cf. Acts 16:37).

(4) He and Judas Barsabbas were sent to Antioch by the Jerusalem Church to inspect the situation.

(5) Paul praises him in II Cor. 1:19 and mentions him in several letters.

(6) Later he is identified with Peter in writing I Peter. (cf. I Pet. 5:12).

(7) Both Paul and Peter call him Silvanus while Luke calls him Silas.

c. Timothy was also a companion and fellow-worker of Paul:

(1) Paul met him at Lystra where he was converted on the first missionary journey. Thus the Jews had him circumcised as a preliminary to his accompanying the Apostle on the remainder of the second missionary journey. Timothy is more closely linked with Paul than is Silas.

(2) Timothy was half Greek (father) and half Jewish (mother). Paul wanted to use him to work with evangelizing the Gentiles.

(3) Timothy is mentioned in the salutation in: II Corinthians, Colossians, I and II Thessalonians and Philemon.

(4) Paul spoke of him as "my son in the ministry" (cf. I Tim. 1:2; II Tim. 1:2; Tit. 1:4).

(5) Paul's general tone throughout his letters implies Timothy was young and timid. Yet Paul has great confidence and trust in him (cf. Acts 19:27; I Cor. 4:17; Phil. 2:19).

d. It is only fitting in the section on Paul's companions that mention is made of the men who

151

came to Thessalonica and accompanied Paul on his later missions. They are Aristarchus (Acts 19:29; 20:4; 27:2) and Secundus (Acts 20:4). Also, Demas could have been from Thessalonica (Philem. 24; II Tim. 4:10).

4. Paul's Ministry in the City

   a. Paul's ministry in Thessalonica followed his usual pattern of going to the Jews first and then turning to the Gentiles. Paul preached on three Sabbaths in the synagogue. His message was "Jesus is the Messiah." He used Old Testament Scriptures to show that the Messiah was to be a suffering Messiah, and not a political temporal Messiah. Paul also emphasized the resurrection and offered salvation to all. Jesus was clearly presented as the Messiah promised of old that would save all men.

   b. The response to this message was that some Jews, many devout Gentiles, and many important women accepted Jesus as Savior and Lord. An analysis of these groups of converts is very meaningful in understanding Paul's later letters to this church.

   c. Gentiles comprised most of the members of the church, a condition evinced by the absence of allusions to the OT in either of the two epistles (Farrar, p. 368). The Gentiles readily accepted Jesus as Savior and Lord for several reasons:

     (1) Their traditional religions were powerless superstition. Thessalonica lay at the foot of Mt. Olympus and all knew its heights were empty.

     (2) The Gospel was free to all.

     (3) Christianity contained no Jewish exclusive nationalism. The Jewish religion had attracted many because of its monotheism and its high morals, but it also repelled many because of its repugnant ceremonics (such as circumcision), and its inherent racial and national prejudices.

d. Many "chief women" accepted Christianity, because of these women's abilities to make their own religious choices. Women were more free in Macedonia and Asia Minor than in the rest of the Greco-Roman world (Sir Wm. M. Ramsay, *St. Paul the Traveller and Roman Citizen*, New York: G. P. Putnam's Sons, 1896, p. 227). Yet the poorer class of women, although free, were still under the sway of superstition and polytheism (Ramsay, p. 229).

e. Many have found a problem in the length of time that Paul stayed at Thessalonica. Acts 17:2 speaks of Paul's reasoning in the synagogue on three Sabbaths while in Thessalonica. I Thes. 2:7-11 tells of Paul's working at his trade. This was tent-making or as some have suggested working with leather. Phil. 4:16 supports the longer residence, when Paul received at least two money gifts from the church at Philippi while in Thessalonica. The distance between the two cities is about 100 miles. Some suggest that Paul stayed about two or three months and that the three Sabbaths only refer to the ministry to the Jews (Shepard, p. 165). The differing accounts of the converts in Acts 17:4 and I Thes. 1:9 and 2:4 support this view, the key difference in the accounts being the rejection of idols by the Gentiles. The Gentiles in Acts were Jewish proselytes and had already turned from idols. The context implies Paul may have had a larger ministry among pagan Gentiles than Jews (Morris, p. 17).

f. When a larger ministry might have occurred is uncertain because Paul always went to the Jews first. After they rejected his message, he turned to the Gentiles. When they responded to the Gospel in large numbers, the Jews became jealous and started a riot among the rabble of the city. They themselves did not riot, however, since Jews throughout the world were under suspicion of the local governmen-

153

tal officials. There had been a major riot in Rome apparently over "Chrestus" or "Christus." Many believe this was a fight between Jews and Christians over Jesus. The Jews were expelled from Rome for a period of time.

g. Because of this riot Paul left Jason's ("Jason" is a Hellenized form of Jesus) house and hid with Timothy and Silas or at least they were not present when the mob stormed Jason's house looking for them. The Politarchs made Jason put up a security bond to insure peace. This caused Paul to leave the city by night and go to Berea. Nevertheless, the church continued its witness of Christ in the face of much opposition.

AUTHOR

A. I Thessalonians. Only modern form critics have seriously doubted Paul's authorship and the authenticity of I Thes., but their conclusions have not convinced many scholars. I Thes. is included in Marcion's canon (A.D. 140) and in the Muratorian Fragment (A.D. 170). Both lists of canonical books of the NT circulated in Rome. Irenaeus quoted I Thes. by name—he wrote around 180 A.D.

B. II Thessalonians.

1. The book of II Thes. has not always been accepted as Pauline and has been attacked on several grounds:

a. The vocabulary poses one problem. The epistle contains "a relatively high proportion of words not found in the genuine Pauline epistles."

b. "The style is stereotyped and at times] curiously formal" (Heard, p. 186).

c. The eschatology of the two letters is supposedly inconsistent.

d. II Thes. contains a view of the anti-Christ evidently unparalleled in the NT, therefore, some conclude that Paul could not be the author.

154

2. The authenticity of II Thes. is based on several premises:
    a. Polycarp, Ignatius, and Justin recognized it;
    b. The Marcionite canon included it;
    c. The Muratorian Fragment included it;
    d. Irenaeus quoted it by name;
    e. The vocabulary, style and theology are as Pauline as I Thes.

C. The Two Compared
    1. The two epistles are very similar, not only in ideas, but also in actual phraseology. If the opening and closing formula language are excluded, resemblances still occur in about one-third of the material.
    2. The general tone of II Thes. is different from the first letter, being colder and more formal. Yet this can easily be understood when one sees the emotional circumstances involved in the writing of the first letter.

D. The Order of the Letters
    1. Another interesting hypothesis is presented by F. W. Manson using Johannes Weiss' notes. They contend that the order of the books is reversed. The reasons for this are:
        a. the trials and tribulations are at their height in II Thes., but are past in I Thes.;
        b. in II Thes. the internal difficulties are spoken of as a new development of which the author of the letter has just learned, whereas in I Thes. the circumstances were familiar to all concerned;
        c. the statement that the Thessalonians have no need to be instructed about times and seasons (I Thes. 5:1) is very relevant if they are acquainted with II Thes. 2;
        d. the formula "Now concerning..." in I Thes. 4:9, 13; 5:1, is like that in I Cor. 7:1,25; 8:1; 12:1; 16:1,12, where the writer is replying to points raised in a letter sent to him. Manson thinks that the replies might concern certain

questions arising from statements in II Thes.

2. Several premises may counteract this argument:
   a. the problems occupying Paul's attention intensify and deepen from I Thes. to II Thes.;
   b. the passages in II Thes. refer to a letter from Paul (2:2, 15; 3:17) and if we assume this letter not to be I Thes., then we have the problem of a lost letter;
   c. the personal reminiscences forming so prominent a part of the first letter are lacking in the second, which seems natural if the letter is a sequel to the first;
   d. the tone of the letters seems completely unnatural to this situation if the order is reversed.

DATE OF LETTERS

A. The date for the writing of the Thessalonian Letters is one of the most certain dates we have involving Paul's Epistles. It is recorded that while Paul was in "Corinth he was arrested and brought before Gallio, the proconsul of Achaia." An inscription discovered at Delphi answers a question referred to the Emperor Claudius by this same Gallio. It was dated in the twelfth year of the Emperor's tribunal power and after his twenty-sixth acclamation as Emperor. This twelfth year was from 25 January A.D. 52 through 24 January A.D. 53. While the date of the twenty-sixth acclamation is not exactly known, the twenty-seventh was before 1 August A.D. 52. Claudius' decision would have been given to Gallio during the first half of 52. Now proconsuls usually took office in early summer and held office for one year. It would seem, therefore, Gallio entered his term of office in the early summer of 51" (Morris, p. 15).

B. This dating of the term of office of the proconsul does not completely solve all the problems of the dating of the Thessalonian Letters. Paul was in Corinth for 18 months (Acts 18:11) but at which time he appeared before Gallio is not known. Most commentators date I and II Thessalonians in 50-51 A.D.

EVENTS SURROUNDING THE THESSALONIAN LETTERS

A. The events that led to Paul's writing of the Thessalonian letters are complex and intertwined. Certain distinctions must be noted, especially concerning the physical setting and the emotional setting. Paul was forced to leave the new Thessalonian believers because the Jews had incited the superstitious, polytheistic rabble of the city to riot at Jason's house in a search for Paul and his companions. After a hearing before the Politarchs, Jason and other Christian leaders were forced to put up a security bond to assure peace. When Paul heard of this he knew he had to move on and leave this young, immature church. He, therefore, went to Berea with Timothy and Silas. Timothy apparently stayed at first (cf. Acts 17:10) then later joined Silas to go to Athens (cf. Acts 17:15). At first the honest reception of the Jews at Berea was a blessing to Paul in contrast to previous Jewish opposition. Yet this did not last long. The Jews from Thessalonica came down to Berea and started causing trouble. Therefore, Paul had to leave again.

B. This time Paul went to Athens where he received a cold and unresponsive welcome. He became a novelty to the academic philosophers. His experience in Macedonia was characterized by persecution and opposition. He was beaten, stripped naked, and chased out of town by night. Scholars mocked him, and pagans and many of his own countrymen hated him (cf. II Cor. 4:7-11; 6:4-10; 11:23-29).

C. Paul had been forced to leave this promising church at Thessalonica at a crucial time. They were immature in the faith and were facing affliction and persecution. Paul could stand the mental anguish no longer. Worried about the young converts, somewhere between Berea and Athens, Paul sent Timothy and Silas back to the new Macedonian churches. Timothy went to Thessalonica. Many feel he stayed and ministered there for six months to a year. The church desperately needed someone to teach them, comfort them and encourage them. Timothy himself was a fairly new convert. He was converted on Paul's first missionary journey, but he had only been with Paul since Paul went to Lystra on his second missionary journey. He was, therefore, new in the ministry but Paul had great confidence in him. This was Timothy's first pastorate.

D. Paul ministered in Athens alone and he became very discouraged and depressed because of the lack of response to the gospel and his incessant concern for the new Christians there. He was concerned about the Thessalonian church in particular. Could a church be founded in such a short time and in difficult circumstances and still endure? (Carter, p. 115) To add to this he had received no word from Timothy and Silas for some time (six months to a year, although some say only one or two months) (Farrar, p. 369). This was the emotional state in which we found Paul as he arrived in Corinth.

E. In Corinth two things happened that greatly encouraged Paul.
   1. The vision that God had many in Corinth who would respond to the Gospel (Acts 18:9-10).
   2. Timothy and Silas arrived and brought good news (Acts 18:5). It was Timothy's message from Thessalonica that would lead Paul to write to them from Corinth. Paul was responding to questions from the church on doctrinal and practical issues in the ministry.

F. The occasion for II Thes. was not long after because the first letter did not achieve all that Paul had hoped it would. Also, he had become aware of more problems. Many scholars believe II Thes. was written about six months after I Thes., though Leon Morris believes it was only a few weeks (Morris, p. 30).

PURPOSE OF THE LETTERS

A. The Thessalonian Letters have a threefold purpose:
   1. to share Paul's joy and thanksgiving to God for the faithfulness and Christlikeness of the Thessalonians.

158

2. to answer the criticism of his motives and character which had been brought against him.
3. to discuss the return of the Lord. This eschatological element of Paul's preaching caused two questions in the minds of the Thessalonian Christians:
    a. What would happen to believers who had died before the Lord's return?
    b. What would happen to the believers in the congregation who had stopped working and were sitting around waiting for the Lord's return (Barclay, pp. 21-22)?

B. The specific purposes of I Thessalonians as listed by Leon Morris in his commentary (pp. 18-19) are:
    1. to answer Jewish opponents in their mean-spirited campaign against Paul,
    2. to help Christians face pagan persecution (2:14ff.),
    3. to exhort Christians not to succumb to old pagan practices (4:4-6),
    4. to dispel the idea of merely waiting for Christ's return and not working for His Kingdom (4:11ff.),
    5. to help comfort and explain to those who had lost loved ones about their deceased's place in Jesus' return (4:13-15),
    6. to dispel the immediate time element of the Parousia (5:1-3),
    7. to ease tension that may have existed between different members of the congregation (5:12ff.),
    8. there may have been some difficulty about the work of the Holy Spirit and the importance of spiritual gifts (5:19ff.).

C. Much of the above can be explained by the fact that this was a young and very zealous church. Yet because of the circumstances, they were imperfectly trained and disciplined. These problems represent what would be expected of a church of this nature. We find the weak, the fainthearted, the idle, the working, the visionary, and the puzzled.

D. The occasion for II Thessalonians was, "It is simply a second prescription for the same case, made after discovering that certain stubborn symptoms had not yielded to the first treatment." (Walker, p. 2968)

BIBLIOGRAPHY OF SOURCES CITED

Barclay, William. *The Letters and the Revelation. The New Testament.* 2 vol. New York: Collins, 1969.

Carter, Thomas. *Life and Letters of Paul.* Nashville: Cokesbury Press, 1921.

Farrar, Dean. *The Life and Work of St. Paul.* New York: Cassell and Company, Limited, 1904.

Heard, Richard. *An Introduction to the New Testament.* New York: Harper and Row Publishers, 1950.

Metzger, Bruce Manning. *The New Testament: Its Background, Growth and Content.* Nashville: Abingdon Press, 1965.

Manson, T. W. *Studies in the Gospels and Epistles.* Philadelphia: Westminster, 1962.

Morris, Leon. *The First and Second Epistles to the Thessalonians.* Grand Rapids: Eerdmans, 1991.

Ramsay, W. M. *St. Paul the Traveller and Roman Citizen.* New York: G. P. Putnam's Sons, 1896.

Shepard, J. W. *The Life and Letters of Paul.* Grand Rapids: Wm. B. Eerdmans Publishing Company, 1950.

Walker, R. H. *The International Standard Bible Encyclopedia.* Vol. V. N. D.

CONTENT OUTLINE
    A. Greeting, 1:1
    B. Prayer of Thanksgiving, 1:2-4
    C. Reminiscences, 1:5-2:16
        1. Response of the Thessalonians to the original preaching, 1:5-10

2. The preaching of the Gospel at Thessalonica, 2:1-16
    a. The purity of the team's motives, 2:1-6a
    b. The team's refusal to accept maintenance, 2:6b-9
    c. The team's behavior had been impeccable, 2:10-12
    d. The team's message of the Word of God, 2:13
    e. Persecution, 2:14-16

D. The Relationship of Paul to the Thessalonians, 2:17-3:13
    1. His desire to return, 2:17,18
    2. Paul's joy in the Thessalonians, 2:19, 20
    3. Timothy's mission, 3:1-5
    4. Timothy's report, 3:6-8
    5. Paul's satisfaction, 3:9, 10
    6. Paul's prayer, 3:11-13

E. Exhortation to Christian Living, 4:1-12
    1. General, 4:1, 2
    2. Sexual purity, 4:3-8
    3. Brotherly love, 4:9, 10
    4. Earning one's living, 4:11, 12

F. Problems Associated with the Second Coming, 4:13-5:11
    1. Believers who died before the Parousia, 4:13-18
    2. The time of the Parousia, 5:1-3
    3. Children of the day, 5:4-11

G. General Exhortations, 5:12-22

H. Conclusion, 5:23-28

READING CYCLE ONE (see p. vi)

(see p. vi)

This is a study <u>guide</u> commentary which means that you are responsible for your own interpretation of the Bible. Each of us must walk in the light we have. You, the Bible and the Holy Spirit are priority in interpretation. You must not relinquish this to a commentator.

Therefore, read the entire biblical book at one sitting. State the central theme of the entire book in your own words.

1. Theme of entire book

2. Type of literature (genre)

READING CYCLE TWO (see pp. vi-vii.)

This is a study <u>guide</u> commentary which means that you are responsible for your own interpretation of the Bible. Each of us must walk in the light we have. You, the Bible and the Holy Spirit are priority in interpretation. You must not relinquish this to a commentator.

Therefore, read the entire biblical book a second time at one sitting. Outline the main subjects and express the subject in a single sentence.

1. Subject of first literary unit

2. Subject of second literary unit

3. Subject of third literary unit

4. Subject of fourth literary unit

5. Etc.

I THESSALONIANS 1

PARAGRAPH DIVISIONS OF MODERN TRANSLATIONS*

UBS⁴	NKJV	NRSV	TEV	JB
Salutation	Greeting	Salutation	Salutation	Address
1:1	1:1	1:1	1:1	1:1
The Thessalonians'	Their Good	Thanksgiving	The Love and Faith	Thanksgiving and
Faith & Example	Example		of the Thessalonians	Congratulations
1:2-10	1:2-10	1:2-10	1:2-10	1:2-3
				1:4-10

READING CYCLE THREE (see p. vii)
*FOLLOWING THE ORIGINAL AUTHOR'S INTENT AT THE PARA-
GRAPH LEVEL*

This is a study <u>guide</u> commentary which means that you are responsible for your own interpretation of the Bible. Each of us must walk in the light we have. You, the Bible and the Holy Spirit are priority in interpretation. You must not relinquish this to a commentator.

Read the chapter in one sitting.   Identify the subjects. Compare your subject divisions with the five translations above. Paragraphing is not inspired but it is the key to following the original author's intent which is the heart of interpretation. Every paragraph has one and only one subject.

1. First paragraph

---

*Although not inspired, paragraph divisions are the key in understanding and following the original author's intent. Each modern translation has divided and summarized chapter one. Every paragraph has one central topic, truth, or thought. Each version encapsulates that topic in its own distinct way. As you read the text, which translation fits your understanding of the subject and verse divisions?

In every chapter you must read the Bible first and try to identify its subjects (paragraphs).   Then compare your understanding with the modern versions. Only when one understands the original author's intent by following his logic and presentation can one truly understand the Bible. Only the original author is inspired—readers have no right to change or modify the message. Bible readers do have the responsibility of applying the inspired truth to their day and their lives.

Note that all technical terms and abbreviations are explained fully in Appendices One, Two and Three.

2. Second paragraph

3. Third paragraph

4. Etc.

CONTEXTUAL INSIGHTS TO VERSES 1-10

A. Verse 1 is a standard letter form of the first century. Paul made it uniquely Christian by substituting "grace" for the similar sounding Greek word "greetings" (*charis* vs. *charein*).

B. Verses 2-10 form one long thanksgiving prayer to God for the believers at Thessalonica:
   1. Verses 2-5 form one sentence that describes Paul's evangelistic witness.
   2. Verses 6-9 describe the Thessalonians' response.

WORD AND PHRASE STUDY

> **NASB (UPDATED) TEXT: 1:1**
>
> **Paul and Silvanus and Timothy to the church of the Thessalonians in God the Father and the Lord Jesus Christ: Grace to you and peace.**

1:1 "Paul" His name meant "little." This may refer either to his physical stature or to his own estimation of his spiritual worth. Paul considered himself the least of the saints because he persecuted the church (cf. I Cor. 15:9; Eph. 3:8; I Tim. 1:15). Notice there is no defense of Paul's apostleship in this introduction to the Thessalonian church.

❖**"Silvanus"** This was his Roman name. He, like Paul, was a Roman citizen (cf. Acts 16:37). Luke called him "Silas." He was a gifted prophet and a respected member of the Jerusalem church like Barnabas (cf. Acts 15:22,27,32; I Pet. 5:12). He replaced Barnabas as Paul's companion on the second and third missionary journeys.

❖**"Timothy"** He was Paul's convert from Lystra on his first missionary journey. Timothy became Paul's team member on the second journey (cf. Acts 16:1-3).

❖**"the Thessalonians"** Acts 17:1-9 describes Paul's encounter with these people.

❖**"church"** *Ekklesia* means "called out ones." It originally meant a town assembly in Greek society. The Greek translation of the OT, the Septuagint, uses this equivalent for the Hebrew *qahal* meaning "congregation." The early church considered themselves the Messianic congregation of Israel.

❖**"in God the Father and the Lord Jesus Christ:"** God and Jesus are combined in a syntactical way by using one preposition to identify them both (cf. 3:11; II Thes. 1:2, 12; 2:16). This is one technique used by the NT authors to theologically assert the deity of Christ. Another was to attribute OT titles and functions of YHWH to Jesus of Nazareth.

❖**"the Lord"** God revealed His covenant name to Moses in Ex. 3:14 —YHWH. It was from the CAUSATIVE FORM of the verb, "to be." The Jews were afraid to pronounce this holy name, lest they take it in vain and break one of the Ten Commandments. Therefore, they substituted another word when they read the Scriptures, *Adonai*, which meant, "husband, owner, master, lord." This is the source of the English translation of YHWH: LORD.

When the NT authors called Jesus, "Lord," they were asserting the deity of Jesus. This affirmation became the early church's baptismal formula, "Jesus is Lord" (cf. Rom. 10:9-13; Phil. 2:6-11).

❖**"Jesus"** This name means "YHWH saves" (cf. Mt. 1:21), equivalent to the OT name "Joshua." "Jesus" is derived from the Hebrew word for salvation, "Hosea," suffixed to the covenant name for God "YHWH."

❖**"Christ"** This is a translation of the Hebrew term for "Anointed One." This refers to the special empowering by the Spirit in the OT. It is the Hebrew term "Messiah."

NOTES

❖**"Grace"** Paul took the secular greeting *charein* [greetings] and changed it to *charis* [grace] making it uniquely Christian.

❖**"peace"** "Peace" reflects the Hebrew greeting *shalom.* The phrase "grace and peace" was possibly intended to combine traditional Greek and Hebrew greetings.

The King James Version adds a typical Pauline phrase from II Thes. 1:1 after "peace." This phrase does not appear in the Greek manuscripts B, F, or G. It appears in manuscripts א and A. A slightly modified form appears in manuscript D. Manuscripts of the Vulgate, Syriac and Coptic translations alternatively include and exclude it. It may be a scribal gloss from II Thes. 1:1.

NASB (UPDATED) TEXT: 1:2-10

We give thanks to God always for all of you, making mention *of you* in our prayers; constantly bearing in mind your work of faith and labor of love and steadfastness of hope in our Lord Jesus Christ in the presence of our God and Father, knowing, brethren beloved by God, His choice of you; for our gospel did not come to you in word only, but also in Spirit and with full conviction; just as you know what kind of men we proved to be among you for your sake. You also became imitators of us and of the Lord, having received the word in much tribulation with joy of the Holy Spirit, so that you became an example to all the believers in Macedonia and in Achaia. For the word of the Lord has sounded forth from you, not only in Macedonia and Achaia, but also in every place your faith toward God has gone forth, so that we have no need to say anything. For they themselves report about us what kind of a reception we had with you, and how you turned to God from idols to serve a living and true God, and to wait for His Son from heaven, whom He raised from the dead, *that* is Jesus, who rescues us from the wrath to come.

1:2 "We" Referring to Paul, Silas and Timothy, Paul used this PLURAL PRONOUN more often in I Thes. than in any other letter. It does not imply Silas and Timothy helped write the letter.

❖**"We give thanks to God"** This is a PRESENT ACTIVE INDICATIVE indicating continuous action. A spirit of thanksgiving characterizes the entire letter (cf. 2:13; 3:9). Paul had a wonderful relationship with this church.

❖**"making mention of you"** This is a PRESENT MIDDLE PARTICIPLE indicating a purposeful decision by Paul to continue to pray. The syntactical structure of Paul's prayer can be seen in the three dependent clauses: (1) making mention (v. 2); (2) constantly bearing in mind (v. 3); and (3) knowing (v. 4).

1:3 "constantly bearing in mind" This is a PRESENT ACTIVE PARTICIPLE. This shows Paul's intense, abiding concern for these believers.

❖	NASB, NRSV	"YOUR WORK OF FAITH AND LABOR OF LOVE AND STEADFASTNESS OF HOPE"
	NKJV	"YOUR WORK OF FAITH AND LABOR OF LOVE AND PATIENCE OF HOPE"
	TEV	"HOW YOU PUT YOUR FAITH INTO PRACTICE, HOW YOUR LOVE MADE YOU WORK SO HARD, AND HOW YOUR HOPE IN OUR LORD JESUS CHRIST IS FIRM."
	JB	"YOUR FAITH IN ACTION, WORKED FOR LOVE AND PERSEVERED THROUGH HOPE"

These characteristics form the basis of Paul's thanksgiving to God. In Eph. 2:8-10, grace and faith are related to good works. These three terms are often linked in the NT (cf. Rom. 5:2-5; I Cor. 13:13; Gal. 5:5-6; Col. 1:4-5; I Thes. 5:8; Heb. 6:10-12; 10:22-24; I Pet. 1:21-22). The order often differs. "Faith," in this context, does not refer to doctrine but to personal trust (cf. v. 8).

❖**"labor"** "Labor" is a very strong word—Christianity is active—not passive.

❖**"steadfastness"** This is not a passive concept but refers to active, voluntary, steadfast endurance in the face of trials. It meant to see a need and then voluntarily help carry the load as long as needed.

❖**"hope...in the presence of our God"** This refers to the *parousia* or Second Coming. This is a major theme of this letter (cf. 1:10; 3:13; 4:13-5:11; 5:32; II Thes. 1:7,10). "Hope" does not have the connotation of a doubtful "maybe" or "could be" as in English, but rather the expectation of a certain event with an ambiguous time element.

1:4 "beloved by God," Literally "divinely loved ones," this PER-FECT PASSIVE PARTICIPLE phrase is theologically linked to their election (cf. Eph. 1:4-5). It emphasizes our continuing status as "loved ones." The agent of love is God. The next phrase in v. 4 also supports this great truth of God's electing, sovereign choice of the Thessalonian believers.

❖   **NASB**   **"His choice of you;"**
         NKJV   **"your election by God."**
         NRSV   **"that he has chosen you,"**
         TEV   **"God...has chosen you"**
         JB   **"that you have been chosen,"**

While no verb appears (just the noun phrase "the choice of you"), the agent of action is obvious: God.

1:5   **NASB, NKJV**   **"did not come to you in word only,"**
       NRSV   **"came to you not in word only,"**
       TEV   **"not with words only,"**
       JB   **"it came to you not only as words"**

More than just an abstract idea, the Gospel has changed lives (cf. Romans 1:16; Jas. 2:14-26).

❖   **NASB, NRSV**   **"in the Holy Spirit and with full conviction;"**
         NKJV   **"in the Holy Spirit and in much assurance,"**
         TEV   **"but also with power and the Holy Spirit,"**
         JB   **"as the Holy Spirit and as utter convictions."**

These two PREPOSITIONAL PHRASES are related syntactically (cf. Rom. 8:15-16). Grammatically, they could refer either to Paul or the Thessalonians. Even in a spiritually powerful setting, Paul was run out of town.

❖**"as you know what kind of men we proved to be among you for your sake"** This is a PERFECT ACTIVE which implies a settled state. The lifestyle of Christian workers is crucial.

NOTES

1:6 "You also" This is an emphatic contrast to the "we" of vv. 2-5.

❖   **NASB, NRSV**   **"You also became imitators of us and of the Lord,"**

    NKJV   **"And you became followers of us and of the Lord,"**

    TEV   **"You imitated us and the Lord;"**

    JB   **"and you were led to become imitators of us, and of the Lord;"**

"Imitators" comes into English as "mimic" (cf. I Cor. 4:16; 11:1; Gal. 4:12; Phil. 3:17; 4:9; I Thes. 2:14; II Thes. 3:7). Christlikeness is God's goal for every believer (cf. Rom. 8:28-20; Gal. 4:19).

❖   **NASB, NKJV**   **"having received the word"**

    NRSV   **"you received the word"**

    TEV   **"you received the message"**

    JB   **"you took to the gospel,"**

This term means "to receive as a welcomed guest." This is an AORIST MIDDLE which could read "received for yourselves." Man must respond to God's offer of love in Christ's finished work by repentance and faith (cf. Mk. 1:15; Jn. 1:12, 3:16; Acts 20:21; Rom. 10:9-13). Salvation is both a message and a person. We receive the gospel message and befriend the Person of Jesus. We must trust completely in both.

❖   **NASB**   **"in much tribulation"**

    NKJV   **"in much affliction,"**

    NRSV   **"in spite of persecution"**

    TEV   **"even though you suffered much,"**

    JB   **"the great opposition all round you."**

This is literally "to press" (cf. Acts 17:55ff.; Rom. 8:17; I Pet. 3:13ff.; 4:12ff.). Becoming a Christian does not guarantee a lack of tension—on the contrary, it is quite the opposite.

❖ **"with the joy of the Holy Spirit,"** This joy given by the Spirit is so encompassing and complete that it is present and sustaining amid great persecution and pain. It is a joy above circumstances (cf. Rom. 5:2-5).

1:7 "you became an example to all the believers" Their joy and perseverance under testing and trial was a source of great encouragement to other believers. This is also how the suffering of Job, the prophets, the Messiah and the Apostles affect us!

❖ **"in Macedonia and in Achaia"** These were Roman provinces. Achaia is located within modern Greece; Macedonia is a political state independent of Greece, though culturally and economically related.

1:8 "has sounded forth" This is literally "trumpeted" or "thundered." It is a PERFECT TENSE which implies "sounded forth and still sounds." In English we get the word "echo" from this Greek word. Verses 8-10 form one sentence in Greek.

❖**"but also in every place"** This is a metaphorical exaggeration similar to verse 2.

❖	NASB	"so that we have no need to say anything."
	NKJV	"so that we do not need to say anything."
	NRSV	"so that we have no need to speak about it."
	TEV	"There is nothing, then, that we need to say."
	JB	"We do not need to tell other people about it:"

An ambiguous phrase, many translations supply the word "faith" from the previous clause. This does not necessarily mean that they understood everything about Christian doctrine or even the theology of suffering. But their lives have shown that the gospel truly took root in their hearts and minds. The Holy Spirit will reveal the basics of the gospel to every receptive heart.

1:9 "turned to God from idols" This refers to their repentance from pagan idolatry. The gospel is both negative and positive—repentance and faith (cf. Mk.. 1:15; Acts 3:16, 19; 20:21). There is a "turning from" as well as a "turning to."

❖ **"to serve"** "As a slave." This portrays God as King and His followers as servants. In one sense, we are slaves, in another, we are sons.

❖**"a living and true God,"** This reflects God's name: YHWH (cf. Ex. 3:14). It comes from the CAUSATIVE FORM of the Hebrew verb "to be." YHWH is the ever-living, only-living God. This is the basis of biblical monotheism.

❖**"to wait"** Paul continued his emphasis on the Second Coming as the theological keynote of the letter. He discussed it in detail in 4:13-18 and II Thes. 2.

❖**"He raised from the dead,"** This was confirmation of God's acceptance of Christ's substitutionary death (cf. I Cor. 15). All three persons of the Trinity were active in Christ's resurrection: the Father (cf. Acts 2:24; 3:15; 4:10; 5:30; 10:40; 13:30, 33, 34, 37; 17:31); the Spirit (cf. Rom. 8:11) and the Son (cf. Jn. 2:19-22; 10:17-18).

❖**"rescues us"** This is a PRESENT TENSE VERB which emphasizes continuous action. Victory is ongoing (cf. Rom. 8:31-39).

❖**"wrath to come."** For some, Jesus' Second Coming is their great hope, but for others it will be their eternal loss (cf. Mt. 25). The believers will experience the wrath of Jews and pagans, but they will never experience the wrath of God.

DISCUSSION QUESTIONS

This is a study guide commentary which means that you are responsible for your own interpretation of the Bible. Each of us must walk in the light we have. You, the Bible and the Holy Spirit are priority in interpretation. You must not relinquish this to a commentator.

These discussion questions are provided to help you think through the major issues of this section of the book. They are meant to be thought provoking, not definitive.

1. Why did Paul not assert his apostleship in this letter?

2. What is significant about verse 1?

173

NOTES

3. Why are faith, hope and love mentioned together so often in the New Testament?

4. How is election linked to the believers' actions?

5. Why do Christians suffer? How does the Second Coming address the problem of suffering?

NOTES

I THESSALONIANS 2

PARAGRAPH DIVISIONS OF MODERN TRANSLATIONS

UBS[4]	NKJV	NRSV	TEV	JB
Paul's Ministry in Thessalonica	Paul's Conduct	Paul's Life and Work at Thessalonica	Paul's Work in Thessalonica	Paul's Example in Thessalonika
2:1-12	2:1-12	2:1-8	2:9	2:1
		2:9-12	2:10-12	2:2-6
				2:7-12
	Their Conversion			The Faith & Patience of the Thessalonians
2:13-16	2:13-16	2:13-16	2:13-16	2:13-16
Paul's Desire to Visit the Church Again (2:17-3:13)	Longing to See Them	Paul's Affection for the Thessalonians (2:17-3:13)	Paul's Desire to Visit Them Again (2:17-3:13)	Paul's Anxiety
2:17-20	2:17-20	2:17-20	2:17-20	2:17-20

READING CYCLE THREE (see p. vii)
FOLLOWING THE ORIGINAL AUTHOR'S INTENT AT THE PARA-GRAPH LEVEL

This is a study <u>guide</u> commentary which means that you are responsible for your own interpretation of the Bible. Each of us must walk in the light we have. You, the Bible and the Holy Spirit are priority in interpretation. You must not relinquish this to a commentator.

Read the chapter in one sitting. Identify the subjects. Compare your subject divisions with the five translations above. Paragraphing is not inspired but it is the key to following the original author's intent which is the heart of interpretation. Every paragraph has one and only one subject.

1. First paragraph

2. Second paragraph

3. Third paragraph

4. Etc

CONTEXTUAL INSIGHTS TO VERSES 1-13

A. This chapter reflects the growing Jewish opposition to the Church in Thessalonica (cf. Acts 17:1-9).

B. This chapter expresses in a wonderful way the characteristics of a true minister. Paul presented these characteristics in three contrasting pairs: first the negative, then the positive (vv. 3-7).

C. Verses 10-12 are a summary of verses 1-9.

D. This chapter reflects some confusion among English translations on where the verses should be divided:
   1. Verses 6-7.
   2. Verses 11-12.

E. Paul digressed in verses 14-16 to discuss his current situation in Corinth and a summary of his first experiences with Jewish opposition. These verses are Paul's strongest comments about the Jews (except for Romans 9-11).

WORD AND PHRASE STUDY

NASB (UPDATED) TEXT: 2:1-12

For you yourselves know, brethren, that our coming to you was not in vain, but after we had already suffered and been mistreated in Philippi, as you know, we had the boldness in our God to speak to you the gospel of God amid much opposition. For our exhortation does not *come* from error or impurity or by way of deceit; but just as we have been approved by God to be entrusted with the gospel, so we speak, not as pleasing men, but God who examines our hearts. For we never came with flattering speech, as you know, nor with a pretext for greed—God is witness—nor did we seek glory from men, either from you or from others, even though as apostles of Christ we might have asserted our authority. But we proved to be gentle among you, as a nursing *mother* tenderly cares for her own children. Having so fond an affection for you, we were well-pleased to impart to you not only the gospel of God but also our own lives, because you had become very dear to us. For you recall, brethren, our labor and hardship, *how* working night and day so as not to be a burden to any of you, we proclaimed to you the gospel of God. You are witnesses, and *so is* God, how devoutly and uprightly and blamelessly we behaved toward you believers; just as you know how we *were* exhorting and encouraging and imploring each one of you as a father would his own children, so that you *would* walk in a manner worthy of the God who calls you into His own kingdom and glory.

2:1 "For you yourselves know," Paul appealed to the experience of the Thessalonian Christians so often that this phrase becomes a characteristic of this book (cf. 1:5; 2:1, 2, 5, 11). Similar phrases are found in vv. 9, 10.

❖ **NASB, NKJV, NRSV "that our coming to you was not in vain,"**
   TEV **"that our visit to you was not a failure."**
   JB **"that our visit to you has not proved ineffectual."**

This is a PERFECT TENSE. This can either mean: (1) not "fruitless" (cf. I Cor. 15:10,58); or (2) not "empty handed" (cf. Mk. 12:2) in spite of much Jewish opposition. Paul does not return to this subject until v. 13.

2:2 "but" This is a strong ADVERSATIVE CONJUNCTION.

❖**"after we had already suffered...in Philippi"** Acts 16:11-48 and II Cor. 11:24-27 describe this episode.

   NASB **"mistreated"**
   NKJV **"spitefully treated"**
   NRSV **"shamefully mistreated"**
   TEV **"insulted"**
   JB **"grossly insulted"**

This was both physical and mental abuse.

❖ **NASB** **"we had the boldness in our God to speak to you the gospel of God"**
   NKJV **"we were bold in our God to speak to you the gospel of God"**

179

NOTES

NRSV	"we had courage in our God to declare to you the gospel of God"
TEV	"Yet God gave us courage to tell you the Good News that comes from him,"
JB	"it was our God who gave us the courage to proclaim his Good News to you"

"Boldness" translates literally "freedom to speak." Paul asserted the truth that his preaching of the gospel always caused problems. He was getting used to it.

❖ **"amid much opposition."** This is an athletic or military term for rough, hand-to-hand fighting (cf. Phil. 1:30; Col. 2:1). The Greek *agoni* entered English as "agony."

2:3 "exhortation" This is literally "to call alongside." This same root is used of the Spirit in Jn. 14:16, 26; 15:26 and 16:7 and of Jesus in I Jn. 2:1 and is translated as "comforter," "advocate" or "helper."

❖
NASB	"does not *come* from error"
NKJV	"*did* not *come* from deceit"
NRSV	"does not spring from deceit"
TEV	"is not based on error"
JB	"because we are deluded,"

Planes was the Greek word for "planet," which referred to heavenly lights that did not follow the usual pattern of constellations. Thus, they were called "wanderers."

❖
NASB	"impurity"
NKJV	"uncleanness"
NRSV, TEV	"impure motives"
JB	"immoral"

This term implied sexual looseness (cf. Rom. 1:24; Gal. 5:19; Eph. 5:3; Col. 3:5). It must be remembered that pagan worship often employed sexual acts.

❖
NASB	"by way of deceit;"
NKJV	"nor *was it* in guile"
NRSV	"or trickery,"

| TEV | "nor do we try to trick anyone" |
| JB | "or trying to deceive anyone;" |

The other two terms in verse 3 speak of Paul's motives, but this phrase indicates an atmosphere of trickery. "Fraud" originally meant "to catch with bait," but later evolved into a metaphor for trickery for profit.

2:4 "we have been approved by God" This PERFECT PASSIVE INDICATIVE has the connotation of testing with a view toward approval. "Approve" in this sense commonly meant testing the genuineness of coins. The missionary team had been and continued to be approved by God.

❖ **"entrusted"** This is an AORIST PASSIVE INDICATIVE. This term comes from the same root as "faith," "believe" or "trust." The basic idea is trustworthiness (cf. I Cor. 9:17; Gal. 2:7; I Tim. 1:11). God has chosen to use human instrumentality (cf. Ex. 3:7-12).

❖ **"so we speak,"** This is a PRESENT ACTIVE INDICATIVE. We are stewards of the gospel.

❖ **"not as pleasing men, but God"** (cf. 2:6; II Cor. 4:5; Gal. 1:10).

❖ **"who examines our hearts."** This reflects the Hebrew usage of "heart," in the sense of the entire personality. God knows our motives (cf. I Sam. 16:7; Ps. 7:9; 26:2; 44:21; 139:1,23; Prov. 21:2; Jer. 11:20; 12:3; 17:10; Lk. 16:15; Acts 1:24; 15:8; Rom. 8:27).

2:5 "we never came with flattering speech," This term implies manipulation by false motives. Opponents, especially at Corinth, often accused Paul of false motives.

❖ **"nor with a pretext for greed"** Paul was often accused of greed or opportunism, possibly because it was characteristic of Greek itinerant teachers (cf. Acts 20:33).

❖ **"God is witness"** Paul was swearing an oath using God as a witness (cf. 2:10; Rom. 1:9; I Cor. 1:23; 11:31; Gal. 1:19; Phil. 2:25).

2:6 "though as apostles of Christ" This includes Silas and Timothy.

This illustrates the wider use of the term. In I Cor. 12:28 and Eph. 4:11, "apostles" are mentioned as an ongoing spiritual gift in the church. Some examples are: (1) Barnabas (cf. Acts 14:4,14); (2) Andronicus and Junias (cf. Rom. 16:6-7); (3) Apollos (cf. I Cor. 4:6); (4) James the Just (cf. Gal. 1:19); and (4) Epaphroditus (cf. Phil. 2:25).

❖ Some English translations put this phrase in verse 6 and others in verse 7.

NASB, 2:6	**"we might have asserted our authority."**
NKJV, 2:6	**"we might have made demands"**
NRSV, 2:7	**"we might have made demands"**
TEV, 2:7	**"we could have made demands"**
JB, 2:7	**"we could have imposed ourselves on you with full weight,"**

Literally, this translates "with weight." The intended meaning could be: (1) authority; (2) honor; or (3) financial compensation (cf. I Cor. 9:3-14; II Cor. 11:7-11).

2:7 "we proved to be gentle among you," There is a manuscript option problem between the use of the terms: (1) "infants," and (2) "gentle." Only their initial letter is different. The Greek manuscripts disagree on which is correct. Origen and Augustine believe Paul spoke to the Thessalonians in baby language so they could understand. Paul used parental language in vv. 7, 8 and 11. He saw himself as their spiritual parent.

❖ **"as a nursing *mother* tenderly cares for her own children."** This is literally "to warm." This was commonly used of mother birds "warming" their young (cf. Eph. 5:29). It was a metaphor for breast feeding.

2:8 NASB	**"Having so fond an affection for you,"**
NKJV	**"So, affectionately longing for you,"**
NRSV	**"So deeply do we care for you"**
TEV	**"Because of our love for you"**
JB	**"we felt so devoted and protective towards you,"**

This word appears nowhere else in the entire New

NOTES

Testament. A strong term of affection related to the nursery, it was used in Greek literature for parents longing for their dead children.

❖"**we were well-pleased to impart to you not only the gospel of God but also our own lives, because you had become very dear to us.**" This shows the costliness of the ministry as well as the love of the Apostle. Ministry is not something we do—it is who we are.

2:9 "our labor and hardship," These are strong synonymous terms (cf. I Thes. 3:8 and II Cor. 11:27). Greek society denigrated labor as only for slaves. Paul often encouraged it, especially in this letter because some in the fellowship had quit their jobs to wait for the Second Coming.

❖ "*how* **working night and day**" All rabbis had to have a trade, or livelihood (cf. Acts 18:3). Paul would not accept money for his ministry because of accusations of greed.

"Night and day" reflects Jewish reckoning of time where the day begins at dusk (cf. Gen. 1:5,8,13,19,23, 21). Paul worked during the day at tent making or leather working and at night he preached the gospel.

2:10 "devoutly and uprightly and blamelessly we behaved toward you believers;" Some in the church, in the community or outsiders must have questioned his motives. Paul was always having to defend his motives.

2:11 "exhorting" This literally means "to call alongside for help." This is the same root as "appeal" of v. 3.

2:12 "walk in a manner worthy" This is a PRESENT INFINITIVE. This metaphor refers to our continuing lifestyle, which must reflect our Master (cf. Eph. 4:1; 5:2, 15).

❖ "**who calls you**" There is a Greek manuscript problem in the TENSE of this phrase: (1) manuscripts א and A have the AORIST, like Gal. 1:6. This would emphasize God's predestinating call; (2) manuscripts B, D, F, G, H, K, L, and P have the PRESENT which would emphasize God's call to holiness (cf. Gal. 4:19).

❖ **"His own kingdom"** Paul does not use this term often. This refers to God's rule in men's hearts now which will one day be consummated over all the earth (cf. Mt. 6:10). This was the burden of Jesus' teaching and preaching. It reflects the "already" but "not yet" tension of the time between the Incarnation and the Second Coming.

NASB (UPDATED) TEXT: 2:13-16

For this reason we also constantly thank God that when you received the word of God which you heard from us, you accepted it not as the word of men, but for what it really is, the word of God, which also performs its work in you who believe. For you, brethren, became imitators of the churches of God in Christ Jesus that are in Judea, for you also endured the same sufferings at the hands of your own countrymen, even as they did from the Jews, who both killed the Lord Jesus and the prophets, and drove us out. They are not pleasing to God, but hostile to all men, hindering us from speaking to the Gentiles so that they may be saved; with the result that they always fill up the measure of their sins. But wrath has come upon them to the utmost.

2:13 "we also constantly thank God" A PRESENT TENSE VERB, it may refer to 1:2-10. This reflected Paul's ongoing prayer life and writing style (cf. 1:2; 5:17-18).

❖ **"received"** This is an AORIST ACTIVE PARTICIPLE. This shows the necessity of our personal response. Here, it refers to the message. In Jn. 1:12 it is to the person of Christ. In I Thes. 4:1, it is to a lifestyle. The gospel focuses around three emphases: (1) personal relationship, (2) doctrinal truth, and (3) lifestyle Christlikeness. The believer must choose to respond to all areas for maturity.

❖ **"received...accepted"** These synonymous terms describe the need for a human response to the divine gospel. Fallen man must repent and believe the gospel (cf. Mk. 1:15; Acts 3:16,19; 20:21), and continue to repent and believe the gospel (content and person).

The former word is a compound term found in Jn. 1:12. The latter means to welcome someone as a guest. In this context, one must welcome the gospel. The NT describes the gospel as both a person and a message.

❖ **"the word of God"** The Bible's message is the self revelation of the only Creator/Redeemer God (cf. II Tim. 3:15-17; II Pet. 1:20-21).

❖

NASB	"the word of God, which also performs its work in you who believe"
NKJV	"the word of God, which also effectively works in you who believe"
NRSV	"God's word, which is also at work in you believers"
TEV	"as God's message, which indeed it is. For God is at work in you who believe"
JB	"God's message...it is still a living power among you who believe it"

This is PRESENT TENSE (cf. Phil. 2:13). "Work" was a favorite word for Paul, related to the English cognate "energy." Paul personified the Bible as energizing believers! This probably reflects the OT understanding of the power of the spoken word, as in Gen. 1 and Isa. 55:11.

❖**"in you who believe"** This is PRESENT TENSE. Again, continuing belief is the key! The gospel is not a product but a personal, growing relationship.

2:14 "the churches" This translates literally "the called out ones." In the Septuagint, the same idea is expressed as "the congregation of Israel." The early church saw itself as the continuation of the OT people of God.

❖ **"in Christ Jesus"** This phrase takes the LOCATIVE OF SPHERE CASE, which means "in" or "surrounded by" an atmosphere, like a fish in water. A very common Pauline expression, it speaks of our union with Jesus. We live and move and have our being in Him.

❖ **"you also endured the same sufferings"** Generally, the reaction to the Christian message in the Roman world was persecution (cf.

187

NOTES

Mt. 5:10-12; I Pet. 4:12-16), because of the message's exclusive nature (cf. Jn. 14:6).

❖ **"at the hands of your own countrymen,"** In context this refers to Gentiles' persecution, but Paul, who was in Corinth at the time of the writing, was confronting Jewish opposition.

2:15 "who both killed the Lord Jesus" (cf. Acts 2:23).

❖ **"and the prophets,"** (cf. Mt. 23:31,37; Acts 7:52).

❖ **"and drove us out."** Possibly this is related to Jason's peace bond (cf. Acts 17:5-9).

❖

NASB	"They are not pleasing to God,"
NKJV	"they do not please God"
NRSV	"they displease God"
TEV	"How displeasing they are to God!"
JB	"acting in a way that cannot please God"

The Jews thought their actions were God's will, defending His covenant with Moses. They believed they were His servants defending against false teachers. Tragically ironic, *they* were the false teachers.

❖ **"but hostile to all men,"** The hostility mentioned here was rooted in Jewish national arrogance and prejudice. They had rejected the Messiah and His universal gospel.

2:16 "hindering us from speaking to the Gentiles" This reflects Paul's experience in Corinth at the time of the writing of I Thes. These sentences were Paul's strongest complaint against the Jews (cf. Rom. 9-11).

❖ **"so that they may be saved;"** This is an AORIST PASSIVE SUB-JUNCTIVE. God wants to save all men (cf. Gen. 3:15; 12:3; Ezek. 18:32; I Tim. 2:4; II Pet. 3:9). But they must repent and believe (cf. Mk. 1:15; Acts 3:16,19; 20:21).

❖

NASB	"they always fill up the measure of their sins."
NKJV	"to fill up *the measure* of their sins;"

NRSV	"they have constantly been filling up the measure of their sins;"
TEV	"This is the last full measure of their sins they have always committed."
JB	"They never stop trying to *finish off the sins they have begun,*"

The exact Greek phrase is found in the Septuagint of Gen. 15:16 (cf. Mt. 23:32). God records the evil deeds of the sons of men and they will give an account.

❖ **"But wrath has come upon them"** This is an AORIST ACTIVE INDICATIVE. This verse seems to relate to Mk. 12:1-12 and Rom. 9-11. God's wrath is present and future (temporal and eschatological).

NASB	"to the utmost"
NKJV	"to the uttermost"
NRSV, TEV, JB	"at last"

This phrase may be translated several ways, so compare your English Bibles to grasp more fully the possible translations. Basic renderings include: (1) looking back and summing up; (2) looking forward to consummation; or (3) used in the Semitic sense of "completely."

NASB (UPDATED) TEXT: 2:17-20

But we, brethren, having been taken away from you for a short while—in person, not in spirit—were all the more eager with great desire to see your face. For we wanted to come to you—I, Paul, more than once—and yet Satan hindered us. For who is our hope or joy or crown of exultation? Is it not even you, in the presence of our Lord Jesus at His coming? For you are our glory and joy.

2:17	NASB, NKJV	"having been taken away from you"
	NRSV	"we were made orphans by being separated from you—"
	TEV	"we were separated from you"
	JB	"we had been separated from you—"

This is an AORIST PASSIVE PARTICIPLE. Highly emotional language fills this whole paragraph. This continues Paul's parenting metaphors of vv. 7 and 11. It is literally "orphaned" by an outside agent.

❖ **"with great desire"** This term is often rendered "lust," in its pejorative sense, but rarely, as it does here, it is used positively.

2:18 "For we wanted to come to you—" (cf. Rom. 1:13; 15:22).

❖ **"Satan"** A personal evil force is active in our world, seeking to thwart God's plans and purposes by the agency of: (1) a fallen world system, (2) fallen angels, and (3) sinful men (cf. Eph. 2:2-3). We can see Satan in the OT in Job 1-2; Zech. 3; Isa. 14 and Ezek. 28. In the OT Satan is a servant of YHWH. According to the NT he is an enemy but still under God's control! For a good discussion of the intensification of evil in the Bible, read A.B. Davidson's *Old Testament Theology*, pp. 330-36.

❖ **"hindered"** This is a military term used for the destruction of roads and bridges in the face of the enemy's advance.

2:19 The mark of genuineness of Paul's apostleship was the success of his ministry among the Gentiles (cf. v. 20).

❖
NASB	**"Is it not even you,"**
NKJV	**"Is *it* not even you"**
NRSV	**"Is it not you?"**
TEV	**"It is you—you, no less than others!"**
JB	**"You are;"**

The problem with this phrase is how it related to Paul's affection and love for the Thessalonian church compared to his other Gentile churches. Were they somehow special? TEV's translation of "you, no less than others" may best represent the thought.

❖ **"at His coming?"** "*Parousia*," literally meaning "presence," by implication means "coming." This is the first use of the term in the NT. It was used in secular literature of the first century for a royal visit by a king. It came to have a technical meaning, in the church, for the Second Coming. This coming of Jesus is the theological focus of I & II Thes.

2:20
NASB, NKJV, NRSV	**"our glory"**
TEV, JB	**"our pride"**

NOTES

This is the use of the term glory as pride. This does not relate to the theological glory used to describe God (cf. v. 12).

DISCUSSION QUESTIONS

This is a study <u>guide</u> commentary which means that you are responsible for your own interpretation of the Bible. Each of us must walk in the light we have. You, the Bible and the Holy Spirit are priority in interpretation. You must not relinquish this to a commentator.

These discussion questions are provided to help you think through the major issues of this section of the book. They are meant to be thought provoking, not definitive.

1. Who was attacking Paul and why?

2. Why was Paul so firm in denying compensation for his preaching?

3. Why does Paul bring in the subject of Jewish opposition to the Gospel?

4. What does verse 16 mean to the Jewish nation as to God's purposes?

5. Why are verses 17 - 20 so emotional?

NOTES

I THESSALONIANS 3

PARAGRAPH DIVISIONS OF MODERN TRANSLATIONS

UBS⁴	NKJV	NRSV	TEV	JB
Paul's desire to Visit the Church again (2:17-3:13)	Concern for Their Faith	Paul's Affection for the Thessalonians (2:17-3:13)	Paul's Desire to Visit Them Again (2:17-3:13)	Timothy's Mission to Thessalonika
3:1-5	3:1-5	3:1-5	3:1-5	3:1-5
	Encouraged by Timothy			Paul Thanks God for the Thessalonians
3:6-10	3:6-10	3:6-10	3:6-10	3:6-10
	Prayer for the Church			
3:11-13	3:11-13	3:11-13	3:11-13	3:11-13

READING CYCLE THREE (see p. vii)
FOLLOWING THE ORIGINAL AUTHOR'S INTENT AT THE PARA-GRAPH LEVEL

This is a study <u>guide</u> commentary which means that you are responsible for your own interpretation of the Bible. Each of us must walk in the light we have. You, the Bible and the Holy Spirit are priority in interpretation. You must not relinquish this to a commentator.

Read the chapter in one sitting. Identify the subjects. Compare your subject divisions with the five translations above. Paragraphing is not inspired but it is the key to following the original author's intent which is the heart of interpretation. Every paragraph has one and only one subject.

1. First paragraph

2. Second paragraph

3. Third paragraph

4. Etc.

BRIEF OUTLINE OF CHAPTER 3

A. Paul sends Timothy to them, 3:1-5
B. Timothy returns with good news, 3:6-10
C. Paul's prayer for the Thessalonian Church, 3:11-13

WORD AND PHRASE STUDY

NASB (UPDATED) TEXT: 3:1-10

Therefore when we could endure *it* no longer, we thought it best to be left behind at Athens alone, and we sent Timothy, our brother and God's fellow worker in the gospel of Christ, to strengthen and encourage you as to your faith, so that no one would be disturbed by these afflictions; for you yourselves know that we have been destined for this. For indeed when we were with you, *we* kept telling you in advance that we were going to suffer affliction; and so it came to pass, as you know. For this reason, when I could endure it no longer, I also sent to find out about your faith, for fear that the tempter might have tempted you, and our labor would be in vain. But now that Timothy has come to us from you, and has brought us good news of your faith and love, and that you always think kindly of us, longing to see us just as we also long to see you, for this reason, brethren, in all our distress and affliction we were comforted about you through your faith; for now we really live, if you stand firm in the Lord. For what thanks can we render to God for you in return for all the joy with which we rejoice before our God on your account, as we night and day keep praying most earnestly that we may see your face, and may complete what is lacking in your faith?

3:1 "could endure it no longer," Paul was worried about this church born in persecution (cf. 2:17-20).

❖ **"to be left behind"** This is a strong PASSIVE VOICE used of: (1) a child leaving his parents, Eph. 5:31; or (2) the death of one's spouse (cf. Mk. 12:19). Paul's depth of feeling for this church is illustrated in 2:17-20.

❖ **"at Athens alone,"** This was the intellectual center of the Hellenistic world. Paul had eye problems (cf. II Cor. 12:7), and it was very hard for him to be alone, especially in an unfamiliar environment such as Athens. The term "alone" is plural but the meaning is uncertain. Acts 18:5 implies both Silas and Timothy were on assignment. This verse may be a key to Paul's use of "we" as an editorial plural, referring only to himself.

3:2	NASB	"God's fellow worker in the gospel of Christ,"
	NKJV	"minister of God, and our fellow laborer in the gospel of Christ,"
	NRSV	"co-worker for God in proclaiming the gospel of Christ,"
	TEV	"who works with us for God in preaching the Good News about Christ."
	JB	"who is God's helper in spreading the Good News of Christ,"

These phrases refer to Timothy. The Greek manuscripts differ: manuscript B has "co-laborer" while manuscript ℵ and A have "minister," the root for "deacon." It denoted lowly service of a slave. Most modern translations follow manuscript B. Possibly a scribe was shocked at Paul calling Timothy "God's co-laborer."

This verse is functioning like a letter of recommendation for Timothy (cf. Acts 18:27; Rom. 16:1; II Cor. 8:18-24; III Jn. 9, 10).

❖ **"to strengthen and encourage you"** (cf. 2:3,11). Paul was worried about this new church under persecution (cf. v. 3; 1:6; 2:14; 3:8).

3:3 "be disturbed by these afflictions;" This is the only use of this term, "disturbed," in the NT. It originally referred to a dog wagging its tail. In classical Greek (Homer), it was used in the sense of "flattered." This may relate to 2:1 or 3:5. True faith perseveres (cf. Mt. 13:1-23; Gal. 6:9).

❖ **"we have been destined for this."** The PASSIVE VOICE implies that God is the active agent. It is not a reference to the pagan idea of an impersonal fate. Suffering is the norm for believers in a fallen world (cf. v. 4; Mt. 5:10-12; Jn.15:18, 20; 16:33; Acts 14:22; Rom. 8:17 II Cor. 4:7-11; 11:23-27; II Tim. 3:12; I Pet. 2:21; 4:12-16). Suffering is a means of spiritual maturity (cf. Heb. 5:8).

NOTES

3:4 "we *kept* telling you in advance" This is an IMPERFECT TENSE which means repeated action in past time. Paul must have warned them several times.

❖ | NASB | "we were going to suffer afflictions;"
| NKJV | "we would suffer tribulation,"
| NRSV | "we were to suffer persecutions;"
| TEV | "that we were going to be persecuted;"
| JB | "we must expect to have persecutions to bear"

This is a PRESENT PASSIVE INFINITIVE. The Williams' translation footnote says "picture of a loaded wagon crushed under its heavy load," p. 450.

3:5 "your faith," This is possibly used in the OT sense of "faithfulness." Were they true to their profession of faith?

❖ **"the tempter might have tempted you,"** A personal, evil force is active in our world and in our lives (cf. 2:18). This Greek word translated "tempt" connotes tempting "with a view toward destruction," the opposite of "approved" in 2:4.

❖ **"our labor would be in vain."** The use of MOODS is important here; the INDICATIVE which is the mood of reality is used of Satan, but the SUBJUNCTIVE which is the mood of possibility is used of Paul's labor. This may relate to 2:1. The question is, "Does 'in vain' relate to their personal conversion or the establishment of a viable functioning church in Thessalonica?"

3:6 "good news" This is the only use of this Greek term in the NT where it does not refer to the Gospel of Christ. The message about this church was "gospel," "good news" to Paul.

❖ **"of your faith and love,"** "Faith" can have several meanings. This refers either to: (1) orthodox doctrine and loving care for one another; or (2) faithfulness and love toward God.

❖ **"think kindly of us, longing to see us just as we also long to see you,"** This shows that neither the persecution nor the false teachers had embittered this church against Paul.

3:7 "in all our distress and affliction" Paul's problems are listed in I Cor. 4:9-13; II Cor. 4:8-12; 6:4-10 and 11:24-27.

3:8 "for now we _really_ live," Paul is using metaphorical language to express his release from his tension at the good news from this church.

❖ **"if you stand firm in the Lord."** This is a Greek CONDITION-AL SENTENCE, combining FIRST CLASS and THIRD CLASS conditions, thereby adding contingency to Paul's statement. He assumed that they would stand firm but that remained for him to see (cf. 2:1 and 3:5).

"Standing firm" relates to our position in Christ. The Bible presents our salvation in a tension-filled pair of truths: (1) it is free, it is in Christ, but (2) it is costly, it is progressive, it is seen in our lifestyle choices. Both are true. This verse emphasizes the first truth (cf. Rom. 5:2; I Cor. 15:1 and Eph. 6:11, 13).

3:9-10 This is a rhetorical question that leads into a prayer, vv. 11-13, concluding the first half of Paul's letter.

3:10 "night and day" This is the Jewish order of time (see note at 2:9). This reflects Paul's prayer life (cf. 1:2; 2:12; II Tim. 1:3).

❖	NASB	"keep praying"
	NKJV	"praying exceedingly"
	NRSV	"we pray most earnestly"
	TEV	"we ask him with all our heart"
	JB	"We are earnestly praying"

This is a very strong, double compound, emotional term. Paul worried about these new churches (cf. II Cor. 11:28).

❖	NASB	"may complete what is lacking in your faith?"
	NKJV	"perfect what is lacking in your faith?"
	NRSV	"restore whatever is lacking in your faith"
	TEV	"supply what is needed in your

	faith."
JB	**"make up any shortcomings in your faith."**

They had done well but they were not yet mature in their understanding, as the misunderstanding of the Second Coming shows. This is the use of faith as doctrine (cf. Acts 6:7; 13:8; 14:22; Gal. 1:23; 6:10; Jude 3,20). It is also possible that with the recurrent emphasis on lifestyle, "what was lacking" had an ethical aspect.

NASB (UPDATED) TEXT: 3:11-13

Now may our God and Father Himself and Jesus our Lord direct our way to you; and may the Lord cause you to increase and abound in love for one another, and for all people, just as we also do for you; so that He may establish your hearts without blame in holiness before our God and Father at the coming of our Lord Jesus with all His saints.

3:11-13 This is one sentence in Greek. OPTATIVE MOOD is the mood of potentiality. This prayer contains three rare OPTATIVE VERBAL FORMS: "direct" (v. 11), "increase" (v.12) and "abound" (v.12). The Galatians' response to Paul's gospel would determine God's blessing.

3:11 "may...direct" This is a rare AORIST ACTIVE SINGULAR OPTATIVE verb, used in some prayers in the NT (cf. 5:23; II Thes. 2:16; 3:5, 16 and in Rom. 15:5-6,13). Note the verb is singular, though it refers to both God the Father and Jesus Christ. This was a way for the NT authors to assert the deity of Jesus of Nazareth (cf. II Thes. 2:16). Another theological point is that in the same way Satan prevented Paul from coming to them, recorded in 2:18, Paul asked the Father and Son to make a way (straight or smooth: cf. Lk. 1:79) for him to visit them!

3:12-13 Paul prayed for himself in v. 11 but now his petition turns toward the church at Thessalonica. He prayed for their love for one another and all men. He also prayed for the believers' holiness (cf. v. 13). God's will for every believer is Christlikeness (cf. Rom. 8:28-29; Gal. 4:19).

3:12 "for all people," God's love is as wide as the world; so too, must be ours who know Him.

NOTES

3:13	NASB	"without blame in holiness"
	NKJV	"blameless in holiness"
	NRSV, JB	"in holiness that you may be blameless"
	TEV	"perfect and holy"

Holiness is both a gift and a task (INDICATIVE and IMPERATIVE). It is characteristic of someone above reproach, against whom no accusation may be brought (cf. Eph. 5:27). This leaves Satan with no basis for criticism (cf. Rom. 8:31,32,33). The exact relationship between the events of the Second Coming, the "Rapture" (cf. I Thes. 4:13-18), the Judgment Seat of Christ (cf. II Cor. 5:10), and the White Throne of Judgment (cf. Mt. 25 and Rev. 20) is uncertain.

❖ **"at the coming of our Lord Jesus"** This shows Paul's continuing concern in his letters to this church about end time events (cf. 2:19; 4:15-17).

This phrase is literally rendered "in the presence of," commonly used in the context of "a legal court setting" (cf. Rom. 8:31-34).

❖ **"His saints"** "Saints" are either: (1) angels who will accompany Jesus (cf. Zech. 14:5; Mk. 8:38); or (2) His people, saints (cf. I Thes. 4:14-16). Paul never called angels "saints" or "holy ones," possibly resolving the interpretive problem. This church was unsure if the dead saints would participate in the endtime events.

DISCUSSION QUESTIONS

This is a study guide commentary which means that you are responsible for your own interpretation of the Bible. Each of us must walk in the light we have. You, the Bible and the Holy Spirit are priority in interpretation. You must not relinquish this to a commentator.

These discussion questions are provided to help you think through the major issues of this section of the book. They are meant to be thought provoking, not definitive.

1. Why was it hard for Paul to be alone?

2. List the different meanings of the term "faith".

3. Is suffering normal for believers? Why?

4. Is sanctification initial or progressive?

5. Does verse 5 refer to one's salvation or fruitfulness? How do 2:1 and 3:5 relate to the parable of the Soils (cf. Mt. 13:1-23)?

I THESSALONIANS 4

PARAGRAPH DIVISIONS OF MODERN TRANSLATIONS

UBS⁴	NKJV	NRSV	TEV	JB
A Life Pleasing to God 4:1-8	Plea for Unity 4:1-8	Exhortations to Purity 4:1-8	A Life that Praises God 4:1-8	Live in Holiness and Charity 4:1-2 4:3-8
	A Brotherly and Orderly Life			
4:9-12	4:9-12	4:9-12	4:9-12	4:9-12
The Lord's Coming 4:13-14	The Comfort of Christ's Coming 4:13-18	Questions Concerning the Coming of the Lord (4:13-5:11) 4:13-18	The Lord's Coming 4:13-14 4:15-18	The Dead and the Living at the Time of the Lord's Coming 4:13-18

READING CYCLE THREE (see p. vii)
FOLLOWING THE ORIGINAL AUTHOR'S INTENT AT THE PARAGRAPH LEVEL

This is a study <u>guide</u> commentary which means that you are responsible for your own interpretation of the Bible. Each of us must walk in the light we have. You, the Bible and the Holy Spirit are priority in interpretation. You must not relinquish this to a commentator.

Read the chapter in one sitting. Identify the subjects. Compare your subject divisions with the five translations above. Paragraphing is not inspired but it is the key to following the original author's intent which is the heart of interpretation. Every paragraph has one and only one subject.

1. First paragraph

2. Second paragraph

3. Third paragraph

4. Etc.

EXPANDED OUTLINE OF VERSES 1-12

A. Introductory remarks, 1-2

B. Warnings about sexual immorality, 3-8
1. be holy, 3a
2. practice abstinence from sexual immorality, 3b
3. be sexually self disciplined, 4-5
4. practice appropriate sexuality by not defrauding your covenant brother's sexual rights

C. Exhortations to other Christians, 9-12
1. Christians are to love one another, 9-10
2. live better and better, 10b
3. live quiet lives, 11a
4. tend to your own affairs, 11b
5. do your own labor, 11c
6. so that you may be a witness to the lost, 12

WORD AND PHRASE STUDY

> **NASB (UPDATED) TEXT: 4:1-8**
>
> **Finally, then, brethren, we request and exhort you in the Lord Jesus, that as you received from us** *instruction* **as to how you ought to walk and please God (just as you actually do walk), that you excel still more. For you know what commandments we gave you by the** *authority* **of the Lord Jesus. For this is the will of God, your sanctification;** *that* **is, that you abstain from sexual immorality; that each of you know how to possess his own vessel in sanctification and honor, not in lustful passion, like the Gentiles who do not know God;** *and* **that no man transgress and defraud his brother in the matter because the Lord is the avenger in all these things, just as we also told you before and solemnly warned** *you.* **For God has not called us for the purpose of impurity, but in sanctification. So, he who rejects this is not rejecting man but the God who gives His Holy Spirit to you.**

4:1 "Finally then," This is literally "for the rest." This begins Paul's practical section. Most of Paul's letters can be divided into a doctrinal section and a practical section. Paul used this phrase to introduce the last major subject, not as an immediate prelude

206

to a closing (cf. II Thes. 3:1).

❖ **"brethren,"** Paul often used this term to start a new subject (cf. 1:4; 2:1,9,14,17; 3:7; 4:1,10,13; 5:1,4,12, 14,25,26,27; II Thes. 1:3; 2:1,13,15; 3:1,6,13).

❖ **"request and exhort"** Paul used these PRESENT TENSE verbs which emphasize continuing action to soften his commands as an Apostle (cf. 4:2,11; II Thes. 3:4,6,10,12).

❖ **"as you received from us** *instruction*" This is an AORIST TENSE. This is the Greek term that means "receive traditional teachings from another" (cf. 2:13; I Cor. 15:1). Paul not only taught them how to be saved but also how to live as saved people.

❖ **"as to how you ought to walk"** This is a PRESENT INFINITIVE. Christianity was originally called "The Way" (cf. Acts 9:2; 19:9,23; 22:4; 24:14,22; 18:25-26). This speaks of abiding lifestyle faith. Our initial response in repentance and faith must be followed by persistent obedience and perseverance.

❖ **"and please God"** God's will for His children is not heaven when they die, but Christlikeness now (cf. Rom. 8:28-29; Gal. 4:19).

❖ | NASB | "(just as you actually do walk)," |
NKJV	[missing]
NRSV	"(as, in fact, you are doing),"
TEV	"This is, of course, the way you have been living."
JB	"as you are already living it."

A Greek manuscript problem is connected to this phrase. This phrase is missing in manuscripts Dᶜ, K, L, and the Textus Receptus texts. It is present in manuscripts א, A, B, D*, F, G and also in the Syriac, Coptic, and Vulgate translations. This is either PRESENT INDICATIVE or IMPERATIVE MOOD. It could be INDICATIVE in that it asserts Paul's confidence in their Christlike lifestyle, as rendered in the NASB, NRSV, TEV, and JB..

| 4:2 | NASB, NKJV | "commandments" |
| | NRSV, JB, TEV | "instructions" |

NOTES

This is a rare military word for authoritative commands handed down through the ranks (cf. I Tim. 1:5, 18).

❖ **"by *the authority* of the Lord Jesus"** These were not Paul's personal thoughts but Jesus' teachings. Paul's Apostolic authority rested on Jesus' authority (cf. v. 8).

4:3-6 This is one sentence in Greek.

4:3 "For this is the will of God," There is no ARTICLE, therefore, this means one of God's wills (cf. Eph. 5:17), after salvation (cf. Jn. 6:40).

❖ **"your sanctification"** This word shares the same root word with "holy" and "saints." Sanctification, like justification, is an initial instantaneous act of grace (cf. I Cor. 1:30; 6:11). Positionally, believers are in Christ. However, it should develop into lifestyle character, progressive sanctification (cf. v. 7; 3:13; Rom. 6:19-23). God's will for every Christian is Christlikeness.

❖ **"abstain from sexual immorality;"** This is literally "fornication." Premarital sex was distinguished from extramarital sex in the OT, but the meaning became generalized in scope in the NT. "Fornication" covered all inappropriate sexual activity, including homosexuality and bestiality. Often pagan worship included sexual activity.

4:4 NASB, NKJV   **"to possess"**
      NRSV   **"to control"**
      TEV   **"how to take"**
      JB   **"to use"**
This is a PRESENT MIDDLE. It is literally "to continually acquire or possess."

❖   NASB, NKJV   **"his own vessel"**
      NRSV   **"your own body"**
      TEV   **"a wife"**
      JB   **"the body that belongs to him"**
This can refer to "his own body" or "his own wife." Theodore of Mopsuestia, Augustine, rabbinical usage, I Pet. 3:7, and the Septuagint interpret this in the sense of "wife." But the early Church Fathers interpreted it as "body" and this fits the con-

text best (cf. NIV). Vessel is used in the sense of "body" in II Cor. 4:7.

❖ **"in sanctification and honor,"** Knowing Jesus changes the way one lives. Believers are stewards, dependent on another's will. God's will is to use every believer to show His transforming power to a lost world.

4:5 "not in lustful passion," This refers to a fallen man's inability to control himself sexually. Self control is a characteristic of a Spirit filled, Spirit led life (cf. Gal. 5:23).

❖ **"like the Gentiles"** This is literally "the nations." Here, however, it does not refer to non-Jews but to all non-Christians. The lifestyle of the pagans of Paul's day was very immoral.

❖ **"who do not know God;"** This does not exclude "natural revelation" (cf. Ps. 19:1-6 and Rom. 1-2) but speaks of personal knowledge. In the OT "know" has the connotation of intimate, personal relationship (cf. Gen.4:1; Jer. 1:5).

4:6 "transgress" This term means "to go beyond bounds."

❖ **"defraud"** This term means "to take advantage of."

❖ **"his brother"** This may relate to taking sexual liberties with another believer's family. But the term "brother" in context could refer to any other man.

❖ **"in the matter"** This has the definite article and therefore refers to vv. 3-5.

❖ **"because the Lord is *the* avenger in all these things,"** This refers to even-handed justice—both temporal (cf. Rom. 1:24,26,28) and eschatological (cf. Mt. 25:31ff.). YHWH is an ethical God (cf. Gal. 6:7.) In vv. 6, 7a and 8a, three different reasons are given why the believers should live holy lives.

❖ **"as we also told you before and solemnly warned you."** This is a strong statement (cf. Heb. 13:4).

4:7 "God...called" God always takes the initiative (cf. Isa. 53:6; Jn. 6:44,65) both in salvation and in sanctification.

4:8 "he who rejects *this* is not rejecting man but the God" This is literally "treat as of little value." Paul asserted that along with the truth of the gospel goes the lifestyle imperatives. These are God's truths, not Paul's, (cf. 2:13; 3:1-2).

❖ **"who gives His Holy Spirit to you."** This is a PRESENT TENSE. This refers to the indwelling Spirit as both an initial and ongoing experience (cf. Rom. 8:9-10).

NASB (UPDATED) TEXT: 4:9-12

Now as to the love of the brethren, you have no need for any-*one* to write to you, for you yourselves are taught by God to love one another; for indeed you do practice it toward all the brethren who are in all Macedonia. But we urge you, brethren, to excel still more, and to make it your ambition to lead a quiet life and attend to your own business and work with your hands, just as we commanded you, so that you will behave properly toward outsiders and not be in any need.

4:9	NASB	"love of the brethren,"
	NKJV	"brotherly love"
	NRSV	"love of the brothers and sisters,"
	TEV	"love for your fellow believers."
	JB	"loving our brothers"

This is the Greek term, *philadelphia*. This refers to love for covenant partners. The balancing statement about loving the lost is in v. 12 (cf. 3:12).

❖ **"you have no need of anyone to write to you,"** This was Paul's tactful way of affirming them and yet encouraging them to greater effort (cf. v. 10c).

❖ **"for you yourselves are taught by God"** This is PRESENT TENSE. The teaching continues as the indwelling Spirit continues (cf. 5:1; Jn. 14:26; 16:13; II Cor. 9:1; I Jn. 2:20,27).

NOTES

4:10 "you do practice" This is another PRESENT TENSE verb which speaks of continuing action (cf. v. 17).

4:11	NASB	"to make it your ambition to lead a quiet life"
	NKJV	"that you also aspire to lead a quiet life,"
	NRSV	"to aspire to live quietly,"
	TEV	"Make it your aim to live a quiet life,"
	JB	"we do urge you, brothers, to go on making even greater progress and to make a point of living quietly,"

Verse 11 is a series of four PRESENT INFINITIVES used as IMPERATIVES, commandments for continuing action. This is probably exhorting patience and normalcy in anticipation of the Second Coming. "Stay ready and stay faithful," not "get ready," is the NT message in this area.

❖ **"work with your hands,"** Remember the historical occasion for the writing was that some in the church misunderstood Paul's preaching on the Second Coming and had quit working (cf. II Thes. 2:1-4 and 3:6-15).

In Greek culture, manual labor was believed to be exclusively the work of a slave. But in Hebrew culture, everyone needed a vocation—a means of supporting themselves, even rabbis (cf. Acts 20:35; I Cor. 4:17).

❖ **"just as we commanded you,"** This is a strong term for "order" (cf. II Thes. 3:4,6,10,12).

4:12	NASB, NRSV	"that you will behave properly toward outsiders"
	NKJV	"that you may walk properly toward those who are outside,"
	TEV	"In this way you will win the respect of those who are not believers,"
	JB	"so that you are seen to be respectable by those outside the Church,"

People are watching. We are witnesses (cf. Mt. 5:13-16;

Col. 4:5).

❖ | NASB | "not be in any need."
| NKJV | "*that* you may lack nothing."
| NRSV | "and be dependent on no one"
| TEV | "and will not have to depend on anyone for what you need"
| JB | "though you do not have to depend on them"

Apparently the Christians who quit work were expecting the other Christians to provide all their needs.

NASB (UPDATED) TEXT: 4:13-18

But we do not want you to be uninformed, brethren, about those who are asleep, so that you will not grieve as do the rest who have no hope. For if we believe that Jesus died and rose again, even so God will bring with Him those who have fallen asleep in Jesus. For this we say to you by the word of the Lord, that we who are alive and remain until the coming of the Lord, will not precede those who have fallen asleep. For the Lord Himself will descend from heaven with a shout, with the voice of *the* archangel and with the trumpet of God, and the dead in Christ will rise first. Then we who are alive and remain will be caught up together with them in the clouds to meet the Lord in the air, and so we shall always be with the Lord. Therefore comfort one another with these words.

4:13 "we do not want you to be uninformed, brethren," This is a common phrase in Paul's writings (cf. Rom. 1:13; 11:25; I Cor. 10:1; 12:1; II Cor. 1:8). Usually it introduced an important statement, like Jesus' "Amen, amen." Knowledge of Christian truth (doctrine) gives believers stability in a fallen world.

❖ **"about"** Timothy might have had some questions from the Church concerning the Second Coming: (1) What about the believers who had already died? Would they participate in the end-time events? (2) Would believers be surprised by the Second Coming and thereby miss participating in the end-time events?

Paul often used this preposition "about" to introduce his answers to the Corinthian Church's questions (cf. I Cor. 7:1; 8:1; 12:1; I Thes. 1:9,13; 5:1).

❖   NASB   "those who are asleep"
     NKJV   "those who have fallen asleep"
     NRSV, TEV, JB   "those who have died"
Greek manuscripts vary here: (1) some manuscripts have
a PRESENT PARTICIPLE, א, A, B, and (2) others have a PERFECT
PARTICIPLE, such as D, F, G, K, and L. Scribes probably changed
the original PRESENT to a PERFECT following the usage in Mt.
27:52 and I Cor. 15:20.

Jesus used the OT term for death, "sleep" (cf. Gen. 47:30;
II Sam. 7:12; I Kgs. 22:40; references in NT: Mt. 27:52; Jn. 11:11-
13; Acts 7:60; 13:26; I Cor. 7:39; 11:30; 15:18; II Pet. 3:4). The
English term "cemetery" is derived from this word.

This does not refer to the doctrine of "soul sleep," that
believers wait unconsciously until Resurrection Day. The NT
speaks of conscious, but limited fellowship, even now (cf. Lk.
16:19-31; 23:43; II Cor. 5:8; Phil. 1:23).

❖ "that you will not grieve as do the rest who have no hope" This
is a PRESENT PASSIVE SUBJUNCTIVE (cf. Eph. 2:12). Believers
must not continue to be grieved by earthly death. The pagan
world was at a loss for comfort at death. Socrates said, "Oh, that
there were some divine word upon which we could more securely
and less perilously sail, upon a stronger vessel."

4:14 "if" This is a FIRST CLASS CONDITIONAL sentence which
is assumed true from the author's perspective or for his literary
purposes.

❖ "we believe" "Faith" here is in the PRESENT TENSE, which
means it is an ongoing reality. Faith is described in AORIST (cf.
Rom. 8:24), PRESENT (cf. I Cor. 1:18; 15:2), PERFECT (cf. Eph.
2:5,8), and FUTURE VERB (cf. Rom. 10:9) TENSES. It is an initial
decision, followed by lifestyle discipleship that will one day be consummated in an eternal body and face-to-face fellowship with the
Triune God. The theological progression can be seen in Rom.
8:29-30, from election, to justification, to sanctification, to glorification.

❖ "Jesus died and rose again" These are both AORIST ACTIVE
INDICATIVES which reflect historical facts. These truths are the
basis for the believer's hope—vicarious substitutionary atonement
(cf. Isa. 53; Mk. 10:45; II Cor. 5:21), and bodily, physical, eternal

NOTES

resurrection (cf. I Cor. 15).

❖ **"God will bring with Him"** This is a difficult phrase because the verb has such a wide semantic field. Does it imply that the dead are with Jesus in heaven or that the dead will be raised at Jesus' coming? The Jerusalem Bible's first edition had "will bring" but its second edition had "will take away." This shows the wide connotations of this term.

In context the pronoun refers to Jesus, at His coming. The Thessalonian believers did not understand Paul's preaching about the Second Coming. They wanted to know if those who had already died would participate in the end-time events. This is Paul's positive response. Not only will they participate, they will receive their new bodies first and will accompany Jesus on the clouds of heaven.

The NT is not clear about the fate of believers between death and Resurrection Day. When this passage is compared to II Cor. 5:8, postulating a disembodied period becomes necessary. Believers are with the Lord, but as yet do not have their resurrection bodies.

4:15 "For this we say to you by the word of the Lord" Paul was not giving his personal opinion but was relating Jesus' teachings. It is uncertain if this refers to: (1) oral tradition (cf. Acts 20:35); (2) Jesus' sermons, like Mt. 24 or Mk. 13 or Lk. 21; (3) if this was part of Jesus' personal revelation to Paul while in Arabia, Gal. 1:17, or (4) later, direct revelation like II Cor. 12:1ff.

❖	NASB, NKJV	"we who are alive *and* remain until the coming of the Lord,"
	NRSV	"we who are alive, who are left until the coming of the Lord"
	TEV	"we who are alive on the day the Lord comes"
	JB	"left alive until the Lord's coming"

Paul expected the Lord to return in his lifetime. This "any moment" return of the Lord is the privilege of every generation of believers. This does not imply that Paul was inaccurate which would question inspiration.

| ❖ | NASB | "will not precede" |

NKJV, NRSV	"will by no means precede"
TEV	"will not go ahead"
JB	"will not have any advantage"

This is a strong DOUBLE NEGATIVE, "never—no, never." Those saints who have died will fully participate in all the endtime events as will the believers who are alive at the Second Coming.

4:16 "the Lord Himself" The Greek text emphasizes the Lord's personal return—not a surrogate (cf. Jn. 5:25-28).

❖ **"will descend from heaven"** Jesus is referring to the Father's right hand. He will leave heaven a second time to retrieve His own.

❖ NASB, NKJV	"with a shout, with the voice of *the* archangel and with the trumpet of God,"
NRSV	"with a cry of command, with the archangel's call and with the sound of God's trumpet,"
TEV	"There will be the shout of command, the archangel's voice, the sound of God's trumpet,"
JB	"at the trumpet of God, the voice of the archangel will call out the command"

The question remains how many heavenly persons are related to these three parallel events. There is a shout, a voice and a trumpet blast. The JB assumes all three are done by the archangel and then Jesus descends. Other translations imply the first "cry," "command" or "shout" is from Jesus and then the archangel calls for the trumpet blast.

Heaven is prepared for this event—it is on the calendar. The uncertainty of when and how the event will occur fades into insignificance with the knowledge of who will be coming. Jesus is coming again to receive His own.

❖ **"*the* archangel"** No ARTICLE appears, thus, it should read "an archangel." Although Dan. 10:13 implies several, the Bible only mentions one: Michael (cf. Jude 9). He is the angel of the nation of Israel.

❖ **"trumpet"** This was a very important means of communication in the OT, used for religious and military events (cf. Ex. 19:16; Isa. 27:13; Joel 2:1; Zech. 9:14; I Cor. 15:52).

Two types of trumpets appear in the OT: (1) silver trumpets (cf. Num. 10:2,8-10; 31:6), and (2) the left ram's horn called the shophar (cf. Ex. 19:16,19; 20:18; Lev. 25:9; Josh. 6).

❖ **"and the dead in Christ will rise first."** This phrase causes confusion about where the dead go between their death and resurrection day. This verse implies that they will remain in the grave (cf. Mt. 27:52-53).

However, II Cor. 5:8 implies that they are with the Lord. The solution may be in postulating a disembodied state. The body remains in the grave, the life force goes to be with the Lord. There are many unanswered questions here. The Bible does not provide a clear teaching passage on this subject.

Most translations translate it as if the saints are with God/Jesus and return with Him (cf. NASB): "God will bring with Him those who have fallen asleep." Another view is found in TEV, "Those who have died believing in Christ will rise to life first."

4:17 "caught up" Our theological concept of "rapture" originates from this verb. "Rapture" is a Latin rendering of the Greek verb here, which implies a forceful "snatching away" (cf. Jn. 6:15; 10:12, 28-29).

Many have disagreed about this endtime event. Some expect a secret rapture of believers before a thousand-year reign of Christ upon the earth. Often a seven-year tribulation period is linked to this. Some theologians have the rapture before, in the middle or after this period. The order and nature of these endtime events are ambiguous at best. Dogmatism is surely inappropriate here.

Believers are going to meet the Lord in the air, because in the NT the air was seen as the realm of Satan (cf. Eph. 2:2). Believers will be reunited with their Lord in the midst of Satan's kingdom to show its complete overthrow.

❖ **"together with them"** This church had misunderstood Paul's preaching about the Second Coming. Paul wrote both I Thessalonians and II Thessalonians to answer these questions.

219

NOTES

The church wanted to know: (1) Would the Christians who had died participate in these end-time events? and (2) When would dead and living believers be reunited?

❖ **"in the clouds"** Clouds were the transportation of deity (cf. Dan. 7:13; Mt. 24:30; 26:64; Acts 1:9-11; Rev. 1:7). The image calls to remembrance the Shekinah cloud of the OT exodus experience (cf. Ex. 13:21,22; 14:19,20,24; 16:10; 19:9,16; 24:15,16,18; 34:5; 40:34-38). It symbolizes God's presence with His people.

❖ **"in the air,"** The air was the dominion of Satan and his followers (cf. Eph. 2:2). We are going to meet the Lord there to show the complete victory.

❖ **"we shall always be with the Lord."** Nothing further can be said (cf. Psalm 23:6). The Second Coming is referred to repeatedly (cf. 1:10); 2:19; 3:13; 4:13-18; 5:1-11. Notice that neither in this book nor II Thes. does Paul mention a thousand-year reign but an eternal reign, like Dan. 7:13-14.

4:18 This, like v. 13, shows the purpose of Paul's presentation of these end-time events. The believers had many concerns about their fellow believers who had died. Would they be involved in the wonderful events of the Lord's return? Paul assured them that all believers, alive and dead, will be ultimately involved in the Second Coming. Remember this passage is primarily pastoral, not didactic. How this fits into other eschatological passages is uncertain.

DISCUSSION QUESTIONS

This is a study guide commentary which means that you are responsible for your own interpretation of the Bible. Each of us must walk in the light we have. You, the Bible and the Holy Spirit are priority in interpretation. You must not relinquish this to a commentator.

These discussion questions are provided to help you think through the major issues of this section of the book. They are meant to be thought provoking, not definitive.

1. Where in the Bible is the most detailed discussion of the Second Coming?

2. What was the reason for Paul writing this passage?

3. What is the Rapture?   Why?   Who?   When?

I THESSALONIANS 5

PARAGRAPH DIVISIONS OF MODERN TRANSLATIONS

UBS⁴	NKJV	NRSV	TEV	JB
The Lord's Coming	The Day of the Lord	Questions Concerning the Coming of the Lord	Be Ready for the Lord's Coming	Watchfulness While Awaiting the Coming of the Lord
(4:13-5:11)		(4:13-5:11)		
5:1-11	5:1-11	5:1-11	5:1-11	5:1-3
				5:4-11
Final Exhortations and Greetings	Various Exhortations	Concluding Exhortations	Final Instructions and Greetings	Some Demands Made by Life in Community
5:12-15	5:12-22	5:12-22	5:12-13	5:12-13
			5:14-15	5:14-18
5:16-22			5:16-18	
			5:19-22	5:19-22
	Blessing & Admonition			Closing Prayer and Farewell
5:23-24	5:23-28	5:23-24	5:23-24	5:23-24
5:25		5:25	5:25	5:25
5:26-27		5:26-27	5:26	5:26-27
			5:27	
5:28		5:28	5:28	5:28

READING CYCLE THREE (see p. vii)
FOLLOWING THE ORIGINAL AUTHOR'S INTENT AT THE PARA-GRAPH LEVEL

This is a study <u>guide</u> commentary which means that you are responsible for your own interpretation of the Bible. Each of us must walk in the light we have. You, the Bible and the Holy Spirit are priority in interpretation. You must not relinquish this to a commentator.

Read the chapter in one sitting. Identify the subjects. Compare your subject divisions with the five translations above. Paragraphing is not inspired but it is the key to following the original author's intent which is the heart of interpretation. Every paragraph has one and only one subject.

1. First paragraph

2. Second paragraph

3. Third paragraph

4. Etc.

CONTEXTUAL INSIGHTS TO VERSES 1-22

    A. Verses 1-11 are closely linked to 4:13-18. Notice the similar ending in 4:18 and 5:11. These passages are primarily pastoral. Their contextual purpose is to comfort, not give doctrine, although surely Paul does.

    B. This continues the discussion of the Second Coming and how Christians should live in light of the Lord's imminent return.

    C. Verses 13-22 have 15 PRESENT IMPERATIVES which speak of ongoing lifestyle characteristics of believers.

WORD AND PHRASE STUDY

NASB (UPDATED) TEXT: 5:1-11

Now as to the times and the epochs, brethren, you have no need of anything to be written to you. For you yourselves know full well that the day of the Lord will come just like a thief in the night. While they are saying, "Peace and safety!" then destruction will come upon them suddenly like labor pains upon a woman with child, and they will not escape. But you, brethren, are not in darkness, that the day would overtake you like a thief; for you are all sons of light and sons of day. We are not of night nor of darkness; so then let us not sleep as others do, but let us be alert and sober. For those who sleep do their sleeping at night, and those who get drunk get drunk at night. But since we are of *the* day, let us be sober, having put on the breastplate of faith and love, and as a helmet, the hope of salvation. For God has not destined us for wrath, but for obtaining salvation through our Lord Jesus Christ, who died for us, so that whether we are awake or asleep, we will live together with Him. Therefore encourage one another and build up one another, just as you also are doing.

5:1 "Now as to" The subject of the Second Coming continues but a new aspect of the event is approached: the judgment of unbelievers.

❖ | NASB | "the times and the epochs," |
NKJV, NRSV	"the times and the seasons,"
TEV	"the times and occasions"
JB	"'times and seasons'"

Although believers are not to seek specific times, they do need to recognize the trends of history (cf. Acts 1:7; Mt. 24:32-36). The Greek *chronoi*, translated "times," answers the question, "How long?"   It speaks of the passing of time.   The English word "chronology" is derived from this Greek root. *Kairo*, translated "epochs," answers the question, "when?"   It speaks of special events.

❖ **"brethren,"** This is often used by Paul to mark a transition to a new subject.

❖ **"you have no need of anything to be written to you."** Paul had not been able to give them extensive and prolonged information about the Second Coming. Remember, he only stayed approximately three weeks in Thessalonica, but he must have preached on this subject several times. This phrase does not mean to imply the Thessalonian believers perfectly understood all aspects of the end-time events but that the Spirit would lead them and inform in the necessary areas, (cf. Jn. 14:26; 16:13; I Jn. 2:20,27) especially those truths that relate to: (1) the gospel, and (2) the Christian life.

5:2 "the day of the Lord" This corresponds to an OT phrase referring to God or His Messiah breaking into history to set up the new age of righteousness (cf. Joel 1:15; 2:11,31; Amos 5:18; Isa. 2:12). In the OT God's coming could be for blessing or for judgment. For believers it will be the culmination of salvation but for unbelievers the consummation of judgment.

❖ **"will come just like a thief in the night"** This is a PRESENT TENSE used as a FUTURE. This "any-moment" return is a recurrent theme in the NT (cf. Mt. 24:42-44; 25:13; Lk. 12:40,45; 21:34-36; II Pet. 3:10; Rev. 3:3; 16:15). There was a Jewish tradition that the Messiah would come at midnight on Passover like the Death

NOTES

Angel of the Exodus.

5:3 "While they are saying, 'Peace and safety!'" This was the message of the false prophets of Jeremiah's day, 6:14; 8:11,28. Human life and society will appear normal before God's intervention (cf. Mt. 24:37-38). They will not be expecting the Messiah. The NT emphasis is that there will be intense suffering before the Second Coming (cf. Mt. 24:21; Mk. 13:19-20).

❖ **"then destruction will come upon them suddenly"** This passage strongly contrasts "them" and "brothers." This destruction does not refer to annihilation, but to God's judgment (cf. II Thes. 1:9; Dan. 12:2).

❖ **"labor pains"** This common OT metaphor of judgment (cf. Isa. 13:6-8; Jer. 4:31) became a common NT metaphor (cf. Mk. 13:8; Rom. 8:22). It speaks of the suddenness and certainty of the event, as well as the severe pain involved.

❖	NASB	"and they will not escape."
	NKJV	"And they shall not escape."
	NRSV	"and there will be no escape!"
	TEV	"They will not escape-"
	JB	"and there will be no way for any body to evade it."

This is an emphatic DOUBLE NEGATIVE: "Never, no, never under any circumstances escape."

5:4 "But you, brethren, are not in darkness" God has revealed—through the OT prophets, Jesus, and NT writers—the basic outline of endtime events so that those believers who are alive will not be surprised by what is occurring. This is one way that God has provided courage to His followers amid the difficulties of this life and the end-time tribulation period.

One reason for the recurrent confusion among believers about these events is that every generation of believers has tried to force these events into their history.

5:5 "sons of light and sons of day." These are two Semitic idioms for the righteous (cf. Lk. 16:8; Jn. 1:4-9; 3:17-21; 8:12; 11:9-10; 12:35-36,46; Eph. 5:8; I Jn. 1:5,7; 2:8-10). This metaphorical dual-

227

ism of light versus darkness is characteristic of the Ancient Near East. It is a recurrent theme in John and the Dead Sea Scrolls.

5:6 "let us not sleep" This is a different word from 4:13ff. It is often used in the NT for moral indifference (cf. Mk. 13:36; Eph. 5:14). Notice the three different uses of "sleep": (1) lack of moral alertness, (v. 6); (2) physical rest, (v. 7); (3) death, (v. 10).

❖ | NASB, NKJV, NRSV | "as others do," |
   |---|---|
   | TEV | "like the others" |
   | JB | "as everyone else does" |

This is literally "the remaining" or "the rest." It is the same term used to describe unbelievers who have no hope in 4:13.

❖ **"let us be alert and sober."** Alertness is a common theme of the NT for Christians concerning the Second Coming (cf. Mt. 24:42-43; 25:13; Mk. 13:34; Lk. 21:34). Both "awake" and "sober" are used metaphorically. "Sober" in vv. 6 & 8 is used of mental alertness or self-control.

5:8 "having put on" This is an AORIST MIDDLE PARTICIPLE which could read "having once for all ourselves put on." This usage is very similar to Eph. 6:13ff. which reflects Isa. 59:12. Paul used this military armor metaphor often but not always using the armor to represent the same Christian attributes. Believers must personally avail themselves of the blessing provided by Christ.

❖ **"faith...love...hope"** This was Paul's favorite triad of Christian virtues (cf. Rom. 5:2-5; Gal. 5:5-6; Col. 1:4-5; I Thes. 1:3; Heb 6:10-12; I Pet. 1:21-22). They form a link from initial faith to consummated faith.

❖ **"hope"** This often is used to refer to the Second Coming, especially in I & II Thes.

5:9 "for obtaining salvation through our Lord Jesus Christ," God's love flows to us only through Christ. He is the only way (cf. Jn. 14:6); the door (Jn. 10:1-3); the mediator (I Tim. 2:5).

5:10 "who died for us," This expresses Jesus' substitutionary vicarious sacrifice on our behalf (cf. Isa. 53; Mk. 10:45; II Cor. 5:21).

❖ **"whether we are awake or asleep,"** The church was concerned about those members of their fellowship who had died.

❖ **"we will live together with Him."** Heaven is being with Jesus (cf. II Cor. 5:8).

5:11 "encourage" "Encourage" is from the same root as "*paraclete*" (cf. Jn. 14-16; I Jn. 2:1). Paul's discussion of the Rapture (cf. 4:13-18) ends in a very similar way (cf. I Cor. 15:53; Eph. 4:13). Doctrine should encourage godly living.

5:12 "brethren" This is often used by Paul to show a transition to a new subject (cf. 4:13; 5:1), though not always (cf. 5:14 and 25, 26). Here it shows that Paul was addressing the whole church.

NASB (UPDATED) TEXT: 5:12-22

But we request of you, brethren, that you appreciate those who diligently labor among you, and have charge over you in the Lord and give you instruction, and that you esteem them very highly in love because of their work. Live in peace with one another. We urge you, brethren, admonish the unruly, encourage the fainthearted, help the weak, be patient with everyone. See that no one repays another with evil for evil, but always seek after that which is good for one another and for all people. Rejoice always; pray without ceasing; in everything give thanks; for this is God's will for you in Christ Jesus. Do not quench the Spirit; do not despise prophetic utterances. But examine everything *carefully*; hold fast to that which is good; abstain from every form of evil.

❖
NASB	"appreciate"
NKJV	"recognize"
NRSV	"respect"
TEV	"to pay proper respect"
JB	"be considerate"

Literally "know," this is a PERFECT INFINITIVE used in the sense of "to appreciate," "to show people respect," "to acknowledge the value of" or "know the value of." "Know" is used to show deep personal relationship in the OT (cf. Gen. 4:1; Jer. 1:5).

NOTES

❖   **NASB**   "those who diligently labor amongst you,"
     NKJV, NRSV   "those who labor among you,"
     TEV   "to those who work among you,"
     JB   "those who are working amongst you"

This term for "labor" means "strenuous effort" (cf. I Cor. 16:16). This entire section seems to refer to an attitude problem in the church toward its leadership (cf. I Tim. 5:17; Heb. 13:17). There is one ARTICLE in the Greek text followed by three descriptive phrases, all referring to the same persons.

❖ **"have charge over you in the Lord"** This is literally "to be set before."

❖ **"give you instruction,"** This is literally "put sense into." It is usually translated "to admonish the unruly."

5:13   **NASB, NKJV, NRSV**   "esteem them very highly in love"
        TEV   "Treat them with the greatest respect and love,"
        JB   "Have the greatest respect and affection for them"

This is a PRESENT INFINITIVE which emphasizes continuing personal action. This verbal root is from the noun for "leader." This is a triple compound term used three times by Paul (cf. Eph. 3:20; I Thes. 3:10). Believers should respect their leaders (cf. I Cor. 16:18; Phil. 2:29; I Tim. 5:17).

❖ **"because of their work."** Leadership is a gift from God (cf. Eph. 4:11-13). When He assigns the task, he honors the task, not necessarily the man who receives it. The term translated "work" in v. 13 is different from the one in v. 12. This hard working group of leaders may have been contrasted with those who refused to work (cf. v. 14 and II Thes. 3:6-11).

❖ **"Live in peace with one another."** This is a PRESENT IMPERATIVE, a continual command for believers and a common NT appeal (cf. Mk. 9:50; Rom. 12:18; II Cor. 13:11). This reflects a common problem in the churches. Christianity embraced men and women from many differing backgrounds.

5:14 "brethren," This could refer primarily to the leaders, but the things mentioned would apply to all believers. This is also true of I Tim. 3. NT Christianity does not make a distinction between "clergy" and "laity." We are all Spirit-gifted, called ministers of Jesus (cf. Eph. 4:11-13). However, God does choose leaders.

❖ NASB   **"admonish the unruly,"**
    NKJV   **"warn those who are unruly,"**
    NRSV   **"to admonish the idlers,"**
    TEV   **"warn the idle,"**
    JB   **"warn the idlers,"**

This begins a series of PRESENT IMPERATIVES, denoting continuous or habitual action. This could have one of two meanings: (1) a military term for disorderly conduct; or (2) used in the Egyptian papyri for "idlers." The latter fits the context of this letter better (cf. II Thes. 3:7-16).

❖ NASB, NRSV   **"encourage the fainthearted,"**
    NKJV   **"comfort the fainthearted,"**
    TEV   **"encourage the timid,"**
    JB   **"give courage to those who are apprehensive,"**

A PRESENT IMPERATIVE, this is literally, "little-minded." KJV has "feeble-minded" but it is really used in the sense of "fainthearted" or "little-faithed."

❖ **"help the weak,"** This PRESENT IMPERATIVE is used in the sense of weak in body and mind. This may designate the same type of Christian as characterized in Rom. 14:1-15:13.

❖ **"be patient with everyone."** This is a PRESENT IMPERATIVE. It is a command to continually be longsuffering, not short-tempered (cf. I Cor. 13:4). This is directed to both leaders and people. It also gives us a window into the problems of the early church.

5:15 "See that no one repays another with evil for evil," This is another PRESENT IMPERATIVE (cf. Mt. 5:44; Rom. 12:17-21; I Pet. 3:9). Believers must respond in a way different than unbelievers. Believers should act in faith not react in anger.

❖	NASB	"always seek after that which is good"
	NKJV	"always pursue what is good"
	NRSV	"always seek to do good"
	TEV	"at all times make it your aim to do good"
	JB	"you must all think of what is best"

This PRESENT IMPERATIVE rendered literally is "pursue good." Goodness is the goal, not selfish desires.

❖ **"for one another and for all people"** This is much like v. 14. Believers must put the good of the community above personal benefit (cf. Rom. 12:10; Phil. 2:1-5). How believers treat other believers should be the same way they treat nonbelievers also.

5:16 "Rejoice always;" This PRESENT IMPERATIVE is the theme of the book of Philippians (cf. 2:18; 3:1; 4:4,10). It is a worldview based on our relationship with Christ and each other, not on circumstances.

5:17 "pray without ceasing;" Another PRESENT IMPERATIVE, this must refer to lifestyle prayer, moment by moment fellowship with God. Paul sensed a need for prayer and believed it affected his ministry (cf. v. 25; Eph. 6:18-19; II Thes. 3:1).

5:18	NASB, NKJV	"in everything give thanks;"
	NRSV	"give thanks in all circumstances;"
	TEV	"be thankful in all circumstances."
	JB	"for all things give thanks to God,"

This is a PRESENT IMPERATIVE. Circumstances must not dictate our thanksgiving or our joy (cf. Rom. 8:26-30, 31-39). Remember that thanksgiving should flow not "for all things," but "in all circumstances."

"God's will" This is literally "a will of God" like Eph. 5:17. The will of God is that fallen man believe in Christ (cf. Jn. 6:29). After this there are several "wills" of God. One is to rejoice and give thanks even during persecution and conflict.

5:19 NASB, NKJV, NRSV "Do not quench the Spirit;"

233

NOTES

TEV	"Do not restrain the Holy Spirit;"
JB	"Never try to suppress the Spirit"

Verses 19 and 20 are both PRESENT IMPERATIVES with the NEGATIVE PARTICLE, meaning to stop an act in process. The Williams translation has "stop stifling the Spirit." The five IMPERATIVES of vv. 19-22 must go together. The first two NEGATIVE IMPERATIVES of vv. 19 & 20 set the boundaries for the three POSITIVE IMPERATIVES of vv. 21-22. "Quench" meant putting out a fire.

5:20

NASB	"do not despise prophetic utterances."
NKJV	"Do not despise prophecies."
NRSV	"Do not despise the words of prophets,"
TEV	"do not despise inspired messages."
JB	"never...treat the gift of prophecy with contempt;"

The definition of "prophecy" in the NT has been much debated. It is included in the list of spiritual gifts in I Cor. 12:28-29 (cf. Eph. 4:11). How the Scripture-writing prophets of the OT are related to the post-apostolic gift of "prophecy" is uncertain. Most scholars want to limit inspiration/revelation to the NT period (cf. Jude 3,20).

Clearly NT prophets are not synonymous with OT prophets. The gift usually relates to practical application issues, not new revelatory information. However, there is a predictive element in Acts 11:27-30 and 21:10-11.

5:21

NASB	"examine everything *carefully*;"
NKJV	"Test all things;"
NRSV	"test everything;"
TEV	"Put all things to the test:"
JB	"think before you do anything-"

This is a PRESENT IMPERATIVE. It is literally, "and all things prove." In context this could refer to: (1) church leaders, (2) spiritual gifts, or (3) doctrine. The word implies "to test with a view toward approval" (cf. I Cor. 12:10; 14:29; I Jn. 4:1ff.). Some things appear spiritual but actually are not (cf. Col. 2:16-23).

❖ **"hold fast to that which is good;"** "Hold fast" is another PRESENT IMPERATIVE (cf. 5:15; Rom. 12:9).

5:22 "abstain from every form of evil." "Abstain" is a PRESENT MIDDLE IMPERATIVE.

"Evil" can be MASCULINE or NEUTER. This causes problems in passages like Mt. 6:13, because the text could refer to Satan or evil in general. In this context it could be evil men or evil in general. There is no emphasis on false teachers in I Thes., therefore, it is probably parallel to the generic "good" in v. 21.

The phrase "every form of" can be understood in two ways: (1) KJV translates it as "every appearance of evil," as in Lk. 9:29. This is also the way the early Church Fathers understood the term; (2) the *Didache* 3:1 seems to use the term in a general sense of "all evil," not just apparent, but real evil.

NASB (UPDATED) TEXT: 5:23-24

Now may the God of peace Himself sanctify you entirely; and may your spirit and soul and body be preserved complete, without blame at the coming of our Lord Jesus Christ. Faithful is He who calls you, and He also will bring it to pass.

5:23 "may the God of peace Himself" This is a common phrase in the closings of Paul's letters (cf. Rom. 15:33; 16:20; II Cor. 13:11; Phil. 4:6; II Thes. 3:16). What a wonderful title for deity!

❖ **"sanctify...be preserved"** These are both AORIST OPTATIVES which is the mood of wishing or praying. Paul prayed that believers be sanctified and preserved by God.

❖ **"sanctify you entirely;"** In this sentence, two Greek words "entirely" and "complete" combine with "spirit, soul and body." This phrase underscores the completeness of our person, not that man is a trichotomous being like the Triune God. In Lk. 1:46-47 the parallelism shows that soul and spirit are synonymous. Man does not *have* a soul—he *is* a soul (cf. Gen. 2:7). This phrase emphasizes our call to holiness (cf. Mt. 5:48).

❖ **"without blame"** This term is only found here in the NT. It has been found in inscriptions at Thessalonica. It means free from blame or accusations, therefore, morally pure. It possibly reflects the OT term "blameless" that meant free of defects and, therefore, available for sacrifice.

❖ **"at the coming of our Lord"** The emphasis of the entire book is on the Second Coming.

5:24 "He who calls...He also will bring it to pass." The descriptive title "He who calls" always refers to God the Father (cf. 2:12; 4:7). This verse refers to the believers' election plus glorification (cf. Rom. 8:29-34). It focuses on the trustworthy God who initiates and perfects (cf. Phil. 1:6; 2:13). Our hope is in God's trustworthiness to keep His promises.

NASB (UPDATED) TEXT: 5:25

Brethren, pray for us.

5:25 "pray for us." Paul felt a need for prayer (cf. Rom. 15:30; Eph. 6:18-19; Col. 4:3-4; Phil. 1:9). Prayer somehow releases the power of God for effective ministry. The sovereign God has chosen to limit Himself in some areas to the prayers of His children (cf. Jas. 4:2).

NASB (UPDATED) TEXT: 5:26-27

Greet all the brethren with a holy kiss. I adjure you by the Lord to have this letter read to all the brethren.

5:26 "holy kiss" The "who," "where," and "how" of the Early Church's use of this type greeting is uncertain. Later, men kissed men and women kissed women on the cheek (cf. Rom. 16:16; I Cor. 16:20; II Cor. 13:23; I Pet. 5:14). The holy kiss was discontinued because of cultural misunderstanding by the pagans.

5:27 This verse is addressed to the leaders. Paul's letters were for public reading and later to be passed around to other churches. Paul understood that his writings had meaning beyond their original setting and time.

NASB (UPDATED) TEXT: 5:28

The grace of our Lord Jesus Christ be with you.

5:28 Paul probably wrote this himself to authenticate the letter (cf. II Thes. 3:17-18).

NOTES

DISCUSSION QUESTIONS

This is a study <u>guide</u> commentary which means that you are responsible for your own interpretation of the Bible. Each of us must walk in the light we have. You, the Bible and the Holy Spirit are priority in interpretation. You must not relinquish this to a commentator.

These discussion questions are provided to help you think through the major issues of this section of the book. They are meant to be thought provoking, not definitive.

1. Should we try to set the date of Jesus' return? Why?

2. Define the phrase "Day of the Lord."

3. Why is the Second Coming described as like: (1) a thief in the night; and (2) a woman in labor?

4. Where else in the Bible is the Christian armor discussed?

5. Which of these verses was written to the congregation and which to leaders?

6. What was the possible background at Thessalonica for this chapter?

7. Why are there so many "present imperatives"? What does this grammatical form mean to us?

NOTES

II THESSALONIANS

II THESSALONIANS 1

PARAGRAPH DIVISIONS OF MODERN TRANSLATIONS

UBS⁴	NKJV	NRSV	TEV	JB
Salutation	Greetings	Salutation	Greetings	Address
1:1-2	1:1-2	1:1-2	1:1	1:1-2
			1:2	
The Judgment at Christ's Coming	God's Final Judgment and Glory	Thanksgiving	The Judgment at Christ's Coming	Thanksgiving & Encouragement. The Last Judgment
1:3-12	1:3-12	1:3-4	1:3-4	1:3-5
		The Judgment of God		
		1:5-12	1:5-10	1:6-10
			1:11-12	1:11-12

READING CYCLE THREE (see p. vii)
FOLLOWING THE ORIGINAL AUTHOR'S INTENT AT THE PARA-GRAPH LEVEL

This is a study <u>guide</u> commentary which means that you are responsible for your own interpretation of the Bible. Each of us must walk in the light we have. You, the Bible and the Holy Spirit are priority in interpretation. You must not relinquish this to a commentator.

Read the chapter in one sitting. Identify the subjects. Compare your subject divisions with the five translations above. Paragraphing is not inspired but it is the key to following the original author's intent which is the heart of interpretation. Every paragraph has one and only one subject.

1. First paragraph

2. Second paragraph

3. Third paragraph

4. Etc.

CONTEXTUAL INSIGHTS TO VERSES 1-10

A. II Thessalonians is similar to I Thessalonians in many ways.

B. Verses 3-10 are one long sentence in Greek. They describe Paul's confidence in the believers and confidence in God's judgment on the unbelievers. This is a very strong passage on God's final judgment. The earthly roles, the blessed and unblessed, of the persecutor and persecuted will be reversed.

C. Verses 11-12 are a summary of verses 3-10.

WORD AND PHRASE STUDY

> **NASB (UPDATED) TEXT: 1:1-2**
>
> **Paul and Silvanus and Timothy to the church of the Thessalonians in God our Father and the Lord Jesus Christ: Grace to you and peace from God the Father and the Lord Jesus Christ.**

1:1 "Paul" This is from the Greek term for "little." All Jews of this period had a Jewish and a Greco-Roman name. This may have always been his Greco-Roman name. If he adopted it later it could have been because: (1) in stature, tradition says he was short, or (2) in his own mind because he persecuted the church (cf. I Cor. 15:9; Eph. 3:8; I Tim. 1:15).

❖ **"Silvanus"** Luke called him "Silas." He was a leader in the church in Jerusalem (cf. Acts 15:22,27,32; I Pet. 5:12). He replaced Barnabas as Paul's missionary companion after the first missionary journey. Paul wanted another leader from the Jerusalem church with him as a witness to what God was doing among the Gentiles.

242

❖ **"Timothy"** He was converted on Paul and Barnabas' first missionary journey. Paul chose him on his second missionary journey to be his helper. He was half-Jewish (cf. Acts 16:1-3).

❖ **"church"** The Greek term *ekklesia* means "the called out ones." The same term signified called town meetings in Greek cities. It was used in the Septuagint to translate *qahal* or "congregation" of Israel. The early Christians saw themselves as the fulfillment and extension of OT Israel.

❖ **"God our Father"** This phrase is one of the few differences between the introduction in I Thes. 1:1 and II Thes. 1:1. We can call God "our Father" (cf. Mt. 6:9). Of course, God is not our father in a physically generative or chronological sense, but in the sense of a familial relationship.

1:2 "Grace to you and peace" Many see this as a combination of the Greek and Jewish greetings. This phrase "from God our Father and the Lord Jesus Christ" occurs in both v. 1 and v. 2. In v. 1 the phrase has the preposition "in" while v. 2 has the preposition "from." The Father and Son are linked by the CONJUNCTION "and" and the SINGLE PREPOSITION, showing Paul's theology of Jesus' deity.

NASB (UPDATED) TEXT: 1:3-12

We ought always to give thanks to God for you, brethren, as is *only* fitting, because your faith is greatly enlarged, and the love of each one of you toward one another grows ever greater; therefore, we ourselves speak proudly of you among the churches of God for your perseverance and faith in the midst of all your persecutions and afflictions which you endure. *This* is a plain indication of God's righteous judgment so that you will be considered worthy of the kingdom of God, for which indeed you are suffering. For after all it is *only* just for God to repay with affliction those who afflict you, and *to give* relief to you who are afflicted and to us as well when the Lord Jesus will be revealed from heaven with His mighty angels in flaming fire, dealing out retribution to those who do not know God to those who do not obey the gospel of our Lord Jesus.

NOTES

> **These will pay the penalty of eternal destruction, away from the presence of the Lord and from the glory of His power, when He comes to be glorified in His saints on that day, and to be marveled at among all who have believed—for our testimony to you was believed. To this end also we pray for you always, that our God will count you worthy of your calling, and fulfill every desire for goodness and the work of faith with power, so that the name of our Lord Jesus will be glorified in you, and you in Him, according to the grace of our God and *the* Lord Jesus Christ.**

1:3 "We ought always to give thanks to God for you," This reflected Paul's prayer life for the churches (cf. I Thes. 1:2; II Thes. 2:13 and Phil. 1:3-4).

❖ | NASB | "because your faith is greatly enlarged,"
| NKJV | "because your faith grows exceedingly,"
| NRSV | "because your faith is growing abundantly,"
| TEV | "because your faith is growing so much"
| JB | "because your faith is growing so wonderfully"

This is a metaphor from agriculture which expresses vigorous plant growth. Paul applauded the development of their faith and love.

❖ **"the love of each one of you toward one another"** In light of the internal fellowship problems (cf. I Thes. 3:12; I Jn. 4:7,11,12,31), the recollection of love was important .

❖ **"grows *ever* greater;"** This expression was used to invoke images of swelling flood waters.

1:4 "we ourselves speak proudly of you" The emphasis of this phrase is on "we ourselves" in contrast to "you." The church itself felt weak (cf. I Thes. 5:14). Paul saw and articulated their strengths. Their Christlikeness under persecution was evidence of Paul's effective ministry and thereby his apostleship (cf. I Thes. 2:19).

❖   NASB   "perseverance"
        NKJV   "patience"
        NRSV   "steadfastness"
        TEV   "about the way you continue to endure"
        JB   "constancy"

This is literally "voluntary, active, steadfast endurance" (cf. I Thes. 1:3). It relates to people and circumstances.

❖ **"faith"** This term in the OT was used of God's trustworthiness and man's response in trust (cf. Hab. 2:4). Here it is used of their faithfulness in the midst of persecution. Paul prayed for their faith in I Thes. 3:10 and praised them here for their faith.

❖ **"in the midst of all your persecutions and afflictions which you endure."** Suffering is normal for believers in a fallen world (cf. Mt. 5:10-12; Acts 14:22; Rom. 8:17-18; I Thes. 2:14; 3:3; Jas. 1:2-4; I Pet. 4:12-16).

1:5 *"This* **is a plain indication of God's righteous judgment"** (cf. Phil. 1:28).

❖   NASB   "so that you will be considered worthy"
        NKJV   "that you may be counted worthy"
        NRSV   "is intended to make you worthy"
        TEV   "because as a result of all this you will become worthy"
        JB   "you may be found worthy"

This is an AORIST PASSIVE INFINITIVE, "to declare worthy." The PASSIVE VOICE implies that God the Father is the agent. This is one purpose of suffering. It builds character (cf. v. 11; Rom. 5:3-4; Heb. 5:8).

❖ **"of the kingdom of God,"** This speaks of God's reign. It is a present reality that will one day be consummated over all the earth (cf. Mt. 6:10).

1:6   NASB   "For after all it is *only* just"
          NKJV   "since *it is* a righteous thing"
          NRSV   "For it is indeed just"

TEV	"God will do what is right:"
JB	"God will very rightly"

This is an implied FIRST CLASS CONDITIONAL SENTENCE, assumed true from the author's perspective or for his literary purposes. God's judgment is just.

❖ **"for God to repay"** This is a moral world order. God will set things right.

1:7 "to us as well" Paul was suffering too (cf. I Cor. 4:9-13; II Cor. 4:8-12; 6:4-10; 11:24-27).

❖ **"when the Lord Jesus will be revealed"** *Apocalypsis* means "to clearly reveal" (cf. I Cor. 1:7). This refers to the Second Coming of Jesus. The PASSIVE VOICE verb implies God the Father is the agent as in v. 5. The time of God's righteous judgment will be the Second Coming/Resurrection Day/Judgment Day.

❖ **"with His mighty angels"** This is a common biblical theme (cf. Deut. 33:2; Zech. 14:5; Mt. 16:27; 25:31; Mk. 8:38; Jude 14; Rev. 19:14). He will also come with His saints (cf. I Thes. 4:13-18). Mt. 13:41 and 24:31 imply the angels will gather and separate mankind.

❖ **"in flaming fire,"** This is a symbol of God's judgment (cf. Isa. 29:6; 30:27-30; 66:14-15; Dan. 7:9-10).

Confusion exists whether this phrase goes with v. 7 or v. 8. If it goes with v. 7 it relates to the angels; if it goes with v. 8 it relates to judgment. The NKJV, NRSV, and REB translations place it in v. 8.

1:8	NASB	"dealing out retribution"
	NKJV	"taking vengeance"
	NRSV	"inflicting vengeance"
	TEV	"to punish"
	JB	"to impose the penalty"

This is a PRESENT ACTIVE PARTICIPLE. This is not an emotional, vindictive reaction but "full justice for all." This word is etymologically related to "righteous" or "just." God's creation reflects God's character.

NOTES

❖ **"on those who do not know God"** (cf. I Thes. 4:5; Rom. 1:18,25; 2:14-15). This word reflects the pagan's willful rejections of light (cf. Jn. 3:17-21). This phrase does not only refer to truth about God but also fellowship with God. The term "know" has the Hebrew connotation of intimate fellowship (cf. Gen 4:1; Jer. 1:5; Mk. 14:71; Tit. 1:16).

❖ **"to those who do not obey the gospel"** Some commentators think this refers to a second group; the first phrase referring to pagans and the second to Jews. However, only one ARTICLE with these two phrases in v. 8 implies the same group willfully rejecting the divine Messiah and the gospel—both a message and a person.

1:9 "the penalty" This is the same root as "retribution" in v. 8.

❖ **"eternal destruction,"** "Eternal" shares the same root with "age" (cf. Mt. 28:20; Heb. 1:2). In Mt. 25:46 it describes both heaven and hell (cf. I Thes. 2:16). Man's response to the gospel in the present seals his future.

❖ **"away from the presence of the Lord"** This is the worse aspect of hell. In Psa. 139:8 it says "God's presence is in hell" but this refers to *Sheol* or *Hades*, not *Gehenna* (cf. Mt. 7:23).

1:10 "when He comes to be glorified in His saints" "In" is emphatic. "Saints" is literally "holy ones." The term "saints" is always plural except once in Phil. 4:21, and even there, it is corporate in nature. To be saved puts us in Christ and in His family.

This is not so much an experience as a position. Hopefully our position is becoming more actualized in our daily lives. When He returns our glorification will be instantaneous and complete (cf. I Jn. 3:2; Romans 8:30). Jesus is glorified in the godly lives of His saints (cf. v. 12).

❖	NASB, NKJV	"to be glorified in His saints"
	NRSV	"to be glorified by his saints"
	TEV	"to receive glory from all his people"
	JB	*"to be glorified among his saints"*

This phrase can be understood in at least two ways: (1) reflecting a Hebrew idiom, the majesty of the Second Coming will cause Jesus to receive glory from His followers, or (2) reflecting the normal meaning of the Greek preposition, in addition to the unusual compound with the preposition repeated with the noun, (vv. 10,12) that Jesus will be glorified among or in believers.

❖ **"on that day,"** This emphatic phrase is an OT metaphor of the time that God will return to His creation either for blessing or judgment.

❖	**NASB**	**"and to be marveled at among all who have believed-"**
	NKJV	**"and to be admired among all those who believe,"**
	NRSV	**"and to be marveled at ... among all who have believed,"**
	TEV	**"and honor from all who believe."**
	JB	**"and** *seen in his glory* **by all who believe in him;"**

There are two ambiguous phrases in v. 10. They can mean: (1) the saints are glorified with Christ and this amazes them, or (2) the angels are amazed at what God does for believers (cf. Eph. 2:7; 3:10).

❖ **"for our testimony to you was believed."** They were opposite of the pagans in verse 8. They had received the gospel as both a message and a person.

1:11 "we pray for you always," Paul continually prayed for these churches (cf. II Thes. 1:3; 2:12; I Thes. 1:2; 5:13-18).

❖	**NASB**	**"God will count you worthy of your calling,"**
	NKJV	**"God would count you worthy of** *this* **calling,"**
	NRSV, JB	**"God will make you worthy of his call"**
	TEV	**"God to make you worthy of the life he called you to live."**

God does it (cf. Phil. 1:6; 2:13; Eph. 4:4), but we must allow Him and cooperate (cf. Phil. 2:12; Eph. 4:1). It is the paradox of God's sovereignty and man's free will in both an initial and a progressive faith response. In this context the emphasis is on the

Christian's new life (cf. Eph. 4:1; 5:2,15).

❖ **"and fulfill every desire for goodness"** Paul was praying that their new intentions be actualized. As with their new heart, they have acquired a new mouth, hands, and feet (cf. Rom. 6:4; II Cor. 5:17; Col. 3:10).

1:12 "the name of our Lord Jesus...in Him" Here it is obvious from the parallel structure that "the name" represents the person.

❖ **"in you, and you in Him,"** Jesus is glorified in believers and believers are glorified in Him. The means for both is the grace of God.

DISCUSSION QUESTIONS

This is a study <u>guide</u> commentary which means that you are responsible for your own interpretation of the Bible. Each of us must walk in the light we have. You, the Bible and the Holy Spirit are priority in interpretation. You must not relinquish this to a commentator.

These discussion questions are provided to help you think through the major issues of this section of the book. They are meant to be thought provoking, not definitive.

1. What is the central theme of chapter 1? How is it different from I Thes. 1?

2. Why is suffering normal for believers? (verse 5)

3. Is God vindictive and vengeful? If not, what does verse 8 mean?

4. Is Hell forever?

NOTES

II THESSALONIANS 2

PARAGRAPH DIVISIONS OF MODERN TRANSLATIONS

UBS⁴	NKJV	NRSV	TEV	JB
The Man of Lawlessness	The Great Apostasy	The Day of the Lord	The Wicked One	The Coming of the Lord and the Prelude to it
2:1-12	2:1-12	2:1-12	2:1-4 2:5-12	2:1-3a 2:3b-8 2:9-12
Chosen for Salvation	Stand Fast	Thanksgiving and Exhortation	You are Chosen for Salvation	Encouragement to Persevere (2:13-3:5)
2:13	2:13-17	2:13-15 2:16-17	2:13-15 2:16-17	2:13-17

READING CYCLE THREE (see p. vii)
FOLLOWING THE ORIGINAL AUTHOR'S INTENT AT THE PARA-GRAPH LEVEL

This is a study guide commentary which means that you are responsible for your own interpretation of the Bible. Each of us must walk in the light we have. You, the Bible and the Holy Spirit are priority in interpretation. You must not relinquish this to a commentator.

Read the chapter in one sitting. Identify the subjects. Compare your subject divisions with the five translations above. Paragraphing is not inspired but it is the key to following the original author's intent which is the heart of interpretation. Every paragraph has one and only one subject.

1. First paragraph

2. Second paragraph

3. Third paragraph

4. Etc.

CONTEXTUAL AND THEOLOGICAL INSIGHTS TO VERSES 1-12

A. This passage is very difficult to interpret as the several theories show.

B. Biblical Background
   1. As chapter 1 dealt with the Second Coming of Christ, chapter 2:1-12 deals with the coming of the Anti-Christ. This is the most detailed description of this person in the NT. Paul does not use the Johannine term "Anti-Christ" (I Jn. 2:18,22; 4:3; II Jn. 7) but called him "the man of lawlessness" in v. 3 and "the lawless one" in v. 8.
   2. The general background of this passage lies in the OT belief in a final confrontation between the people of God and the people of the evil one (cf. Ps. 2, Ezek. 38-39, Zech. 12-14). This conflict became personalized into individual leaders of both camps: God's Messiah and the Anti-Messiah (cf. Gen. 3:15; Dan. 7-12; Isaiah 14; Ezek. 28).
   3. The specific background of the passage in the NT is Mt. 24, Mk. 13, Lk. 21, I Jn. 2 and Revelation.
   4. Three time elements are involved in vv. 1-12:
      a. current events
      b. future events but preceding the Second Coming
      c. future events concerning the Day of the Lord

C. It must be remembered that the whole subject of the return of Christ is presented in the Bible in a dialectical tension. On one hand, the imminent return of the Lord is balanced with the references that several events must happen first. One of these poles does not eliminate or contradict the other. Some examples of the necessary preliminary events would be:
   1. The apostasy (cf. Mt. 24:1-13,21; I Tim. 4:1; II Tim. 3:1ff. and II Thes. 2:3ff).
   2. Gospel preached to all nations (cf. Mt. 24:24).
   3. Revealing of Anti-Christ (cf. Mt. 24, II Thes. 2; and Rev. 13).
   4. Salvation of the full number of Gentiles and Jews (cf. Rom. 11:11-36).

WORD AND PHRASE STUDY

NASB (UPDATED) TEXT: 2:1-12

Now we request you, brethren, with regard to the coming of our Lord Jesus Christ and our gathering together to Him, that you not be quickly shaken from your composure or be disturbed either by a spirit or a message or a letter as if from us, to the effect that the day of the Lord has come. Let no one in any way deceive you, for *it will not come* unless the apostasy comes first, and the man of lawlessness is revealed, the son of destruction, who opposes and exalts himself above every so-called god or object of worship, so that he takes his seat in the temple of God, displaying himself as being God. Do you not remember that while I was still with you, I was telling you these things? And you know what restrains him now, so that in his time he will be revealed. For the mystery of lawlessness is already at work; only he who now restrains *will do so* until he is taken out of the way. Then the lawless one will be revealed whom the Lord will slay with the breath of His mouth and bring to an end by the appearance of his coming; *that is*, the one whose coming is in accord with the activity of Satan, with all power and signs and false wonders, and with all the deception of wickedness for those who perish, because they did not receive the love of the truth so as to be saved. For this reason God will send upon them a deluding influence so that they will believe what is false, in order that they all may be judged who did not believe the truth, but took pleasure in wickedness.

2:1 "with regard to the coming" This is the Greek term *parousia* meaning "presence." The cultural background of the term was royal visits for which this word was regularly employed. Three words are used in the NT to describe the Second Coming: (1) *parousia* (cf. vv. 1&8), (2) *epiphany* (cf. v. 8), a visible radiant coming and (3) *apocalypsis* (cf. 1:17), meaning "an unveiling" for the purpose of revealing. The last word is also employed at the manifestation of the Anti-Christ in vv. 3,6,8. "Second Coming" is not a biblical term. It was first used by Justin Martyr.

❖**"our gathering together to Him,"** This is a reference to the "rap-

255

NOTES

ture" of I Thes. 4:13-18.   From the context, one coming is intended (cf. Mt. 24:31; 25:31ff.), not two. Verse 3 speaks of the saints experiencing tribulation and the revelation of the Anti-Christ. These two verses, 1 and 3, contradict the view of a pret-ribulational, secret rapture.

Usually Mt. 24:32-44 is used as support for a secret rapture of believers while the unredeemed are left. However, in context, the unredeemed are taken to be judged. In Mt. 24:39, "took them all away" describes those destroyed in the Flood (cf. vv. 37-38).

The real theological purpose of a secret rapture distinct from a later, visible return is to remove the tension between the imminent return of Jesus and the necessity that some prophesied events must occur before the return.

2:2	NASB	"not be quickly shaken from your composure"
	NKJV	"not to be soon shaken in mind"
	NRSV	"not to be quickly shaken in mind"
	TEV	"do not be so easily confused in your thinking"
	JB	"please do not get excited too soon"

This is an AORIST PASSIVE INFINITIVE which speaks of an act by an outside agent, here a spirit, or a message. This word described a ship becoming loosened from its moorings (cf. Eph. 4:13-14). "Quickly" implies (1) Paul's surprise that so soon after he talked to them about these things that so much confusion, fear and speculation had occurred, or (2) their ready acceptance of every person's opinion on this subject.

❖"or be disturbed" This is a PRESENT PASSIVE INFINITIVE which speaks of a continuing occurrence by an outside agent, here a spirit or message. If the first term in v. 2 refers to their thinking process, this rare term refers to their feelings (cf. Mt. 24:6; Mk. 13:7).

❖	NASB	"either by a spirit or"
	NKJV, NRSV	"either by spirit or"
	TEV	"by the claim...Perhaps this was said by someone prophesying"
	JB	"by any prediction or"

This is literally "a spirit," used in the sense of a prophet's message or another supernatural revelation (cf. I Jn. 4:1).

❖   **NASB**   "or a message"
       NKJV, NRSV   "or by word"
       TEV   "or by someone preaching"
       JB   "or rumour"

Amplified, this phrase could be rendered "by means of someone's personal interpretation."

❖   **NASB**   "or a letter as if from us,"
       NKJV   "or by letter, as if from us,"
       NRSV   "or by letter, as though from us,"
       TEV   "Or it may have been said that we
                              wrote this in a letter."
       JB   "or any letter claiming to come from
                              us,"

Paul began to personally autograph his letters to insure their genuineness (cf. 3:17). This could refer to someone's false interpretation of I Thessalonians or Paul's preaching.

❖**"to the effect that the day of the Lord has come."** This is a PER-FECT ACTIVE INDICATIVE. This was the major problem Paul was trying to clear up. The remainder of vv. 3-12 are an explanation why this statement cannot be true (cf. Mt. 24:23,26). The events that accompany the Second Coming had not yet begun.

2:3   **NASB**   "Let no one in any way deceive you,"
       NKJV   "Let no one deceive you by any
                            means;"
       NRSV   "Let no one deceive you in any way;"
       TEV   "Do not let anyone fool you in
                            any way."
       JB   "Never let anyone deceive you in this
                            way."

This is a strong DOUBLE NEGATIVE with an AORIST ACTIVE SUBJUNCTIVE implying a personal agency. Apparently purposeful deception was occurring.

❖**"for it will not come unless"** Some events must happen first (cf. Introduction, C). In this context, two events are mentioned: (1) the great apostasy, and (2) the revealing of "the man of sin."

❖   **NASB**   **"the apostasy comes first,"**
         NKJV   **"the falling away comes first,"**
         NRSV   **"the rebellion comes first"**
         TEV   **"the final Rebellion takes place"**
         JB   **"the Great Revolt has taken place"**

This word can be used of political or military rebellion, but in the Septuagint and Apocrypha, it always refers to spiritual rebellion. Who is rebelling is uncertain but they are rejecting God. It could be the pagans, the Jews or part of the visible church (cf. Mt. 24:1-12; I Tim. 4:1; II Tim. 3:1ff., I Jn. 2:18-19).

❖   **NASB**   **"the man of lawlessness is revealed,"**
         NKJV   **"the man of sin is revealed,"**
         NRSV   **"the lawless one is revealed"**
         TEV   **"the Wicked One appears,"**
         JB   **"the Rebel,...has appeared."**

There is a Greek manuscript problem here. "Lawlessness" is found in the Greek manuscripts א and B while "sin" is found in manuscripts A, D, G, K, L, and P. "Man of sin" is very rare and scribes may have substituted the familiar term "lawlessness." Satan is not intended as in v. 9, but his yielded servant, this man of sin. Paul never used the term "Anti-Christ," but I Jn. 2:18 and 4:3 refer to the same person. The root "lawlessness" is also used in vv. 7 and 8. In I Jn. "sin" and "lawlessness" are equated.

❖   **NASB**   **"the son of destruction,"**
         NKJV   **"the son of perdition,"**
         NRSV   **"the one destined for destruction."**
         TEV   **"who is destined to hell."**
         JB   **"the Lost One,"**

This Hebraic idiom literally translates "the son of perdition." In Jn. 7:12, Judas Iscariot is meant. This person will be lost and doomed to eternal punishment although deeply involved in religion (cf. v. 4).

2:4   **NASB**   **"who opposes and exalts himself above every so-called god or object of worship,"**
         NKJV   **"who opposes and exalts himself above all that is called God or that is**

NOTES

	worshipped,"
NRSV	"He opposes and exalts himself above every so-called god or object of worship,"
TEV	"He will oppose everything which men worship and everything which men consider divine."
JB	"This is the Enemy, the one who claims to be so much *greater than all* that men call 'god,' so much greater than anything that is worshipped,"

This is a PRESENT PARTICIPLE. What is represented here is an evil counterfeit of monotheism (cf. Isaiah 14:13-14; Ezek. 28:2; Dan. 7:25; 8:9-14; 9:27; 11:36-37; Mt. 24:15; Mk. 13:14; Rev. 13).

❖"so that he takes his seat in the temple of God," This strongly specific and personal image suggests a future historical fulfillment. Yet it is also ambiguous. Notably this language fits the Seleucid and Roman invasions of Jerusalem during which pagan gods were enthroned in the Temple area. This end-time figure also resembles the pride and arrogance of the kings of Babylon (Isa. 14) and Tyre (Ezek. 28) which are seen as types of Satanic apostasy.

This Greek term for "temple" was used for the Holy of Holies in the Jewish Temple, though no seat was in it. The term was also employed for pagan temples where deities were enthroned. This may imply that the Jewish temple must be physically rebuilt, possibly following Ezek. 40.

Chrysostom interpreted "a temple" as a common Pauline metaphor for the Church (cf. I Cor. 3:16-17; 6:19; II Cor. 6:16; Eph. 2:21). This view sees the Anti-Christ as manifesting himself in the visible church.

❖"displaying himself as being God." The lawless one actually claims deity. He is in a sense a personification of Satan.

2:5 "I was telling you these things?" This is an IMPERFECT TENSE signifying that these believers had repeatedly heard preachers or teachers about this subject. They had information about this subject that we do not have (cf. v. 5 "do you not remember" and v. 6 "you know.") Therefore, all modern interpretations, to some extent, are incomplete and suppositional. Dogmatism must be avoided though careful exegesis is helpful. It is uncertain if this phrase is referring to the information given in vv. 1-5 or vv. 6-12.

2:6 "you know" This implies that (1) these believers knew who/what Paul was referring to, or (2) they were currently experiencing the power/person in their lives.

❖	NASB	**"what restrains him now,"**
	NKJV	**"what is restraining,"**
	NRSV	**"what is now restraining him,"**
	TEV	**"there is something that keeps this from happening now,"**
	JB	**"what is still holding him back"**

This verb can mean (1) "hold back" (cf. Lk. 4:24; Philem. 13), (2) "hold fast" (cf. I Thes. 5:21; Lk. 8:15), or (3) "hold away" (no biblical example). The context favors "hold back" or "restrains." The real question is: who or what is this restrainer? An interesting grammatical change occurs from the NEUTER in vv. 6 & 7 to the MASCULINE in vv. 7 & 8. This implies an influence capable of personification. Because of this, at least three interpretations are plausible: (1) law vs. anarchy, personified in the Roman emperor, (2) angelic authority, personified in a specific angel(s) (cf. Rev. 7:1-3), or (3) God, in the person of His Spirit or the Spirit's empowering the preaching of the gospel.

The first theory is very old and pervasive, first stated by Tertullian. It fits the contextual criteria that the Thessalonian Christians would have understood. Paul also spoke of his experiences with and the benefit of law (cf. Rom. 13:1ff., Acts 17-18). The second theory is closely related. It uses Dan. 10 as evidence for angelic control and authority over nations and their law systems. The third theory is of a more recent vintage. It has much to commend it but is also very presuppositional. This is employed mostly by particular dispensationalists to support a secret rapture.

The spirit of the Anti-Christ has always been in the world (cf. I Jn. 2:18; 4:3; II Jn. 7), but one day he will be ultimately personified. This restraining force is ultimately supernatural and under God's control and plan (cf. vv. 6b-7). Theory number two fits best.

❖ **"so that in his time he will be revealed."** The person/power referred to is apparently being restrained by God. At the appointed time in the future, he will be allowed to manifest himself.

2:7 "the mystery" Paul often used this term for God's plans once hidden but now revealed to believers (cf. Col. 1:26). It is in a sense the full gospel of Christ. It has several different special usages (cf. Rom. 11:25; 16:25; I Cor. 2:7; 4:1; 13:2; 14:2; 15:51; Eph. 1:9; 3:3,4,9; 6:19; Col. 1:26; 2:2; 4:3; I Tim. 3:9,16).

This term may also be used in the sense that God has a "mystery plan" for the future, so too, Satan has a "mystery plan." These verses reveal how the personification of evil will mimic Christ.

❖ **"of lawlessness is already at work;"** (cf. I Jn. 2:18-29; 4:3). This compound form of the term "work" is used exclusively of supernatural agencies (cf. Eph. 1:9; 3:7; 4:16; Phil. 3:21; Col. 1:29; II Thes. 2:9). This spiritual rebellion has been occurring since the Fall. The rebellion will one day be personified. Currently God is restraining his influence. The Scriptures see an end-time confrontation between evil and God (cf. Psalm 2).

❖	NASB	**"only he who now restrains *will do so* until he is taken out of the way."**
	NKJV	**"only He who now restrains will do so until He is taken out of the way."**
	NRSV	**"but only until the one who now restrains it is removed."**
	TEV	**"until the one who holds it back is taken out of the way."**
	JB	**"and the one who is holding it back has first to be removed."**

This is a PRESENT ACTIVE PARTICIPLE with an AORIST SUBJUNCTIVE. God is still continuing to restrain but sometime in the future this restraining influence will be removed. For a list of the theories as to the identity of "the one restraining," see v. 6. Whatever or whoever it is, God is in control of history, not the lawless one.

2:8 "Then that lawless one will be revealed" The time element is the question. The text implies immediately, but the following vers-

NOTES

es detail his activity (cf. Dan. 7:13; 8:29; 9:24-27).

❖ NASB   "whom the Lord will slay"
    NKJV   "whom the Lord will consume"
    NRSV   "whom the Lord Jesus will destroy"
    TEV   "the Lord Jesus will kill him"
    JB   "The Lord *will kill him*"

There are two Greek manuscript problems in this verse. The first is the name "Lord" or "Lord Jesus." The single title is in manuscripts B, D^c, and K. The double title is in manuscripts ℵ, A, D*, G, and P and the Vulgate, Syrian, and Coptic translations.

The second problem is the verb. "Destroy" is in manuscripts ℵ, A, D*, G and P as well as the Vulgate, Syrian and Coptic translations. Paul was possibly alluding to Isa. 11:4 where this same verb occurs in the Septuagint. The unusual term "consume" is found in manuscripts F and G and a variant form in D^c and K. The Second Coming will end this period of rebellion.

❖"with the breath of His mouth" The OT background for this is Job 4:9 or Isa. 11:4; the NT usage is Rev. 2:16; 9:15. The Hebrew and Greek terms can refer to wind, breath or spirit as Jn. 3:8 shows, but here the context demands "breath." This may refer to: (1) the power of His words, (John Calvin) or (2) the power of the spoken word in the OT (cf. Gen. 1; Isa. 55:11).

❖ NASB   "bring to an end"
    NKJV, NRSV   "destroy"
    TEV   "kill him"
    JB   "will annihilate him"

This phrase means "to make inoperative" not "to eliminate" or "to destroy" (cf. Rom. 3:3; 6:6).

❖ NASB   "the appearance"
    NKJV   "the brightness"
    NRSV   "the manifestation"
    TEV   "his glorious appearing"
    JB   "his glorious appearance"

This term has many possible translations: "brightness," "radiance," "splendor," "glory." This is strong affirmation of a visible manifestation of Christ's physical return to earth. The English "epiphany" is a transliteration of this Greek term.

❖**"of His coming;"** This is the Greek term *parousia* which means "presence." It is used of Jesus in vv. 1 & 8 but of Satan's pawn in v. 9.

2:9 "with the activity of Satan," The lawless one is empowered and directed by Satan. Since the time of Theodore of Mopsuestia, the Anti-Christ has been seen as an ape or imitator of Christ. Notice in this context how much like Christ this one is: "revealed" or "unveiled," vv. 3,6,8; "coming," v. 9; "signs" v. 9; "he will have a committed following," vv. 10,12.

❖	NASB	"with all power and signs and false wonders,"
	NKJV, NRSV	"with all power, signs, and lying wonders,"
	TEV	"with the power of Satan and perform all kinds of miracles and false signs and wonders,"
	JB	"there will be all kinds of miracles and a deceptive show of signs and portents,"

Miracles are not automatically a sign of God (cf. Mt. 24:24; Rev. 13). Verse 9 seems to precede verse 8 chronologically. Also, verses 9-10 may involve a considerable time.

2:10 "with all the deception of wickedness" Satan tricks unbelievers (cf. Mt. 13:19; II Cor. 4:4) as well as believers (Eph. 4:14) if they remain spiritually immature.

❖**"they did not receive the love of the truth"** This is not in the abstract sense, but a reference to: (1) the person and work of Jesus (cf. Jn. 14:6); (2) the Spirit (cf. Jn. 14:17; 15:16; 16:13); and (3) the message about Jesus (cf. Jn. 17:17).

"Receive" was used in I Thes. 1:6 and 2:13 in the sense of personally welcome as a guest. These unbelievers refused to believe the gospel and welcome Jesus.

❖**"so as to be saved."** In the OT this term meant "physical deliverance" (cf. James 5:15). However, in the NT it takes on spiritual/eternal significance.

266

2:11	NASB	"For this reason God will send upon them a deluding influence"
	NKJV	"And for this reason God will send them strong delusion"
	NRSV	"For this reason God sends them a powerful delusion"
	TEV	"For this reason God sends the power of error to work in them"
	JB	"The reason why God is sending a power to delude them"

This is a PRESENT ACTIVE INDICATIVE used as a FUTURE. The major truth here is that God is in control of all things, even Satan (cf. Job 1-2; Zech 3). This sending is either: (1) God's actively sending judgment on them who reject the truth; or (2) God's passively allowing the consequences of their unbelief to become manifested in their lives (cf. Ps. 81:12; Hos. 4:17; Rom. 1:24, 26, and 28). This ambiguity exists also in the OT account of Pharaoh, where it is said, Pharaoh hardened his own heart (cf. Ex. 7:14; 8:15, 32), as much as God did (Ex. 4:21; 7:3,13; 9:12,35; 10:1,20,27; 14:4,8).

The plural pronouns refer to the wicked men of v. 10.

❖	NASB	"so that they will believe"
	NKJV	"that they should believe"
	NRSV	"leading them to believe"
	TEV	"so that they believe"
	JB	"and make them believe"

The man who refuses God is rejected by God (cf. Hos. 5:6c; Jn. 3:17-21). This is not double predestination but the consequences of active unbelief (cf. I Kings 22:19-23).

❖	NASB, NRSV, TEV	"what is false,"
	NKJV	"the lie,"
	JB	"what is untrue"

This is literally "the lie" (cf. Jn. 8:44; Rom. 1:25). It is in contrast to "the truth" of verse 10.

2:12	NASB	"in order that they all may be judged"
	NKJV	"that they all may be condemned"

NOTES

NRSV	"so that all...will be condemned"
TEV	"The result is that all...will be condemned"
JB	"to condemn all"

The KJV translated this as "damned." This term means "to be fairly judged."

"but took pleasure in wickedness." They were not only cold to the truth but warm to evil (cf. Heb. 11:25).

CONTEXTUAL INSIGHTS TO VERSES 13-17

A. This context is a prayer to God for His initiating and electing grace in the lives of the Thessalonian Christians. As 1:3-4 is a prayer of thanksgiving for the believers, this is a prayer for God's activity in their lives.

B. In many ways the close of chapter 2 is similar to the close of chapter 1.

C. Verses 13ff. are in obvious contrast to the doom of the unbelievers in verses 11-12.

D. Three thought units appear in this section:
1. Verses 13-14, the believer and sanctification
2. Verse 15, the believer's perseverance
3. Verses 16-17, the believer's encouragement and hope issues in "good things"
   (in each section God's initiating grace is balanced by man's appropriate response.)

WORD AND PHRASE STUDY

NASB (UPDATED) TEXT: 2:13-15

But we should always give thanks to God for you, brethren beloved by the Lord, because God has chosen you from the beginning for salvation through sanctification by the Spirit and faith in the truth. It was for this He called you through our gospel, that you may gain the glory of our Lord Jesus Christ. So then, brethren, stand firm and hold to the traditions which you were taught, whether by word *of mouth* or by letter from us.

2:13 "God...Lord...Spirit" Paul often alluded to the Trinity (cf. I Cor. 12:4-6; II Cor. 1:21; 13:14; Eph. 1:3-14; 4:4-6; I Thes. 1:2-5;

Titus 3:4-6). It is also assumed by other NT authors (cf. Mt. 28:19; I Pet. 1:2 and Jude 20-21).

❖ **"brethren beloved by the Lord,"** "Beloved" is the PERFECT PASSIVE form of *agapao*. This implies election (cf. Rom. 1:7; Col. 3:12; I Thes. 1:4).

❖	NASB	'because God has chosen you from the beginning for salvation"
	NKJV	"because God from the beginning chose you for salvation"
	NRSV	"because God chose you as the first fruits for salvation"
	TEV	"For God chose you as the first to be saved"
	JB	"because God chose you from the beginning to be saved"

This is an AORIST MIDDLE meaning God Himself has chosen believers. The doctrine of election is often articulated in the NT (cf. Rom. 9; I Cor. 7:7; Eph. 1:4-13; II Tim. 1:9). It was alluded to in I Thes. 2:12; 5:9. God's control of salvation and history is the focus of this context. Evil exists in the spiritual and physical realms, but there is no dualism. Although believers cannot fully understand the mystery of election, they have confidence that the Father of our Lord Jesus Christ is in complete and loving control of all things.

The phrase "from the beginning" is from the Greek manuscripts ℵ, D, K, and the Peshitta Syriac translation. But manuscripts B, F, G, and P and the Vulgate and Harclean Syriac have "first fruits." The problem is that the phrase, "from the beginning," is not used by Paul elsewhere. He used, "from the ages," (cf. Col. 1:26) or "before the ages," (cf. I Cor. 2:7). However, Paul never used the concept of "first fruits" to illustrate election.

❖ **"through sanctification by the Spirit"** Two aspects of the concept of holiness present themselves: (1) initial holiness is positional in Christ, and (2) progressive holiness is growth toward Christlikeness (cf. Rom. 8:28-29; Gal. 4:19). The Spirit woos us to Christ, convicts us of sin and convinces us of the truth of the gospel, baptizes us into Christ and forms Christ in us.

❖**"and faith in the truth."** Two aspects of man's God-given salvation can be determined: (1) the Spirit always approaches man first
(cf. Jn. 6:44, 65); and (2) man must respond to this by repentance
and faith (cf. Mk. 1:15; Acts 3:16,19 and 20:21). "Truth" in v. 13 is
parallel to "gospel" in v. 14.

2:14 "It was for this He called you" This is an AORIST TENSE. It
is another emphasis on election (cf. I Thes. 2:12; 5:24). This
small, persecuted, discouraged group of believers was the chosen
people of God.

❖**"through our gospel,"** The gospel is both a message to be
believed and a person to be trusted. It is the mechanism of God's
blessing flowing to fallen man. There is no other channel.

❖**"that you may gain the glory of our Lord"** This is a restatement
of 1:12. "Glory" is difficult to define. It is used many different
ways in the OT. In this context it reflects the believers' call from
the Father to be sanctified by the Spirit through the work of
Christ.

❖**"Lord"** The covenant name for God in the OT is YHWH which
is a CAUSATIVE FORM of the verb "to be" (cf. Ex. 3:14). This
verb may be alternately rendered "I will be what I cause to be" or
"I am what I am." The Jews were reluctant to pronounce this
name aloud when they read the Scriptures, in fear of taking God's
name in vain (cf. Ex. 20:7). Therefore, they substituted the
Hebrew word *adonai* which meant, "owner, husband, master or
lord." Our English Bible translates YHWH in all capitals, LORD.
When the NT authors use this term for Jesus, it was one of their
ways to identify Him with the God of the OT.

❖**"Jesus"** When used by itself this term was the NT author's way to
refer to the humanity of Jesus of Nazareth.

❖**"Christ"** This is a transliteration of the Hebrew term for
"Messiah" which is literally "an anointed one." In the OT three
different types of offices were anointed: prophets, priests and
kings. It was a symbol of God's calling and equipping for special
service. Jesus fulfilled all three OT offices (cf. Heb. 1:2-3).

NOTES

2:15 "brethren," This shows a transition to a summary statement.

❖**"stand firm"** This is a PRESENT IMPERATIVE (cf. I Cor. 16:13; Eph. 6:11,13; I Thes. 3:8). This emphasizes the need for man to persevere in the face of physical and mental persecution and false teaching. This brings a balance to the above emphasis on election. The same balance can be seen in v. 13.

❖**"hold to"** This is a PRESENT IMPERATIVE. Believers are to continue to cling to the truth that Paul preached (cf. I Cor. 11:2).

"the traditions which you were taught," This term is used in several senses: (1) in I Cor. 11:2 for gospel truths, (2) in Mt. 15:6; 23:1ff. & Mk. 7:8 of Jewish traditions, (3) in Col. 2:6-8 of gnostic speculations and (4) Roman Catholics use this verse as a biblical proof-text for Scripture and tradition being equal in authority. However, in this context it refers to Apostolic truth either spoken or written (cf. 3:6).

NASB (UPDATED) TEXT: 2:16-17

Now may our Lord Jesus Christ Himself and God our Father, who has loved us and given us eternal comfort and good hope by grace, comfort and strengthen your hearts in every good work and word.

2:16 "our Lord Jesus Christ Himself and God our Father, who has loved us and given us" In the Greek text there are two SUBJECTS but with an intensive SINGULAR PRONOUN, "himself" and two SINGULAR AORIST PARTICIPLES. Also notice that Jesus is mentioned first. This shows the equality and unity of the subjects (cf. I Thes. 3:11). The Son and the Father have given us eternal comfort and good hope.

2:16	NASB, NRSV	"eternal comfort"
	NKJV	"everlasting consolation"
	TEV	"eternal courage"
	JB	"inexhaustible comfort"

This is the same term in Greek as "comfort" in v. 17. These two verses form one sentence in Greek. Notice that we are encouraged to do and say "good things." We are not saved <u>by</u> doing good things but we are saved <u>for</u> doing good things. Our relationship with Christ must lead to Christlikeness. We were called unto good works (cf. Eph. 2:10). The goal of every believer is not only heaven when we die but Christlikeness now.

❖**"hope"** This term is often used in the NT in the sense of the Second Coming. This is especially true in the Thessalonian letters which focuses on this theological subject.

2:17 "hearts" The OT uses this as a metaphor for the entire person.

DISCUSSION QUESTIONS

This is a study <u>guide</u> commentary which means that you are responsible for your own interpretation of the Bible. Each of us must walk in the light we have. You, the Bible and the Holy Spirit are priority in interpretation. You must not relinquish this to a commentator.

These discussion questions are provided to help you think through the major issues of this section of the book. They are meant to be thought provoking, not definitive.

1. Why is the subject of the Second Coming so debated in the Church?

2. Is the Second Coming imminent or must certain events occur first?

3. Does God cause people not to believe?

4. What is "the lie"?

II THESSALONIANS 3

PARAGRAPH DIVISIONS OF MODERN TRANSLATIONS

UBS[4]	NKJV	NRSV	TEV	JB
Pray for Us	Pray for Us	Closing Appeals, Rebukes and Prayers	Pray for Us	Encouragement to Perseverance (2:13-3:5)
3:1-5	3:1-5	3:1-5	3:1-2 3:3-4 3:5	3:1-5
Warnings Against Idleness	Warnings Against Idleness		The Obligation to Work	Against Idleness and Disunity
3:6-15	3:6-15	3:6-13	3:6-10 3:11-12 3:13-15	3:6 3:7-9 3:10-12 3:13-15
		3:14-15		
Benediction	Benediction		Final words	Prayer and Farewell
3:16	3:16-18	3:16	3:16	3:16
3:17-18		3:17-18	3:17 3:18	3:17-18

READING CYCLE THREE (see p. vii)
FOLLOWING THE ORIGINAL AUTHOR'S INTENT AT THE PARA-GRAPH LEVEL

This is a study <u>guide</u> commentary which means that you are responsible for your own interpretation of the Bible. Each of us must walk in the light we have. You, the Bible and the Holy Spirit are priority in interpretation. You must not relinquish this to a commentator.

Read the chapter in one sitting. Identify the subjects. Compare your subject divisions with the five translations above. Paragraphing is not inspired but it is the key to following the original author's intent which is the heart of interpretation. Every paragraph has one and only one subject.

1. First paragraph

2. Second paragraph

3. Third paragraph

4. Etc.

CONTEXTUAL INSIGHTS TO VERSES 1-18

A. Paul asked for prayer for his gospel preaching. He sought the blessing of God in his future preaching as it occurred among the Thessalonians, vv. 1-5.

B. Paul warned of the disruptive consequences of false teachings about the Second Coming as seen in the believers who had refused to work.

WORD AND PHRASE STUDY

> **NASB (UPDATED) TEXT: 3:1-5**
>
> **Finally, brethren, pray for us that the word of the Lord will spread rapidly and be glorified, just as *it did* also with you; and that we will be rescued from perverse and evil men; for not all have faith. But the Lord is faithful, and He will strengthen and protect you from the evil *one*. We have confidence in the Lord concerning you, that you are doing and *will continue* to do what we command. May the Lord direct your hearts into the love of God and into the steadfastness of Christ.**

3:1 "Finally" This term is used by Paul to mark off his last major truth or subject (cf. I Thes. 4:1). It is the beginning of the conclusion. It is also used to introduce his closing statements (cf. II Cor. 13:11).

❖**"pray for us"** This is a PRESENT IMPERATIVE (cf. I Thes. 5:25; Eph. 6:19). Paul felt the need for prayer and believed it affected the effectiveness of his ministry.

❖**"that the word of the Lord"** Paul asked prayer for the sake of the gospel, not himself.

❖   NASB, NRSV   **"will spread rapidly and be glorified,"**

276

NKJV	"may have *free* course and be glorified,"
TEV	"may continue to spread rapidly and receive glory,"
JB	"may spread quickly, and be received with honour"

There are two PRESENT TENSE verbs. The term "spread" is literally "run a race." This may be an allusion to Ps. 147:15. "Glory" in this context must be understood as "honor." It refers to receiving and rejoicing in the gospel. The gospel is honored when fallen men respond to it appropriately (cf. v. 2) and are changed.

3:2 "will be rescued from perverse and evil men;" This is an AORIST TENSE. This tense and the ARTICLE with a COMPOUND ADJECTIVE, shows that a specific incident is being referred to in Paul's life. This church understood what incident was intended (cf. I Thes. 2:16).

❖**"faith"** This is literally "the faith." This can refer to: (1) the personal experience of receiving the gospel, or (2) the truth of the gospel in a doctrinal sense.

3:3 "But the Lord is faithful," This term "faith" is used in its OT sense of faithfulness. God is exactly opposite of the evil men of v. 2.

❖**"protect"** This is one of many military terms in this chapter (cf. I Pet. 1:3-12; I Jn. 5:18).

❖**"from the evil *one*."** This inflected Greek form can be NEUTER or MASCULINE. The Eastern Church Fathers and Tertullian interpret it as MASCULINE while the Western Church Fathers interpret it as NEUTER. The NT seems to support the MASCULINE (cf. Mt. 5:37; 6:13; 13:19,38; Jn. 17:15; Eph. 6:11; I Jn. 2:13-14; 3:12; 5:18-19). The context is eschatological which implies the work of the Anti-Christ and/or his followers, who were referred to in v. 2.

3:4 "We have confidence in the Lord concerning you," This is a PERFECT TENSE VERB, an action that occurred in the past and has now become a state of being. Paul's confidence was "in the

NOTES

Lord" but also in true believers. This same balance can be seen in Phil. 2:12-13. Salvation is both from a sovereign God and a responsive human being. All God's dealings with man involve unconditional yet conditional covenant promises.

❖"command" This is a military term. It is used repeatedly in this context (cf. vv. 4,6,10,12). This shows Paul's authority as an Apostle. This term refers to: (1) Paul's preaching, (2) his first letter, I Thes., or (3) his current instructions, II Thes.

3:5 "May the Lord...of God...of Christ" The ambiguity of the term "Lord" is obvious. In the OT it is always YHWH. NT authors often quote OT passages where they attribute actions of YHWH to Jesus. The fluidity may be purposeful because the original, inspired NT author wanted to affirm the deity of Jesus and the unified action of the Triune God.

❖"direct" This is literally "make straight by removing obstacles." It is another military term. It was used in the OT in the sense of "well-worn paths of righteousness" (cf. Lk. 1:79; I Thes. 3:11). Notice the two aspects of this prayer: (1) knowledge of God's love, and (2) patient endurance like Christ's.

❖"hearts" This is used in the OT for the entire person but can be used more specifically of the mind which fits this context best.

❖"the love of God" This GENITIVE phrase can be understood as OBJECTIVELY or SUBJECTIVELY, that is, God's love for us and our love for Him. One of the most stabilizing influences for the believers is to understand and experience this gospel. Once God's love in Christ, continued love in the Spirit, and consummated love in eternal fellowship with the Triune God are realized, life can be lived in freedom and joy.

❖"the steadfastness of Christ," This phrase is used nowhere else in Paul's writings. It is somewhat ambiguous. It is an active term for "voluntary, steadfast endurance." Because He loves us and/or we love Him, our lives will be lived differently.

This GENITIVE phrase can mean the believers' patience like Christ's patience or the patience that Christ gives to believers. In either case this patience relates to: (1) their current persecution, (2) their response to false teaching and its resulting idleness on the part of some church members, or (3) the believers' patience, trust, and expectant faith-living in light of the any-moment return or delayed return of Jesus.

NASB (UPDATED) TEXT: 3:6-15

Now we command you, brethren, in the name of our Lord Jesus Christ, that you keep away from every brother who leads an unruly life and not according to the tradition which you received from us. For you yourselves know how you ought to follow our example, because we did not act in an undisciplined manner among you, nor did we eat anyone's bread without paying for it, but with labor and hardship we *kept* working night and day so that we would not be a burden to any of you; not because we do not have the right *to this*, but in order to offer ourselves as a model for you, so that you would follow our example. For even when we were with you, we used to give you this order: if anyone is not willing to work, then he is not to eat, either. For we hear that some among you are leading an undisciplined life, doing no work at all, but acting like busybodies. Now such persons we command and exhort in the Lord Jesus Christ to work in quiet fashion and eat their own bread. But as for you, brethren, do not grow weary of doing good. If anyone does not obey our instruction in this letter, take special note of that person and do not associate with him, so that he will be put to shame. *Yet* do not regard him as an enemy, but admonish him as a brother.

3:6 "we command you, in the name of our Lord" This is the polite plural including Silas and Timothy, but in reality it is a word from Paul the Apostle. He recognizes his inspiration and authority in Christ to lead and command the church (cf. vv. 10,12). "In the name of" is a Hebrew idiom referring to one's character or person.

❖**"keep"** This is a PRESENT MIDDLE INFINITIVE, often used in Koine Greek as an IMPERATIVE, "you, yourselves, continue to keep away from" (cf. v. 14).

❖**"away from"** Believers should not enter into intimate personal relationships with these people (cf. Rom. 16:17; I Cor. 5:11; II Thes. 3:14).

❖	NASB	"leads an unruly life"
	NKJV	"walks disorderly"
	NRSV	"living in idleness"
	TEV	"who are living a lazy life,"
	JB	"who refuses to work"

This is literally "disorderly conduct" (cf. vv. 6,7,11). This is another military term. It is used here for idle uncooperative believers (cf. I Thes. 4:11-12; 5:14). The apparent closeness of the Second Coming had caused many believers to quit the normal affairs of life. They expected to be supported by other church members.

❖	NASB	"which you received from us."
	NKJV	"which he received from us."
	NRSV	"that they received from us."
	TEV	"that we gave them."
	JB	"we passed on to you."

A Greek manuscript problem is connected with the pronoun. "You" fits the context best.

3:7 "ought to follow our example," There was no NT at this time. Believers had to (1) receive Paul's gospel, and (2) walk in his example (cf. v. 9).

3:8 "nor did we eat anyone's bread without paying for it," Paul, like all rabbis, worked for his daily needs (cf. I Cor. 9:12,18; 11:7; II Cor. 11:9; 12:13-14; I Thes. 2:9). In the ancient world many traveling tricksters and con-men preyed upon people. Paul had often been accused of preaching for money. Being sensitive to this charge, he never took money from those who heard him preach.

❖**"with labor and hardship we *kept* working"** To the Greeks manual labor was for slaves only, but the Bible affirms work as from God. In Genesis work is both before the Fall and after (cf. Gen. 2:15; 3:19; Ex. 31:3; 35:35; Deut. 5:13; Isa. 54:16). The concept of working for one's own needs is crucial to this context. Some believers had rejected work as a spiritual option.

❖**"night and day"** This is the Jewish order of time (cf. Gen. 1:5,8,13,19,23,31). This is an idiom meaning "worked full time,"

NOTES

not literally 24 hours a day.

3:9 "not because we do not have the right to *this*," Paul was affirming the concept that believers should support their leaders (cf. I Cor. 9:4-17; Gal. 6:6). However, in this specific situation he acted (1) to set an example, and (2) to avoid criticism.

3:10 "we used to give you this order:" This is an IMPERFECT TENSE. In context it must mean we told you over and over when we were with you. This command was not new information. This problem must have surfaced early in this church, not after Paul had left.

❖**"if"** This is a FIRST CLASS CONDITIONAL SENTENCE. There *were* people like this in the church.

❖**"anyone is not willing to work, then he is not to eat, either,"** This is a PRESENT ACTIVE INDICATIVE followed by a PRESENT IMPERATIVE. This is the point of the entire chapter. It addresses lifestyle inactivity, not temporary unemployment. One must balance this with Paul's other letters on his care for the poor (cf. Acts 24:17; Rom. 15:26-29; II Cor. 8-9; Gal. 2:10). This command can be understood as (1) not feeding those who refused to work, or (2) excluding them from the common meal or love feast (cf. vv. 13,14).

3:11 "we hear" This is a PRESENT TENSE, which is literally, "keep hearing."

❖**"but acting like busy-bodies."** This is a play in the Greek text on the word "work"—"not working but working around." Their "work" had become interfering with everyone else's business (work).

3:12 "to work in quiet fashion" This is the goal of the Christian life (cf. I Thes. 4:11; I Tim. 2:2).

❖	NASB, NKJV	"eat their own bread."
	NRSV	"do their own work"
	TEV	"work to earn their own living."
	JB	"earning the food that they eat"

This is an idiom which means to support yourself with your own labor.

3:13 "do not grow weary of doing good." This refers to the church's attitude toward these "shirkers" (cf. Lk. 18:1; II Cor. 4:1; Gal. 6:9).

3:14 "if" This is a FIRST CLASS CONDITIONAL SENTENCE which is assumed to be true from the author's perspective or for his literary purposes.

❖   **NASB**   **"take special note of that person"**
       NKJV   **"note that person"**
       NRSV   **"take note of those"**
       TEV, JB   **"take note of him"**
This is a PRESENT MIDDLE IMPERATIVE. This is literally "tag" or "mark." This is not excommunication but internal church discipline (cf. 3:6).

❖**"so that he will be put to shame."** The purpose of church discipline is redemptive as well as disciplinary (cf. v. 15; Gal. 6:1; I Thes. 4:15).

NASB (UPDATED) TEXT: 3:16

Now may the Lord of peace Himself continually grant you peace in every circumstance. The Lord be with you all!

3:16 "the Lord of peace" This is a common title for God the Father (cf. Rom. 15:33; 16:20; II Cor. 13:11; Phil. 4:9; I Thes. 5:23; Heb. 13:20).

❖**"The Lord be with you all!"** The Greek term "all" is in this verse and v. 18. Paul's admonition involves even those erring ones. "Lord" could refer to Jesus or the Father. See parallel in I Thes. 3:11.

NASB (UPDATED) TEXT: 3:17-18

I, Paul, write this greeting with my own hand, and this is a distinguishing mark in every letter; this is the way I write. The grace of our Lord Jesus Christ be with you all.

3:17 "write this greeting with my own hand," Paul dictated his letters to a scribe but he wrote the closing sentences in his own hand to verify his authorship (cf. 2:2; I Cor. 16:21; Gal. 6:11; Col. 4:18; Philem. 19).

3:18 This closing is very similar to I Thes. 5:28.

DISCUSSION QUESTIONS

This is a study <u>guide</u> commentary which means that you are responsible for your own interpretation of the Bible. Each of us must walk in the light we have. You, the Bible and the Holy Spirit are priority in interpretation. You must not relinquish this to a commentator.

These discussion questions are provided to help you think through the major issues of this section of the book. They are meant to be thought provoking, not definitive.

1. How is the church to treat others in their midst who reject the Scriptures?

2. What does this chapter say to our modern welfare state?

3. Why is the truth of verse 16 so important?

NOTES

APPENDIX ONE

BRIEF DEFINITIONS OF GREEK GRAMMATICAL TERMS

Koine Greek, often called Hellenistic Greek, was the common language of the Mediterranean world beginning with Alexander the Great's (336-323 B.C.) conquest and lasting about eight hundred years (300 B.C. - A.D. 500). It was not just a simplified, classical Greek but in many ways, a newer form of Greek that became the second language of the ancient near east and Mediterranean world.

The Greek of the New Testament was unique in some ways because its users, except Luke and the author of Hebrews, probably used Aramaic as their primary language. Therefore, their writing was influenced by idioms and structural forms from Aramaic. Also, they read and quoted the Septuagint (Greek translation of the OT) which was also written in Koine Greek. However, the Septuagint was also written by Jewish scholars whose mother tongue was not Greek.

This serves as a reminder that we cannot push the New Testament into a tight grammatical structure. It is unique and yet has much in common with: (1) the Septuagint; (2) Jewish writings such as those of Josephus; and (3) the papyri found in Egypt. How then do we approach a grammatical analysis of the New Testament?

The grammatical features of Koine Greek and New Testament Koine Greek are fluid. In many ways it was a time of simplification of grammar. Context will be our major guide. Words only have meaning in a larger context, therefore, grammatical structure can only be understood in light of: (1) a particular author's style; and (2) a particular context. No conclusive definitions of Greek forms and structures are possible.

Koine Greek was primarily a verbal language. Often the key

to interpretation is the type and form of the verbs. In most main clauses the verb will occur first showing its preeminence. In analyzing the Greek verb three pieces of information must be noted: (1) the basic emphasis of the tense, voice and mood (accidence or morphology); (2) the basic meaning of the particular verb (lexicography); and (3) the flow of the context (syntax).

I. TENSE

A. Tense or aspect involves the relationship of the verbs to completed action or uncompleted action. This is often called "perfective" and "imperfective":
1. Perfective tenses focus on the occurrence of an action. No further information is given except that something happened! Its start, continuation or culmination is not addressed.
2. Imperfective tenses focus on the continuing process of an action. It can be described in terms of linear action, durative action, progressive action, etc.

B. Tenses can be categorized by how the author sees the actionas progressing:
1. It occurred = AORIST
2. It occurred and the results abide = PERFECT
3. It was occurring in the past and the results were abiding, but not now = PLUPERFECT
4. It is occurring = PRESENT
5. It was occurring = IMPERFECT
6. It will occur = FUTURE

A concrete example of how these tenses help in interpretation would be the term "save." It was used in several different tenses to show both its process and culmination:
1. AORIST - "saved" (cf. Rom. 8:24)
2. PERFECT - "have been saved and the result continues" (cf. Eph. 2:5,8)
3. PRESENT - "being saved" (cf. I Cor. 1:18; 15:2)
4. FUTURE - "shall be saved" (cf. Rom. 5:9, 10; 10:9)

C. In focusing on verb tenses, interpreters are looking for the reason the original author chose to express himself in a certain tense. The standard "no frills" tense was the AORIST. It was the regular "unspecific," "unmarked," or "unflagged" verb form. It can be used in a wide variety of ways which the context must specify. It simply was stating that something occurred. The past time aspect is only intended in the INDICATIVE MOOD. If any other tense was used something more specific was being emphasized. But what?

1. PERFECT TENSE - This speaks of a completed action which has abiding results. In some ways it was a combination of the AORIST and PRESENT TENSES. Usually the focus is on the abiding results or the completion of an act. Example: Eph. 2:5 & 8, "you have been and continue to be saved."

2. PLUPERFECT TENSE - This was like the PERFECT except the abiding results have ceased. Example: Jn. 18:16 "Peter was standing at the door outside."

3. PRESENT TENSE - This speaks of a unit of incomplete action or imperfect action. The focus is usually on the continuation or repetition of the event. Example: I Jn. 3:6 & 9, "Everyone abiding in Him does not continue sinning." "Everyone having been begotten of God does not continue to commit sin."

4. IMPERFECT TENSE - In this tense the relationship to the PRESENT TENSE is analogous to the relationship between the PERFECT and the PLUPERFECT. The IMPERFECT speaks of incomplete action that was occurring but has now ceased or the beginning of an action in the past. Example: Mt. 3:5, "then all Jerusalem were continuing to go out to him." or "then all Jerusalem began to go out to him."

5. FUTURE TENSE - This speaks of a unit of action that was usually projected into a future time frame. It focused on the potential for an occurrence rather than an actual occurrence. It often speaks of the certainty of the event. Example: Mt. 5:4-9, "Blessed are...they will...."

II.   VOICE

A. Voice describes the relationship between the action of the verb and its subject.

B. ACTIVE VOICE was the normal, expected, unemphasized way to assert that the subject was performing the action of the verb.

C. The PASSIVE VOICE means that the subject was receiving the action of the verb which was being produced by an outside agent. The outside agent producing the action was indicated in the Greek NT by the following prepositions and cases:
1. a personal direct agent by "*hupo*" with the ABLATIVE CASE (cf. Mt.1:22; Acts 22:30)
2. a personal intermediate agent by "*dia*" with the ABLATIVE CASE (cf. Mt. 1:22)
3. an impersonal agent usually by "*en*" with the INSTRUMENTAL CASE
4. sometimes either a personal or impersonal agent by the INSTRUMENTAL CASE alone.

D. The MIDDLE VOICE means that the subject produces the action of the verb and was also directly involved for personal interest in the action of the verb. It is often called the voice of heightened personal interest. This construction emphasized the subject of the clause or sentence in some way. This construction is not found in English. It has a wide possibility of meanings and translations in Greek. Some examples of the form are:
1. the direct action of the subject on itself - REFLEXIVE. Example: Mt. 27:5 "hanged himself."
2. the subject produces the action for itself - INTENSIVE. Example: II Cor. 11:14 "Satan himself masquerades as an angel of light."
3. the interplay of two subjects - RECIPROCAL. Example: Mt. 26:4 "they counseled with one another."

III. MOOD (or, "Mode")

A. There are four moods in Koine Greek. They indicate the relation of the verb to reality, at least within the author's own mind. The moods are divided into two broad categories: that which indicated reality (INDICATIVE) and that

which indicated potentiality (SUBJUNCTIVE, IMPERA-
TIVE and OPTATIVE).

B. The INDICATIVE MOOD was the normal expected mood
to express action that had occurred or was occurring, at
least in the author's mind. It was the only Greek Mood that
expressed a definite time, and even here this aspect was secondary.

C. The SUBJUNCTIVE MOOD expressed probable future
action. Something had not yet happened but the chances
were likely that it would. It had much in common with the
FUTURE INDICATIVE. The difference was that the SUB-
JUNCTIVE expresses some degree of doubt. In English this
is often expressed by the terms: "could," "would," or "may,"
"might."

D. The OPTATIVE MOOD expressed a wish which was theo-
retically possible. It was considered one step further from
reality than the SUBJUNCTIVE which expressed probability. The OPTATIVE expressed possibility under certain conditions. The OPTATIVE was rare in the New Testament.
Its most frequent usage is Paul's famous phrase, "May it
never be," (KJV, "God forbid", used fifteen times, cf. Rom.
3:4, 6, 31; 6:2, 15; 7:7, 13; 9:14; 11:1, 11; I Cor. 6:15; Gal.
2:17; 3:21; 6:14). Other examples are found in Lk. 1:38;
20:16; Acts 8:20 and I Thess. 3:11.

E. The IMPERATIVE MOOD emphasized a command which
was possible but the emphasis was on the intent of the
speaker. It asserted only volitional possibility and was conditioned on the choices of another. There was a special use
of the IMPERATIVE in prayers and third person requests.
These commands were found only in the PRESENT and
AORIST tenses in the NT.

F. PARTICIPLES are categorized by some grammars as another type of mood. They are very common in the Greek NT,
usually defined as a verbal adjective. They are translated in
conjunction with the main verb to which they relate. A
wide variety was possible in translating participles. It is best
to consult several English translations. The *Bible in Twenty*

Six Translations published by Baker is a great help here.

IV. For the person not familiar with Greek the following study aids will provide the needed information:

A. Friberg, Barbara and Timothy Friberg. *Analytical Greek New Testament.* Grand Rapids; Baker, 1988.

B. Marshall, Alfred. *Interlinear Greek-English New Testament.* Grand Rapids: Zondervan, 1976.

C. Mounce, William D. *The Analytical Lexicon to the Greek New Testament.* Grand Rapids: Zondervan, 1993

D. Summers, Ray. *Essentials of New Testament Greek.* Nashville: Broadman, 1950.

E. Academically accredited Koine Greek correspondence courses are available through Moody Bible Institute in Chicago, IL.

V. NOUNS

A. Syntactically, nouns are classified by case. Case was that inflected form of a noun that showed its relationship to the verb and other parts of the sentence. In Koine Greek many of the case functions were indicated by prepositions. Since the case form was able to identify several different relationships, the prepositions developed to give clearer separation to these possible functions.

B. Greek cases are categorized in the following eight ways:

1. The NOMINATIVE CASE was used for naming, usually the subject of the sentence or clause. It was also used for predicate nouns and adjectives with the linking verbs "to be" or "become."
2. The GENITIVE CASE was used for description and usually assigned an attribute or quality to the word to which it was related. It answered the question, "What kind?" It was often expressed by the use of the English preposition "of."

3. The ABLATIVE CASE used the same inflected form as the GENITIVE but it was used to describe separation. It usually denoted separation from a point in time, space, source, origin or degree. It was often expressed by the use of the English preposition "from."

4. The DATIVE CASE was used to describe personal interest. This could denote a positive or negative aspect. Often this was the indirect object. It was often expressed by the English preposition "to."

5. The LOCATIVE CASE was the same inflected form as the DATIVE but it described position or location in space, time or logical limits. It was often expressed by the English prepositions "in, on, at, among, during, by, upon, and beside."

6. The INSTRUMENTAL CASE was the same inflected form as the DATIVE and LOCATIVE cases. It expressed means or association. It was often expressed by the English prepositions, "by" or "with."

7. The ACCUSATIVE CASE was used to describe the conclusion of an action. It expressed limitation. Its main use was the direct object. It answered the question, "How far?" or "To what extent?"

8. The VOCATIVE CASE was used for direct address.

VI. CONDITIONAL SENTENCES

A. A CONDITIONAL SENTENCE is one that contains one or more conditional clauses. This grammatical structure aids interpretation because it provides the conditions, reasons or causes why the action of the main verb does or does not occur. There were four types of conditional sentences. They move from that which was assumed to be true from the author's perspective or for his purpose to that which was only a wish.

B. The FIRST CLASS CONDITIONAL SENTENCE expressed action or being which was assumed to be true from the writer's perspective or for his purposes even though it was expressed with an "if." In several contexts it could be translated "since," (cf. Mt. 4:3; Rom. 8:31). However, this does not mean to imply that all FIRST CLASSES are true to reality. Often they were used to make a point in an argument or to highlight a fallacy (cf. Mt. 12:27).

C. The SECOND CLASS CONDITIONAL SENTENCE is often called "contrary to fact." It states something that was untrue to reality to make a point. Examples:
   1. Lk. 7:39, "If He were really a prophet (which He is not), He would know who and of what character the woman is who is clinging to Him (but He does not)."
   2. Jn. 5:46, "If you really believed Moses (which you do not), you would believe me (which you do not)."
   3. Gal. 1:10, "If I were still trying to be pleasing to men (which I am not), I would not be a slave of Christ at all (which I am)."

D. The THIRD CLASS speaks of possible future action. It often assumes the probability of that action. Examples from I Jn.: 1:6,7,8,9,10; 2:4,6,9,15,20,21,24,29; 3:21; 4:20; 5:14,16.

E. The FOURTH CLASS is the farthest removed from possibility. It is rare in the NT. As a matter of fact there is no complete FOURTH CLASS CONDITIONAL SENTENCE in which both parts of the condition fit the definition. Examples of partial FOURTH CLASS CONDITIONS are the opening clause in I Pet. 3:14 and the concluding clause is Acts 8:31.

VII. PROHIBITIONS

A. The PRESENT IMPERATIVE with NEGATIVE PARTICLE denotes stopping an act already in process. Examples: Mt. 6:19, "stop storing up your riches on earth"; Mt. 6:25, "stop worrying about your life"; Rom. 6:13, "stop offering to sin the parts of your bodies as instruments of wrongdoing"; Eph. 4:30, "you must stop offending the Holy Spirit of God"; and 5:18, "stop getting drunk on wine."

B. The AORIST SUBJUNCTIVE with NEGATIVE PARTICLE denotes "do not even begin or start an act." Example: Mt. 5:17, "Do not even begin to suppose that"; Mt. 6:31, "never start to worry"; II Tim. 1:8, "you must never be ashamed"

C. The DOUBLE NEGATIVE with the SUBJUNCTIVE MOOD is a very emphatic negation: "Never, no never" or "not under any circumstance." Examples: Jn. 8:51, "he will never, no never experience death"; I Cor. 8:13, "I will never, no, never" or "I will never ever under any circumstances."

VIII. THE ARTICLE

A. In Koine Greek the definite article "the" had a use similar to English. Its basic function was that of "a pointer," a way to draw attention to a word, name or phrase. The use varies from author to author in the New Testament. The definite article could also function:
   1. as a contrasting device like a demonstrative pronoun;
   2. as a sign to refer to a previously introduced subject or person;
   3. as a way to identify the subject in a sentence with a linking verb. Examples: Jn. 4:24, "God is Spirit;" I Jn. 1:5, "God is light;" 4:8,16, "God is love."

B. Koine Greek did not have an indefinite article like the English "a" or "an". The absence of the definite article could mean:
   1. a focus on the characteristics or quality of something;
   2. a focus on the category of something.

C. The NT authors varied widely as to how the article was employed.

IX. WAYS TO SHOW EMPHASIS IN THE GREEK NEW TESTAMENT

A. The techniques for showing emphasis vary from author to author in the New Testament. The most consistent and formal writers were Luke and the author of Hebrews.

B. We have stated earlier that the AORIST ACTIVE INDICATIVE was standard and unmarked for emphasis but any other tense, voice or mood had significance for interpretation. This is not to imply that the AORIST ACTIVE INDICATIVE was not often used in a significant grammatical sense. Example: Rom. 6:10 (twice) meaning "once for all."

C. Word order in Koine Greek
    1. Koine Greek was an inflected language which was not dependent, like English, on word order. Therefore, the author could vary the normal expected order to show:
        a. what the author wanted to emphasize to the reader;
        b. what the author thought would be surprising to the reader;
        c. what the author felt deeply about.
    2. The normal word order in Greek is still an unsettled issue. However, the supposed normal order is:
        a. for linking verbs:
            (1) verb
            (2) subject
            (3) complement
        b. for transitive verbs:
            (1) verb
            (2) subject
            (3) object
            (4) indirect object
            (5) prepositional phrase
        c. for noun phrases:
            (1) noun
            (2) modifier
            (3) prepositional phrase

    3. Word order can be an extremely important exegetical point. Examples:
        a. Gal. 2:9, "right hand they gave to me and Barnabas of fellowship." The phrase "right hand of fellowship" is split and fronted to show its significance.
        b. Gal. 2:20, "with Christ" was placed first. His death was central.
        c. Heb. 1:1, "It was bit by bit and in many different ways" was placed first. It was how God revealed Himself that was being contrasted, not the fact of revelation.

D. Usually some degree of emphasis was shown by:
1. The repetition of the pronoun which was already present in the verb's inflected form. Example: Mt. 28:20, "I, myself, will surely be with you"
2. The absence of an expected conjunction, or other connecting device between words, phrases, clauses or sentences. This is called an asyndeton ("not bound"). The connecting device was so expected, its absence would draw attention. Examples:
   a. The Beatitudes, Mt. 5:3ff (emphasized the list)
   b. Jn. 14:1 (new topic)
   c. Romans 9:1 (new section)
   d. II Cor. 12:20 (emphasize the list)
3. The repetition of words or phrases present in a given context. Examples: "to the praise of His glory," Eph. 1:6, 12 & 14. This phrase was used to show the work of each person of the Trinity.
4. The use of an idiom or word (sound) play between terms:
   a. euphemisms - substitute words for taboo subjects like "sleep" for death (Example: Jn. 11:11-14) or "feet" for male genitalia (Examples: Ruth 3:7-8; I Sam. 24:3).
   b. circumlocutions - substitute words for God's name like "Kingdom of heaven" (Example: Mt. 3:21) or "a voice from heaven" (Example: Mt. 3:17).
   c. igures of speech:
      (1) impossible exaggerations. Examples: Mt. 3:9; 5:29-30; 19:24.
      (2) mild overstatements. Example: Mt. 3:5; Acts 2:36.
      (3) personifications. Examples: I Cor. 15:55.
      (4) irony. Example: Gal. 5:12.
      (5) poetic passages. Example: Phil. 2:6-11.
      (6) sound plays between words
         (a) "church"
            ❖ Eph. 3:21 - "church"
            ❖ Eph. 4:1,4 - "calling"

     ❖ Eph. 4:1,4 - "called"
    (b) "free"
        ❖ Gal. 4:31 - "free woman"
        ❖ Gal. 5:1 - "freedom"
        ❖ Gal. 5:1 - "free"
d. idiomatic language - language which is usually cultural and language specific:
    (1) Jn. 4:31-34. This was the figurative use of "food."
    (2) Jn. 2:19; Mt. 26:61. This was the figurative use of "Temple."
    (3) Gen. 29:31; Dt. 21:15; Lk. 14:36; Jn. 12:25; Rom. 9:13. This was a Hebrew idiom of compassion, "hate."
    (4) "All" versus "many." Compare Is. 53:6 "all" with 53:11 & 12 "many." The terms are synonymous as Rom. 5:18 and 19 show.

5. The use of a full linguistic phrase instead of a single word. Example: "The Lord Jesus Christ."
6. The special use of "autos"
    a. when with the article (attributive position) it was translated "same."
    b. when without the article (predicate position) it was translated as in intensive reflexive pronoun "himself," "herself" or "itself."

E For the non-Greek reading Bible student emphasis can be identified in several ways:
1. The use of an Analytical Lexicon and Interlinear Greek/English text.
2. The comparison of English translations, particularly from the differing theories of translations. Example: comparing a "Word for Word" translation (KJV, ASV, NASB, RSV, NRSV) with a "dynamic equivalent" (Williams, NIV, NEB, JB, TEV). A good help would be *The Bible in Twenty-Six Translations* published by Baker.
3. The use of *The Emphasized Bible* by Joseph Bryant Rotherham published by Kregel, 1994.
4. The use of a very literal translation such as:

a. *The American Standard Version* of 1901

b. *Young's Literal Translation of the Bible* by Robert Young published by Guardian Press, 1976.

The study of grammar is tedious but necessary for proper interpretation. These brief definitions, comments and examples are meant to encourage and equip non-Greek reading persons to use the grammatical notes provided in this volume. Surely these definitions are oversimplified. They should not be used in a dogmatic, inflexible manner but as stepping stones toward a greater understanding of New Testament syntax. Hopefully these definitions will also enable readers to understand the comments of other study aids such as technical commentaries on the New Testament. A very good help at this point would be *How to Use New Testament Greek Study Aids* by Walter Jerry Clark, published by Loizeaux Brothers, 1983.

We must be able to verify our interpretation based on items of information found in the texts of the Bible. Grammar is one of the most helpful of these items; other items would include: historical setting, literary context, contemporary word usage, and parallel passages.

APPENDIX TWO

TEXTUAL CRITICISM

This subject will be dealt with in such a way as to explain the textual notes found in this commentary. The following outline will be utilized:
I. The textual sources of our English Bible
   A. Old Testament
   B. New Testament
II. Brief explanation of the problems and theories of "lower criticism" also called "textual criticism."
III. Suggested sources for further reading

I. The textual sources of our English Bible
   A. Old Testament
      1. Masoretic text (MT) - The Hebrew consonantal text was set by Rabbi Aquiba in A.D. 100. The vowel points, accents, marginal notes, punctuation and apparatus points started being added in the sixth century A.D. and were finished in the ninth century A.D. It was done by a family of Jewish scholars known as the Masoretes. The textual form they used was the same as the one in the Mishnah, Talmud, Targums, Peshitta, and Vulgate.
      2. Septuagint (LXX) - Tradition says the Septuagint was produced by 70 Jewish scholars in 70 days for the Alexandria library under the sponsorship of King Ptolemy II (285-246 B.C.) The translation was supposedly requested of Ptolemy by a Jewish leader living in Alexandria. This tradition comes from "Letter of Aristeas." The LXX provides a differing Hebrew textual tradition from the text of Rabbi Aquiba (MT).
      3. Dead Sea Scrolls (DSS) - The Dead Sea Scrolls were written in the Roman B.C. period, close to New Testament times by a sect of Jewish separatists called the "Essenes." The Hebrew manuscripts, found in several sites around the Dead Sea, show both a Hebrew textual family behind the MT and the LXX.

4. Some specific examples of how the comparison of these texts have helped man understand the Old Testament:
   a. The LXX has helped translators and scholars understand the MT:
      (1) the LXX of Is. 52:14, "As many shall be amazed at *him*."
      (2) the MT of Is. 52:14, "Just as many were astonished over *you*."
      (3) in Isa. 52:15 the pronoun distinction of the LXX is confirmed
         (a) LXX, "so will many nations marvel at him"
         (b) MT, "so he sprinkles many nations"
   b. The DSS have helped translators and scholars understand the MT:
      (1) the DSS of Is. 21:8, "then the seer cried, Upon a watchtower I stand..."
      (2) the MT of Isa. 21:8, "and I cried a lion! My Lord, I always stand on the watch tower by day..."
   c. Both the LXX and DSS have helped the understanding of Isa. 53:11
      (1) LXX & DSS, "after the travail of his soul he will see light, he will be satisfied"
      (2) MT, "he shall see...of the travail of his soul, He shall be satisfied"

B. New Testament
   1. Over 5,300 manuscripts of all or parts of the Greek New Testament are extant. About 85 of these are written on papyri and 268 of these are manuscripts written in all capital letters (uncials). Later, about the ninth century A.D., a running script (minuscule) was developed. The Greek manuscripts in written form number about 2,700. We also have about 2,100 copies of lists of Scripture texts used in worship that we call lectionaries.
   2. The Papyri. About 85 Greek manuscripts containing parts of the New Testament, written on papyrus are housed in museums. Some are dated from the second century A.D., but most are from the third and

fourth centuries A.D. None of these MSS contain the whole New Testament. Just because these are the oldest copies of the New Testament does not automatically mean they have less variants. Many of these were copied rapidly for a local use. Care was not exercised in the process. Therefore, they contain many variants.

3. Codex Sinaiticus, known by the Hebrew letter "A," א, or (01). It was found at St. Catherine's monastery on Mt. Sinai by Tischendorf. It dates from the fourth century A.D. It contains both the LXX of the Old Testament and the Greek New Testament. It is of "the Alexandrian Text" type.

4. Codex Alexandrinus, known as "A" or (02). It is a fifth century Greek manuscript which was found in Alexandria, Egypt.

5. Codex Vaticanus, known as "B" or (03). It was found in the Vatican's library in Rome and dates from the middle of the fourth century A.D. It contains both LXX of the Old Testament and Greek New Testament. It is of "the Alexandrian Text" type.

6. Codex Ephraemi, known as "C" or (04). It is a fifth century Greek manuscript which was partially destroyed.

7. Codex Bezae, known as "D" or (05). It is a fifth or sixth century Greek manuscript. It is the chief representative of what is called "The Western Text." It contains many additions and was the main Greek New Testament which was the Greek witness for the King James translation.

8. The NT MSS can be grouped into three, possibly four, families of MSS that share certain characteristics.

    a. Alexandrian text, which includes:

        (1) P^{75}, P^{66}, (about A.D. 200) which record the Gospels

        (2) P^{46} (about A.D. 225) records Paul's letters

        (3) P^{72} (about A.D. 225-250) records Peter and Jude

        (4) Code B, called Vaticanus (about A.D. 325), includes the whole OT and NT

   (5) Origen quotes from this text type

   (6) other MSS which show this text type are
    א , C, L, W, 33

  b. Western text from North Africa which
   includes:

    (1) quotes from North African church
     fathers, Tertullian, Cyprian, and the
     Old Latin translation

    (2) quotes from Irenaeus

    (3) quotes from Tatian and Old Syriac
     translation

    (4) Codex D "Bezae" follow this text type

  c. Byzantine text

    (1) this text type is reflected in over 80% of
     the 5,300 MSS

    (2) quoted from Antioch of Syria church
     fathers, Cappadoceans, Chrysostom,
     and Therdoret

    (3) Codex A, in the Gospels only

    (4) Codex E (eighth century) for full NT

  d. the fourth possible type is "Caesarean"

    (1) it is primarily seen only in Mark

    (2) some witnesses to it are: P^{45} and W

II. Brief explanation of the problems and theories of "lower criticism" or "textual criticism."

 A. How the variants occurred

   1. inadvertent or accidental (vast majority of occur-
    rences)

    a. slip of the eye in handcopying which reads the
     second instance of two similar words and,
     thereby, omits all of the words in between
     (homoioteleuton)

     (1) slip of the eye in omitting a double let-
      ter word or phrase (haplography)

     (2) slip of the mind in repeating a phrase
      or line of a Greek text (dittography)

    b. slip of the ear in hand copying by oral dictation
     where a misspelling occurs (itacism). Often
     the misspelling implies or spells a similar
     sounding Greek word.

    c. the earliest Greek texts had no chapter or verse
     divisions, little or no punctuation and no divi-

sion between words. It is possible to divide letters into different words.

2. intentional
   a. changes were made to improve the grammatical form of the text copied
   b. changes were made to bring the text into conformity with other biblical texts (harmonization of parallels)
   c. changes were made by combining two or more variant readings into one long combined text (conflation)
   d. changes were made to correct a perceived problem in the text (cf. I Cor. 11:27 and I Jn. 5:7-8)
   e. some additional information as to the historical setting or proper interpretation of the text was placed in the margin by one scribe but placed into the text by a second scribe (cf. Jn. 5:4)

B. The basic tenets of textual criticism are:
   1. the most awkward or grammatically unusual text is probably the original
   2. the shortest text is probably the original
   3. the older text is given more weight because of its historical proximity to the original, everything else being equal
   4. MSS that are geographically diverse usually have the original reading
   5. doctrinally weaker texts, especially those relating to major theological discussions of the period of manuscript changes like the Trinity in I Jn. 5:7-8, are to be preferred.
   6. two quotes that help show the balance in these troubling variants:
      a. J. Harold Greenlee's book, *Introduction to New Testament Textual Criticism*, p. 68:
      "No Christian doctrine hangs upon a debatable text; and the student of the NT must beware of wanting his text to be more orthodox or doctrinally stronger than is the inspired original."
      b. W. A. Criswell told Greg Garrison of *The*

304

Birmingham News that he (Criswell) doesn't believe every word in the Bible is inspired, "at least not every word that has been given to the modern public by centuries of translators." Criswell said: "I very much am a believer in the textual criticism. As such, I think, the last half of the 16th chapter of Mark is heresy: it's not inspired, it's just concocted...When you compare those manuscripts way back yonder, there was no such thing as that conclusion of the Book of Mark. Somebody added it..."

The patriarch of the SBC inerrantists also claimed that "interpolation" is also evident in Jn. 5, the account of Jesus at the pool of Bethesda. And he discusses the two different accounts of the suicide of Judas (cf. Mt. 27 and Acts 1): "It's just a different view of the suicide," Criswell said. "If it is in the Bible, there is an explanation for it. And the two accounts of the suicide of Judas are in the Bible." Criswell added, "Textual criticism is a wonderful science in itself. It is not ephemeral, it's not impertinent. It's dynamic and central..."

III. Manuscript problems (textual criticism)
    A. Suggested sources for further reading:
        1. *Biblical Criticism: Historical, Literary and Textual,* by R.H. Harrison
        2. *The Text of the New Testament: Its Transmission, Corruption and Restoration* by Bruce M. Metzger
        3. *Introduction to New Testament Textual Criticism,* by J. H Greenlee

APPENDIX THREE

GLOSSARY

Alexandrian School. This method of biblical interpretation was developed in Alexandria, Egypt in the second century A.D. It uses the basic interpretive principles of Philo who was a follower of Plato. It is often called the allegorical method. It held sway in the church until the time of the Reformation. Its most able proponents were Origen and Augustine.

Alexandrinus. This Greek manuscript of the fifth century A.D. from Alexandria, Egypt includes both the Old Testament and most of the New Testament. It is one of our major witnesses to the entire Greek New Testament (except parts of Matthew, John, and II Corinthians). When this manuscript, which is designated "A," and the manuscript designated "B" (Vaticanus) agree on a reading, it is considered to be original by most scholars in most instances.

Allegory. It is a type of Biblical interpretation which developed originally within Alexandrian Judaism. It was popularized by Philo of Alexandria. Its basic thrust is the desire to make the Scripture relevant to one's culture or philosophical system by removing the Bible's historical setting and/or literary context. It seeks a hidden or spiritual meaning behind every text of Scripture. It must be admitted that Jesus, in Matthew 13, and Paul, in Galatians 4, also used symbolism to communicate truth. This was in the form of typology, not strictly allegory.

Analytical lexicon. This is a type of research tool which allows one to identify every Greek form in the New Testament. It is a compilation, in Greek alphabetical order, of forms and basic definitions. In combination with an interlinear translation, it allows non-Greek reading believers to analyze New Testament Greek forms.

Analogy of Scripture. This is the phrase used to describe the view that all of the Bible is inspired by God and is, therefore, not contradictory but complementary. This presuppositional affirmation is the basis for the use of parallel passages in interpreting a biblical text.

Ambiguity. This refers to the uncertainty that results in a written document when there are two or more possible meanings or when two or more things are being referred to at the same time. This often occurs when interpreters do not fully understand the historical or cultural setting.

Anthropomorphic. This term is used to describe our religious language about God. It comes from the Greek term for mankind. It means that we speak about God as if He were a man. God is described in physical and psychological terms which relate to human beings (cf. Gen. 3:8; I Kgs. 22:19-23). This, of course, is only an analogy. However, there are no categories or terms other than human ones for us to use. Therefore, our knowledge of God, though true, is limited and incomplete.

Antiochian School. This method of Biblical interpretation was developed in Antioch, Syria in the third century A.D. as a reaction to the allegorical method of Alexandria, Egypt. Its basic thrust was to focus on the historical meaning of the Bible. It interprets the Bible as normal, human literature. This school became involved in an overemphasis on the humanity of Christ (nestorianism) and was disciplined by the Roman Catholic Church. It continued in Persia but at a very limited level. Its principles were the hermeneutics of the classical reformers (Luther and Calvin).

Antithetical. This is one of three descriptive terms used to denote the relationship between lines of Hebrew poetry. It relates to lines of poetry which are opposite in meaning (cf. Prov. 10:1, 15:1).

Apologist (Apologetics). This is from the Greek root for "legal defense." This is a specific discipline within theology which seeks to give evidence and rational arguments for the Christian faith.

A priori. This is basically synonymous with the term "presupposition." It involves reasoning from previously accepted definitions, principles or positions which are assumed to be true. It is that which is accepted without examination or analysis.

Aristotle. He was one of the philosophers of ancient Greece, a pupil of Plato and teacher of Alexander the Great. His influence, even today, reaches into many areas of modern studies. This is because he emphasized knowledge through observation and classification. This is one of the tenets of the scientific method.

Autographs. This is the name given to the original writings of the New Testament. These original, handwritten manuscripts on papyrus have all been lost. Only copies of copies remain. This is the source of many of the textual variants in the Greek manuscripts.

Bezae. This is a Greek and Latin manuscript of the sixth century A.D. It is designated by "D." It contains the Gospels and Acts and some of the General Epistles. It is characterized by numerous scribal additions. It forms the basis for the "Textus Receptus" which is the major Greek manuscript tradition behind the King James Version.

Bias. This is the term used to describe a strong predisposition toward an object or point of view. It is the mindset in which impartiality is impossible regarding this particular object or point of view. It is a prejudiced position.

Biblical Authority. This term is used in a very specialized sense. It is defined as understanding what the original author said to his day and applying this truth to our day. Biblical authority is usually defined as viewing the Bible itself as our only authoritative guide. However, in light of current, improper interpretations, I have limited the concept to the Bible as interpreted by the tenets of the historical-grammatical method.

Canon. This is a term used to describe the writings which make up the Bible which are believed to be uniquely inspired. It is used regarding both the Old and New Testament Scriptures.

Christocentric. This is a term used to describe the centrality of Jesus. It is used by this author in connection with the concept that Jesus is Lord of all the Bible. The Old Testament points toward Him and He is its fulfillment and goal (cf. Mt. 5:17-48).

Commentary. This is a specialized type of research book. It gives the general background of a Biblical book. It then tries to explain the meaning of each section of the book. Some major on the application aspect while others deal with the text in a more technical way. These books are helpful but must only be used after one has done his own preliminary study. The commentator's interpretations should never be accepted uncritically. Comparing several commentaries from differing theological perspectives is usually helpful.

Dead Sea Scrolls. This refers to a series of ancient texts written in Hebrew and Aramaic which were found near the Dead Sea in 1947. They were the religious libraries of sectarian Judaism of the first century. The pressure of Roman occupation caused them to conceal the scrolls in hermetically sealed pottery jars in caves or holes. They have helped us understand the historical setting of first century Palestine and have confirmed the Masoretic Text as being very accurate, at least as far back as the early B.C. era. They are designated by the abbreviation "DSS."

Deductive. This method of logic or reasoning moves from general principles to specific application premises by means of reason. It is opposite from inductive reasoning which is the heart of the scientific method.

Dialectical. This is the process of reasoning whereby that which seems contradictory or paradoxical is held together in a tension, seeking a unified answer which includes both sides of the paradox. Many biblical doctrines have dialectical pairs, predestination—free will; security—perseverance; faith—works; decision—discipleship; Christian freedom—Christian responsibility.

Diaspora. This is the technical term used by Palestinian Jews to describe other Jews who live outside the geographical boundaries of the Promised Land.

Eclectic. This term is used in connection with textual criticism. It refers to the practice of choosing readings from different Greek manuscripts in order to arrive at a text which is supposed to be close to the original autographs. It rejects the view that any one family of Greek manuscripts captures the originals.

Eisegesis. This is the opposite of exegesis. If exegesis is a "leading out" of the original author's intent, this term implies a "leading in" of a foreign truth.

Etymology. This is an aspect of word study that tries to ascertain the original meaning of a word. From this root meaning then specialized usages are more easily identified. In interpretation, etymology is not the focus but the contemporary meaning of a word.

Exegesis. This is the technical term for the practice of interpreting a specific passage. It means "to lead out" implying that our purpose is to understand the original author's intent.

Existential. This word is used in the sense of our daily circumstances not in its philosophical definition.

Genre. This is a French term that denotes different types of literature. The thrust of the term is the division of literary forms into categories which share common characteristics: historical narrative, poetry, proverb, apocalyptic and legislation.

Hermeneutics. This is the technical term for the principles which guide exegesis. It is both a set of specific guidelines and an art/gift. Biblical, or sacred, hermeneutics is usually divided into two categories: general principles and special principles. These relate to the different types of literature found in the Bible. Each different type (genre) has its own unique guidelines but also shares some common assumptions and procedures of interpretation.

Higher Criticism. This is the procedure of biblical interpretation which focuses on the historical setting and literary structure of a particular Biblical book.

Idiom. This word is used for the phrases found in different cultures which have specialized meaning not connected to the usual meaning of the individual terms. Some modern examples are: "that was awfully good," or "you just kill me." The Bible also contains these types of phrases.

Inductive. This is a method of logic or reason which moves from the particulars to the whole. It is the empirical method of modern science. This is basically the approach of Aristotle.

Interlinear. This is a type of research tool which allows those who do not read a biblical language to be able to analyze its meaning and structure. It places the English translation on a word for word level immediately under the original biblical language. This tool, combined with an "analytical lexicon," will give the forms and basic definitions of Hebrew and Greek.

Language of description. This is used in connection with the idioms in which the Old Testament is written. It speaks of our world in terms of the way things appear to the five senses. It is not a scientific description nor was it meant to be.

Legalism. This is characterized by an over-emphasis on rules or ritual. It tends to rely on the human performance of regulations as a means of acceptance by God. It depreciates relationship to performance. Both aspects are an important part of a covenantal relationship.

Literal. This is another name for the textually-focused method of hermeneutics from Antioch. It means that interpretation involves the normal and obvious meaning of human language. It does recognize the presence of figurative language.

Literary genre. This refers to the distinct forms that human communication can take such as poetry or historical narrative. Each different type of literature has its own special hermeneutical procedures in addition to general principles for all ancient literature.

Literary unit. This refers to the major thought divisions of a biblical book. It can be made up of a few verses, paragraphs or chapters. It is a self-contained unit with a unified central subject.

Lower criticism. See "textual criticism."

Manuscript. This term relates to the different copies of the Greek New Testament. Usually they are divided into the different types by: (1) material on which they are written, or (2) the form of the writing itself. It is abbreviated by "MS" or "MSS" (plural).

Masoretic Text. This refers to the ninth century A.D. Hebrew manuscript of the Old Testament which contains vowel points and other textual notes. It forms the basic text for our English Old Testament. Its text has been confirmed by the Hebrew MSS, especially Isaiah, known from the Dead Sea Scrolls. It is abbreviated by "MT."

Muratorian Fragments. This is a list of the canonical books of the New Testament. It was written from Rome before AD 200. It gives the same twenty-seven books as the Protestant NT. This clearly shows the canon was set before the major church councils by local churches in different parts of the Roman Empire.

Natural revelation. This is one category of God's self-disclosure to man. It involves the natural order (Rom. 1:19-20) and the moral consciousness (Rom. 2:14-15). It is spoken of in Ps. 19:1-6. It is distinct from special revelation which is God's specific self-disclosure in the Bible and supremely in Jesus of Nazareth.

Nestorianism. This is the heresy which emphasized the humanity of Jesus to the point of depreciating His deity. It was condemned by the early church. The Historical-Grammatical School of Antioch was involved in this error and was disciplined by Rome.

Original author. This refers to the writers of Scripture.

Papyri. This is a type of writing material from Egypt. It is made from river reeds. It is the material upon which our oldest copies of the Greek New Testament are written.

Parallel passages. They are part of the concept that all of the Bible is God-given and, therefore, is its own best interpreter and balancer of paradoxical truths. This is also helpful when one is attempting to interpret an unclear or ambiguous passage. They also help one find the clearest passage on a given subject as well as all other Scriptural aspects of a given subject.

Paragraph. This is the basic interpretive literary unit in prose. It contains one central thought and its development. If we stay with its major thrust we will not major on minors or miss the original author's intent.

Parochialism. This relates to biases which are locked into a local mental/cultural setting. It does not see the transcultural nature of biblical truth or its application.

Paradox. This refers to those truths which seem to be contradictory, but yet, both are truth. Much biblical truth is presented in paradoxical pairs.

Plato. He was one of the philosophers of ancient Greece. His philosophy greatly influenced the early church through the scholars of Alexandria, Egypt, and Augustine. He posited that everything on earth was illusionary and a mere copy of a spiritual archetype.

Presupposition. This refers to our preconceived understanding of a matter. Often we form opinions or judgments about issues before we approach the Scriptures themselves. This predisposition is also known as: bias, an *a priori* position, assumption, preunderstanding, or presupposition.

Proof-texting. This is the practice of interpreting Scripture by quoting a verse without regard for its immediate context or larger context in its literary unit. This removes the verses from the original author's intent and usually involves the attempt to prove a personal opinion while asserting biblical authority.

Rabbinical Judaism. This stage of the life of the Jewish people began in Babylonian Exile. As the influence of the Priests and the Temple was removed, local synagogues became the focus of Jewish life. These local centers of Jewish culture, fellowship, worship and Bible study became the focus of the national religious life. In Jesus' day this "religion of the scribes" was parallel to that of the priests. At the fall of Jerusalem in 70 A.D. the scribal form, dominated by the Pharisees, controlled the direction of Jewish religious life. It is characterized by a practical, legalistic interpretation of the Torah as explained in the oral tradition (Talmud).

Revelation. This is the name given to the concept that God has spoken to mankind. The full concept is usually expressed by three terms: (1) revelation—God has acted in human history; (2) inspiration—He has given the proper interpretation of His acts and their meaning to certain chosen men to record for mankind; and (3) illumination—He has given His Spirit to help mankind understand His self-disclosure.

Semantic field. This refers to the total range of meanings associated with a word. It is basically the different connotations a word has in different contexts.

Septuagint. This is the name given to the Greek translation of the Hebrew Old Testament. Tradition says that it was written in seventy days by seventy Jewish scholars for the library of Alexandria, Egypt. The traditional date is around 250 B.C. This translation is significant because: (1) it gives us an ancient text to compare with the Masoretic Hebrew text; (2) it shows us the state of Jewish interpretation in the third century B.C.; (3) it gives us the Jewish Messianic understanding before the rejection of Jesus. Its abbreviation is "LXX."

Sinaiticus. This is a Greek manuscript of the fourth century A.D. It was found by Tischendorf at St. Catherine's monastery on Jebel Musa, the traditional site of Mt. Sinai. This manuscript is designated by the Hebrew "A" [א]. It contains both the Old and New Testaments. It is one of our most ancient uncial MSS.

Spiritualizing. This term is synonymous with allegorizing in the sense that it removes the historical and literary context of a passage and interprets it on the basis of other criteria.

314

Synonymous. This refers to terms with exact or very similar meanings. They are so closely related that they can replace each other in a sentence without loss of meaning. It is also used to designate one of the three forms of Hebrew poetic parallelism. In this sense it refers to two lines of poetry that express the same truth (cf. Ps. 103:3).

Syntax. This is a Greek term which refers to the structure of a sentence. It is synonymous with our "grammar."

Synthetical. This is one of the three terms that relates to types of Hebrew poetry. This term speaks of lines of poetry which build on one another in a cumulative sense (cf. Ps. 19:7-9).

Systematic theology. This is a stage of interpretation which tries to relate the truths of the Bible in a unified and categorized manner. It is a logical, rather than an historical, presentation of Christianity.

Talmud. This is the title for the codification of the Jewish Oral Tradition. The Jews believe it was given orally by God to Moses on Mt. Sinai. In reality it appears to be the collective wisdom of the Jewish teachers through the years. There are two different written forms of the Talmud, the Babylonian and the shorter, unfinished Palestinian version.

Textual criticism. This is the study of the original manuscripts of the Bible. It attempts, by means of scholarship, to arrive at the original wording of the autographs of the Old and New Testaments. It is often called "lower criticism."

Torah. This is the Hebrew term for "teaching." It came to be the official title for the writings of Moses, Genesis through Deuteronomy. It is, for the Jews, the most authoritative division of the Hebrew canon.

Typological. This is a specialized type of revelation. Usually it involves New Testament truth found in Old Testament passages by means of an analogical symbol. Because of the abuse of this type of interpretation, one should limit its use to specific examples recorded in the New Testament. This category of hermeneutics was a major element of the

Alexandrian method.

Vaticanus. This is the Greek manuscript of the fourth century A.D. It was found in the Vatican's library. It originally contained all the Old Testament, Apocrypha and New Testament. However, some parts were lost (Genesis, Psalms, Hebrews, the Pastorals, Philemon and Revelation). It is a very helpful manuscript in determining the original wording of the autographs. It is designated by a capital "B."

Vulgate. This is the name of the Latin translation of Jerome. It became the basic or "common" translation for the Roman Catholic Church. It was done in the 380's A.D.

World picture and worldview. These are companion terms. They are both philosophical concepts related to creation. The term "world picture" refers to "the how" of creation while "worldview" relates to "the Who." These terms are relevant to the interpretation that Gen. 1-2 deals primarily with the Who, not the how, of creation.

YHWH. This is the Covenant name for God in the Old Testament. It is defined in Ex. 3:14. It is the CAUSATIVE form of the Hebrew term "to be." The Jews were afraid to pronounce the name, lest they take it in vain; therefore, they substituted the Hebrew term Adonai, "Lord." This is how this covenant name is translated in English.

APPENDIX FOUR

DOCTRINAL STATEMENT

I do not particularly care for statements of faith or creeds. I prefer to affirm the Bible itself. However, I realize that a statement of faith will provide those who are unfamiliar with me a way to evaluate my doctrinal perspective. In our day of so much theological error and deception, the following brief summary of my theology is offered.

1. The Bible, both the Old and New Testament, is the inspired, infallible, authoritative, eternal Word of God. It is the self-revelation of God recorded by men under supernatural leadership. It is our only source of clear truth about God and His purposes. It is also the only source of faith and practice for His church.

2. There is only one eternal, creator, redeemer God. He is the creator of all things, visible and invisible. He has revealed Himself as loving and caring although He is also fair and just. He has revealed Himself in three distinct persons: Father, Son and Spirit; truly separate and yet the same.

3. God is actively in control of His world. There is both an eternal plan for His creation that is unalterable and an individually focused one that allows human free will. Nothing happens without God's knowledge and permission, yet He allows individual choices both among angels and men. Jesus is the Father's Elect Man and all are potentially elect in Him. God's foreknowledge of events does not reduce man to a determined pre-written script. Man is responsible for his thoughts and deeds.

4. Man, though created in God's image and free from sin, chose to rebel against God. Although tempted by a supernatural agent Adam and Eve were responsible for their willful, self-centeredness. Their rebellion has affected all men and creation. We are all in need of God's mercy and grace both for our corporate condition in Adam and our individual volitional rebellion.

5. God has provided a means of forgiveness and restoration for fallen man. Jesus Christ, God's unique son, became a man, lived a sinless life and by means of his substitutionary death, paid the penalty of man's sin. He is the only way to

restoration and fellowship with God. There is no other means of salvation except through faith in His finished work.

6. Man must personally receive God's offer of forgiveness and restoration in Jesus. This is accomplished by means of volitional trust in God's promises through Jesus and a willful turning from known sin.

7. Man is fully forgiven and restored based upon his trust in Christ and repentance from sin. However, the evidence for this new relationship is seen in a changed, and changing, life. The goal of God for man is not only heaven someday but Christlikeness now. Those who are truly redeemed, though occasionally sinning, will continue in faith and repentance throughout their lives.

8. The Holy Spirit is "the other Jesus." He is present in the world to lead the lost to Christ and develop Christlikeness in the saved. The gifts of the Spirit are given at salvation. They are, in reality, the life and ministry of Jesus divided among His body, the Church. The gifts of the Spirit need to be motivated by the fruit of the Spirit. The Spirit is active in our day as He was in the biblical times.

9. The resurrected Jesus Christ has been made the Judge of all things by the Father. He will return to earth to judge all men. Those who have trusted Jesus and whose names are written in the Lamb's book of life will receive their eternal glorified bodies at His return. They will be with Him forever. However, those who have refused to respond to God's truth will be separated eternally from the joys of fellowship with the Triune God. They will be condemned along with the Devil and his angels.

This is surely not complete or thorough but I hope it will give you the theological flavor of my heart. I like the statement:

> "In essentials—unity,
> In peripherals—freedom,
> In all things—love."

This Commentary reflects the theory and practice of Bob's method of interpretation. You will find it very helpful as you study the Bible. However, the very nature of printed material fails to capture Bob's humor and practical applications of these Bible studies. Bible Lessons International believes you will benefit from both hearing (audio) or seeing (video) Bob's actual presentations of this material in a local church setting.

Also, Bob's worldwide Bible study ministry produces a periodic newsletter. This includes articles about mission trips, overseas letters, special offers of new studies,and family updates. This newsletter is available free. Just fill out the card at the bottom and mail it to our office or call 1-800-785-1005 or fax 1-903-935-2532.

BIBLE LESSONS INTERNATIONAL

P.O. Box 1289
Marshall, TX 75671

I would like to receive:

❏ The Bible Lessons International Catalog, *FREE*

❏ The Bible Lessons International Newsletter, *FREE*

❏ The audio of Galatians, 12 lessons for $24.^{00}

❏ The video of Galatians, 7 lessons for $49.^{00}

❏ The video of I & II Thessalonians, 8 lessons for $56.^{00}

❏ The audio of I & II Thessalonians, 12 lessons for $24.^{00}

Name _____

Address _____

_____

❏ Bill me later   ❏ I have enclosed $ _____ .

❏ We accept MasterCard/Visa/Discover

(When ordering, please call us with your number for security purposes at:
1-800-785-1005)